A Collector's History of English Pottery

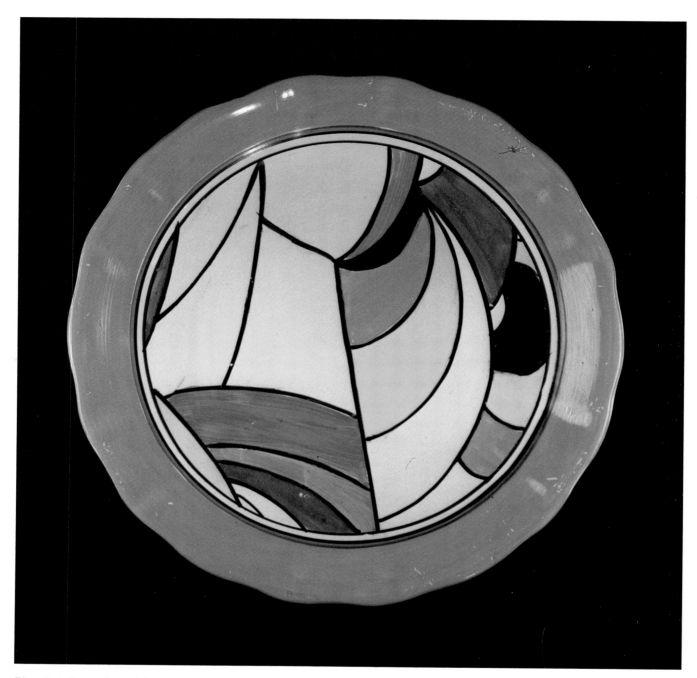

Plate I. A large plate with an early example of geometric
landscape. 'Bizarre' design by Clarice Cliff for the Newport
Pottery. *c.* 1929. 250mm wide. *Courtesy Castle Antiques,
(Warwick's Art Deco Shop) Warwick.*

The drawing on the title page of Stoke-on-Trent is by
Edward Bawden, C.B.E., R.A. It was originally used as a
Shell Press Advertisement in 1934.
Reproduced by kind permission of Shell U.K. Ltd.

A Collector's History of
English Pottery

Griselda Lewis

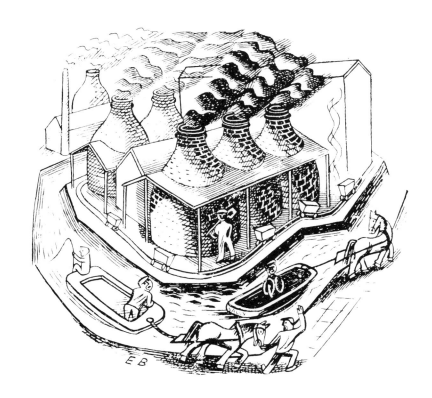

Antique Collectors' Club

Fourth revised edition
© 1987 Griselda Lewis
First published in 1969 by
Studio Vista Ltd.
Second edition published in 1977 by
Barrie & Jenkins Ltd.
Third enlarged edition published in 1985 by
Antique Collectors' Club
World copyright reserved

ISBN 1 85149 056 6

British Library CIP Data
Lewis, Griselda
    A collector's history of English pottery. — 4th ed.
    1. Pottery, English — History
    I. Title   II. Antique Collectors' Club
    738.3′0942   NK4085

Published for the Antique Collectors' Club
by the Antique Collectors' Club Ltd.

Designed by John Lewis FCSD
Printed in England by the Antique Collectors' Club Ltd., Woodbridge, Suffolk.

Antique Collectors' Club

The Antique Collectors' Club was formed in 1966 and now has a five figure membership spread throughout the world. It publishes the only independently run monthly antiques magazine *Antique Collecting* which caters for those collectors who are interested in widening their knowledge of antiques, both by greater awareness of quality and by discussion of the factors which influence the price that is likely to be asked. The Antique Collectors' Club pioneered the provision of information on prices for collectors and the magazine still leads in the provision of detailed articles on a variety of subjects.

It was in response to the enormous demand for information on 'what to pay' that the price guide series was introduced in 1968 with the first edition of *The Price Guide to Antique Furniture* (completely revised 1978), a book which broke new ground by illustrating the more common types of antique furniture, the sort that collectors could buy in shops and at auctions rather than the rare museum pieces which had previously been used (and still to a large extent are used) to make up the limited amount of illustrations in books published by commercial publishers. Many other price guides have followed, all copiously illustrated, and greatly appreciated by collectors for the valuable information they contain, quite apart from prices. The Antique Collectors' Club also publishes other books on antiques, including horology and art reference works, and a full book list is available.

Club membership, which is open to all collectors, costs £15.95 per annum. Members receive free of charge *Antique Collecting*, the Club's magazine (published every month except August), which contains well-illustated articles dealing with the practical aspects of collecting not normally dealt with by magazines. Prices, features of value, investment potential, fakes and forgeries are all given prominence in the magazine.

Among other facilities available to members are private buying and selling facilities, the longest list of 'For Sales' of any antiques magazine, an annual ceramics conference and the opportunity to meet other collectors at their local antique collectors' clubs. There are over eighty in Britain and more than a dozen overseas. Members may also buy the Club's publications at special pre-publication prices.

As its motto implies, the Club is an amateur organisation designed to help collectors get the most out of their hobby: it is informal and friendly and gives enormous enjoyment to all concerned.

For Collectors — By Collectors — About Collecting

The Antique Collectors' Club, 5 Church Street, Woodbridge, Suffolk

Acknowledgements

I have had unstinted help from so many people over the preparation of this third edition that it is impossible to name them all individually. I would like everyone concerned to know how grateful I am for the parts they have played in making this book possible. To people from museums all over the country who have helped me with their knowledge and photographs, to people from the big auction houses and from pottery firms who have provided me with photographs and in some cases actual pottery; to all the dealers, collectors and friends who have helped me in so many ways and to all the dozens of present day potters who have sent me photographs of their work and have given me much helpful advice, I would like to express my grateful thanks.

There are three people I must thank particularly, Ian Craig, for all his help with the chapter on Victorian tiles and for supplying me with so many photographs from his own collection, John Smith of Stourbridge who generously gave me the benefit of all his knowledge of Mocha ware, in spite of the fact that he is writing a book on the subject himself; and last but by no means least my husband, John, for taking hundreds of photographs, helping me with the text and designing the book.

Contents

List of colour plates

To Arnold Mountford, C.B.E.
in gratitude for so many years of
unstinted help and encouragement

Introduction

Fashions in everything including collecting change with the passing of time. When this book was first published, it was still possible to buy, at fairly modest prices, pieces made in the eighteenth century and even before.

Now, partly due to the interest and knowledge of the general public in things antique – inspired without doubt by so many excellent programmes both on the radio and television, there is a whole new generation of collectors.

The prices of early pottery have increased so much that the younger collectors and those of modest means have naturally turned to the products of the nineteenth and even twentieth centuries – including modern studio pottery – the antiques of the future.

Collectors approach their chosen subject from many angles. Some like to acquire pieces from all periods and styles, making a representative collection of English pottery as a whole – others choose one particular facet – delft ware or tiles or nineteenth century stoneware jugs – some people only collect white toast racks, or teapots, or meat dishes. Others prefer to collect only marked pieces while others like to acquire pieces that reflect the social history of some aspect of life, be it railways or ships or commemorative pieces of a political nature. Yet others collect the work of one particular factory, or even one period of the factory's production, or the work of one individual artist.

Though it would be impossible now to amass a vast collection like those of Lady Charlotte Schreiber or Dr. Glaisher without being a millionaire, there is still a wealth of material worth collecting made in this century alone.

The recent interest in Art Deco shows how fashions change – a few years ago it would have been cleared out of the attic and sent to the local jumble sale. Today the work of such Art Deco designers as Clarice Cliff is eagerly sought.

I feel that whatever one is collecting, the object should be good of its kind, in fine condition and preferably not restored, or if restored that one knows precisely what has been done. Any reputable dealer will point this out. If buying at an auction, it may be well worth while to view the object under an infra red lamp, which will reveal most kinds of restoration.

Collectors are ultimately dependant on the goodwill of the dealers from whom they buy their pieces. To establish a relationship, even friendship with dealers in one's particular area is one of the pleasures of collecting.

My main purpose in producing this pictorial history is to show not only the trends and developments of English pottery through the years but also to show how these have influenced modern work. To open one's eyes to these recurring themes is just one of the factors that makes the contemplation of modern pottery so much more understandable and enjoyable. Collecting can be so much more that mere acquisition. The research involved in finding out more about one's chosen pieces is infinitely rewarding. To help this there is a brief list of books for further reading at the end of each chapter as well as a general bibliography at the end of the book.

One use for a pot. Decoration from the Luttrell Psalter. *c.* 1340. *Reproduced Courtesy of the Trustees of the British Musuem.*

INTRODUCTION TO THE FOURTH EDITION

This new edition has given me the opportunity of adding a few more pictures and of amending the text where necessary. As a result of the recent research work done by Mrs. Pat Halfpenny, Keeper of Ceramics at the City Museum, Stoke-on-Trent, the chapter on the Woods of Burslem has been largely re-written and the chapter on enamel coloured figures has been considerably modified.

I would like to thank Pat Halfpenny, also Terence Lockett and Rodney and Eileen Hampson for the help they have given me over these and other revisions.

1. Early pottery in England

Small almost black irregularly shaped cooking pot. New Stone Age *c.* 3000-2000 BC. An example of the earliest and most primitive pottery found in England. Found at Dales Road brickfields, Ipswich. 76mm high. *Ipswich Museum.*

Flat bottomed shallow plant-pot shaped bowl with incised decoration dating from *c.* 2000 BC. The clay is reddish brown in colour and the shape is inspired by that of a wooden vessel. Found at Creeting St. Mary, Suffolk. 144mm high. *Ipswich Museum.*

Because of its enduring quality, pottery-making is the oldest surviving craft practised by man – except for the making of weapons. The basic necessity for survival was food; omnivorous man made spears and arrows in order to kill animals to eat, and when tired of eating them raw, made primitive pots in which to cook them, to store his food and to drink from. So, where clay was to be found, pots could be made. They were probably first made by the women as part of the household chores, while the men did the hunting.

The earliest English pottery to survive belongs to the first Neolithic period or New Stone Age (*c.* 3000-2000 BC). Though pieces are seldom found in anything but a fragmentary state, it has been possible for skilled archaeologists to restore them sufficiently for us to see what they were like. And they were just about as primitive as it was possible to be, for the earliest pots are small round-bottomed bowls made of very coarse clay, dark in colour, shaped by hand and hardened by burning on an open fire. This kind of pottery has been found in East Anglia and in the hill forts of southern England. Sometimes the shapes were a little less basic, for the rims were sometimes rolled or beaded and occasionally handles occur in the form of loops or lugs.

Some slightly later pottery dating from about 2000 BC is of quite a different shape, being flat-bottomed and in the form of a shallow bucket or plant-pot. These are thought to have been this shape because the people who made them probably used wooden vessels before, and this is the shape those wooden vessels could have been.

The pottery that survives from the Bronze Age (*c.* 1900-450 BC) is often in a well-preserved state, for it was buried deliberately with the ashes of the dead. The Bronze Age cinerary urns made to hold these cremated remains probably did not differ very much from the household cooking and storage pots of the time. The beakers and urns of this period, though shaped by hand, were well-formed and decorated with incised patterns of herring-bone or cross-hatched bands, made with a pointed stick; or sometimes with lines made by the impressing of a thong or cord in the damp clay, or patterns made with a finger nail.

The potter's wheel was introduced into this country during the last phase of the Early Iron Age (somewhere about 75 BC) and, dating from this period, are well-thrown, though rather clumsy shapes, ornamented with wheel-turned decorations.

When the Romans first came to Britain, they imported a quantity of red-gloss pottery from Gaul, Italy and the Rhineland, but by the second century AD, Roman potters, (no doubt aided by the native British) were at work in England and the red-gloss ware was certainly produced at Colchester in Essex, where some pieces of moulds and some hundreds of fragments have been found. It was of a much poorer quality than that made on the continent.

Early Bronze Age beaker with incised decoration
c. 1900-1400 BC. Found at Goodmanham, East Riding,
Yorkshire. 172mm high. *Crown copyright Victoria and Albert
Museum.*

Middle Bronze Age burial urn with overhanging rim and
incised bands of decoration. c. 1400-1000 BC. Found at
Kempston, Bedfordshire. 203mm high. *Crown copyright
Victoria and Albert Museum.*

Early Iron Age butt beaker. c. 75 BC. Wheel thrown and
with wheel turned and rouletted decoration. Found at
Sutton Courtenay, Berks. 172mm high. *Crown copyright
Victoria and Albert Museum.*

Early Iron Age (third period) pedestal urn. c. 75 BC. This
has been thrown on a wheel. From the cremation
cemetery at Aylesford, Kent. 249mm high. *Crown copyright
Victoria and Albert Museum.*

Known as The Colchester Vase. *c.* AD 200. The decoration shows a combat between two gladiators, Memnon and Valentinus. It is not absolutely certain whether this was made in Colchester, but similar ware was made there. 216mm high. *Colchester and Essex Museum.*

Castor ware vase or beaker, black with white slip decoration. *c.* AD 400. Found in Broad Street, London. 143mm high. *Museum of London.*

At about the beginning of the second century AD a distinctive type of pottery was made at Castor, near Peterborough in Northamptonshire. Some of this was a light-bodied earthenware of varying hardness, and a dark purplish red colour; it was often decorated with slip of the same colour trailed on the surface like cake icing, in abstract scroll patterns or animal forms. But the most attractive ware made at Castor had a smooth black body and was decorated with white slip. Judging by contemporary standards, it was surprisingly thin and delicately potted. Castor ware was made until the late fourth or early fifth century AD. At the same time, pottery of a similar type was made in other places, notably in the New Forest; but useful ware of all kinds including storage jars, cooking pots, mortars for grinding corn, feeding bottles and burial urns must have been made in considerable quantities wherever potteries existed, for a large amount of Romano-British pottery survives. Twenty-five kilns were found in Colchester alone.

15

Romano-British burial urns dating from the second century AD, from the Roman cemeteries at Colchester. 228-254mm high. *Colchester and Essex Museum.*

Pagan Saxon burial urn. Hand-shaped and decorated with stamps and incised lines. Late 6th century AD. Urns very similar in every way to this one have been found at West Stow Heath, Icklingham and near Cambridge. All obviously made by the same hand, known as the 'Lackford Potter'. Found at Lackford. 228mm high. *Ashmolean Museum, Oxford.*

16

After the retreat of the Romans from these islands in the early fifth century, a period of disorder and lawlessness prevailed. The British seem to have spent all their energies on keeping alive and defending their families and property from a series of foreign invaders. What pottery survives from this time is of a strictly utilitarian nature and coarsely made. The influence of the Roman potters declined, the use of the potters' wheel lapsed and the Anglo-Saxons shaped all their pottery by hand. They had almost reverted to the standards of the Stone Age. They lived in a very primitive way in wooden buildings, of which only traces of post holes in the ground remain.

The pagan Saxons, living in south-eastern England, cremated their dead and put the ashes of the bones into urns which they made for the purpose. Though hand-shaped, sometimes these urns were decorated with quite complicated patterns made by the use of stamps (which they carved from bones) and incised lines. Sometimes the decoration was in the form of raised 'blisters', either pushed up from the interior of the pot, or else applied on top as an extra layer, though this type of decoration was more usual on the continent.

In the late sixth century, there is the first evidence (since the Roman occupation) of a professional potter at work, who must have traded his wares. This potter's work has been found at Lackford, not far from Thetford in Suffolk, and his pots have also been found at Icklingham, West Stow Heath and as far away as Cambridge. The ware can be indentified by the similarity of basic material, of shape and by his very characteristic use of decoration, consisting of horizontal bands of incised lines and pendant triangles of small stamped marks (rather like bunches of grapes, probably made by impressing the cross-section of a bird's legbone) outlined by more incised lines. (See opposite page).

By the mid-seventh century the wheel was back in use again. In East Anglia some kilns were in production at Ipswich, and later a wheel was being used again at Thetford, where a pottery was established for the making of ware similar to that found at Ipswich. This was in about the year 850 and the production continued into the twelfth century. This Thetford ware (so-called because the kilns at Thetford happened to be discovered first) is grey in colour and has very marked grooves round the outside made by the tips of the fingers of the potter. The shapes are simple with relatively thin walls; urns, jars, jugs or pitchers with slightly turned over rims were made, not so very different in character from the coarser pottery made at the time of the Roman occupation.

The pottery at Ipswich must have had high standards, for a good many slightly deformed but usable pieces had been discarded as wasters. Among these were some pieces fired to a brownish red instead of the characteristic ashy grey. The wrong colour was enough to class them as seconds.

'Thetford' ware storage jar. 7th-9th century. Although the potters' wheel was in use again, the pottery at this time was more primitive than that made in the second century AD. 223mm high. *Ipswich Museum.*

17

Although it is unlikely that any early pottery will turn up in a sale-room or a shop, it is not at all unlikely that discoveries of buried pottery, even if fragmentary, will still be made. Important finds have recently been made during the clearing of building sites. The deeper than usual ploughing of farm land can unearth a Roman or Saxon cemetery, and even the process of digging a garden or the clearing of a moat can be rewarded by the finding of pieces of pottery from which we can learn something of our predecessors.

The domestic pottery of mediaeval England was much less refined than that produced at the time of the Roman occupation. The most usual pottery vessels were jugs or pitchers, for at this time the ordinary people ate off wooden platters and drank from vessels made of horn or wood, whereas the nobility and the rich merchants used metal plates, jugs and cups. Pottery was mostly confined to the kitchen or the peasant's hut. Even so, the pieces that have been preserved to this day can hardly be dismissed as uninteresting. They may be crude, but they are remarkable for their bold shapes and the diversity of their decoration. The jugs and pitchers of the thirteenth century were rather tall and attenuated, whereas those of the later fourteenth or fifteenth centuries became broader in the base and less high. Some of the ware

Baluster jug, with traces of a yellowish lead glaze. *c.* 1275. Found in Blossoms Inn yard, Lawrence Lane, London. 457mm high. *Museum of London.*

Left: Jug decorated with incised and rouletted patterns and covered with a yellowish green lead glaze. *c.* 1300. Found at Scarborough. 372mm high. *Fitzwilliam Museum, Cambridge.*

Right: Rope-handled jug, elaborately decorated with knights in armour in high relief round the neck, and stags attacked by hounds round the body. *c.* 1275-1325. Made of buff coloured clay, glazed with a dark apple green lead glaze. Found in Friars Lane, Nottingham. 355mm high. *Castle Museum, Nottingham.*

Plate 2. Mediaeval jug with a bright mottled green glaze. It
was found in London in a rotten cask where it must have
been dropped centuries earlier. 14th-15th century. 114mm
high. *Reproduced by courtesy of the Trustees of the British Museum.*

Left: Buff earthenware pitcher with a bearded face each side and a brownish yellow glaze merging to light apple green, three quarters of the way down. The vertical stripes are purplish black. Found on a kiln site in Nottingham. *c. 1300.* 509mm high. *Castle Museum, Nottingham.*

Centre: Very beautiful red earthenware jug with trailed white slip decoration under a yellow lead glaze. *c. 1300.* Found at Austin Friars, London. 375mm high. *Museum of London.*

Right: Buff earthenware jug with a bearded face, a forerunner of the Toby jug; the decoration is green and brown under a yellow lead glaze. *c. 1350.* Found in Bishopsgate Street, London. *Museum of London.*

Jug decorated with painted streaks and spots of white slip, covered on the front with a thin yellow glaze. Found at Moyes's Farm, Cambridge. *c. 1380.* 225mm high. *Fitzwilliam Museum, Cambridge.*

Jug of reddish earthenware with applied and moulded
decoration and traces of brown glaze. 14th century. 337mm
high. *Crown copyright, Victoria and Albert Museum.*

Puzzle jug of light red earthenware with a coating of white slip, covered with a dark green glaze. The date, 1571, is made of applied strips of clay. 386mm high. *Fitzwilliam Museum, Cambridge.*

Top left: Red earthenware pitcher with white slip applied decoration and a lead glaze. *c.* 1350. 222mm high. *Fitzwilliam Museum, Cambridge.*

Late fifteenth-century watering pot of dark red-brown earthenware decorated with white slip. It was filled by submersion; a thumb was then put over the hole in the top and the pot swung, base upwards. The watering was then done by swinging the pot back and forth, when the water sprinkled out through the holes in the base. 386mm. *Museum of London.*

Encaustic tile with inlaid heraldic decoration in white clay, from Keynsham Abbey, Avon. Early 14th century. 130mm square. *Crown copyright Victoria and Albert Museum.*

Encaustic tile of red clay with inlaid decoration of white clay coated with a greenish yellow transparent glaze. This design of the interlacing quatrefoils enclosing the radiating floral ornament is part of a four tile repeat. 14th century. 104mm square. *Reproduced by courtesy of the Trustees of the British Museum.*

was left unglazed and undecorated, but much was patterned with a different coloured slip, or with incised lines, or decorated with reliefs stamped in different coloured clays, which were made with a wooden stamp cut in intaglio. The only known glaze at that time had a lead basis and developed a yellowish colour in the firing. Sometimes the glaze was stained with copper, giving it a variety of greens and some of the later ware was stained with manganese and oxide of iron, which produced various rich browns. The glaze was sprinkled or dusted on to the surface with a rag. Sometimes it was confined to only a part of a vessel; many mediaeval jugs have only a bib of glaze under the spout. Owing to the primitive methods of firing pottery, impurities were always present in the kilns and this accounts for the generally dark appearance of the ware. In addition to domestic pottery, tiles were made for the decoration of churches and abbeys. The designs on these tiles were either incised or impressed, modelled in low relief or inlaid, or occasionally decorated with slip. They were often glazed.

Much of the ware of Tudor times, though rather coarse, was glazed either with a plain lead glaze giving a yellow effect, or else with a green- stained lead glaze. The objects that have been found range from candle-sticks to chamber-pots and included costrels or pilgrims' bottles.

During the first half of the sixteenth century, that is up to 1539 when Henry VIII ordered the dissolution of the monasteries, a particularly good ware was much used by the monks. This has been given somewhat loosely the name of 'Cistercian' ware, merely because so many pieces were found in the ruins of the Cistercian Abbeys in Yorkshire, though pieces of similar pottery have been found all over the country as far apart as Ely in East Anglia and Abergavenny on the borders of Wales. This ware is quite smooth and thin, made of red clay and glazed with a dark brown or almost black glaze.

A similar ware was made in Burslem from the beginning of the seventeenth century for about a hundred years. This was glazed with the usual lead glaze with the addition of crude oxide of iron and though always very dark in colour, the tone varies, as does the brilliance of the glaze due to the degree of reduction during firing and the amount of iron in the glaze. This ware was made in other places in Staffordshire and in Shropshire during the nineteenth century.

Drinking vessels with one or more handles known as tygs are typical of this ware. They were probably used in some taverns during the eighteenth century, for there is one in the City Museum at Stoke-on-Trent with the excise mark of Queen Anne upon it.

It is difficult to present the history of English pottery in an orderly chronological pattern. Until the middle of the sixteenth century developments were very slow, and then tin-glazing was introduced.

23

Towards the end of the seventeenth century the production of stoneware began. Throughout the eighteenth century one improvement or invention followed another with almost bewildering rapidity, it was the great age of change and growth in the pottery industry. But because a new technique was introduced, it did not mean that old ways were superseded at once; tradition dies hard, and thus we have an overlapping of techniques that is sometimes extremely confusing.

Two-handled tyg. *c.* 1660. Made in Staffordshire and glazed with a dark shiny iron glaze. Similar to the ware found in the ruins of the Yorkshire monastries and called loosely 'Cistercian' ware. 165mm high. *City Museum and Art Gallery, Stoke-on-Trent.*

For further reading

R.J. Charleston. *Roman Pottery*. Faber 1953.

Anon. *English Prehistoric Pottery*. Victoria and Albert Museum 1952.

Vivian G. Swan. *Pottery in Roman Britain*. Shire Publications 1975.

Llewellynn Jewitt. *The Ceramic Art of Great Britain*. 2nd. Edn. London and New York 1883.

David K. Kennett. *Anglo-Saxon Pottery*. Shire Publications 1978.

Bernard Rackham. *Mediaeval English Pottery*. Faber 1948.

R.L. Hobson. *A Guide to the English Pottery and Porcelain*. British Museum 1923.

2. Slipware

LEAD-GLAZED SLIP-DECORATED EARTHENWARE OF THE
SEVENTEENTH AND EIGHTEENTH CENTURIES

Slip is clay mixed with water to the consistency of cream. It can be used in various ways to decorate pottery. Slip of one colour can be applied in a thin all-over coating to the clay body of another colour either by brushing or immersion, and a design can then be trailed on to the surface through a narrow tube (originally a quill) using slips of different colours, or the slip can be applied in lines or stripes, then combed to make a marbled or feathered effect. Or the design can be scratched through the top layer of slip to expose the body of a different colour beneath (*sgraffito*) or the slip can be inlaid (in the same way as on the mediaeval tiles).

Although slip decoration was used by the Romans and also in mediaeval times, this method of decoration was not fully exploited until the seventeenth century. Slipware was made throughout the eighteenth century and was still made by various country potters in the nineteenth century. The traditional methods of slip decoration have been used to the present day by many studio potters, with varying degrees of success.

The early slipware was made in many places, but principally at Wrotham in Kent and in Staffordshire. Most of the slipware found in and around London and loosely termed 'Metropolitan' is now known to have been made at Harlow in Essex.

Slipware of a very characteristic kind was made in Devonshire, at potteries at Bideford, Fremington and Barnstaple (from about 1600), and inlaid slip decoration was used at Rye and Chailey in Sussex in the late eighteenth and early nineteenth century. Other centres where slipware was made include Gestingthorpe and Castle Hedingham in

Tyg. The red body is decorated with moulded applied ornaments made of white clay, as well as trailed and dotted slip. Made at Wrotham and dated 1695. 178mm high. *Fitzwilliam Museum, Cambridge.*

Large circular dish decorated with a pattern of inn signs. The white slip has been cut away to make the design, exposing the light red of the clay body beneath. Glazed with a yellowish lead glaze, slightly mottled with green. Made by John Livermore at the Wrotham pottery in 1647. 442mm diameter. *Fitzwilliam Museum, Cambridge.*

Slip-decorated dish. The design shows a mermaid with a large comb and looking-glass. Made by Ralph Toft in Staffordshire. *c.* 1670. 438mm diameter. *Fitzwilliam Museum, Cambridge.*

Essex (in the nineteenth century); Tickenhall in Derbyshire and Bolsover near Chesterfield; in Buckinghamshire, Cambridgeshire, and at Fareham and Fordingbridge in Hampshire; High Halden in Kent; in Nottingham; in Somerset at Donyatt and Pill near Bristol; Polesworth in Warwickshire and in Wiltshire near Salisbury; in Yorkshire at Midhope, Burton-in-Lonsdale and Halifax as well as near Wakefield. Also at Bridgend and Ewenny in Glamorganshire.

The known history of the pottery at Wrotham dates from the beginning of the seventeenth century, the earliest dated piece known to have come from here being dated 1612. Production continued well into the eighteenth century. John Livermore, who died in 1658 (and who made the dish illustrated on page 26) was working here and also Henry Ifield (who died in 1673) and George Richardson (who died 1687) and who was known to have marked the ware with the word 'Wrotham'. A characteristic of the decoration from this pottery was the use of 'sprigged' designs. That is, the application of a design stamped out in a different coloured clay from separate small moulds. Most of the known pieces from Wrotham are tygs and jugs.

Without doubt the most spectacular pieces of slipware were made in Staffordshire during the last thirty years of the seventeenth century and the first decade of the eighteenth. These were large circular dishes or chargers some 460mm to 560mm in diameter and made by Thomas Toft and his son of the same name, Ralph Toft, and James Toft (the brother of Thomas the younger); John and William Wright, George Taylor, William Talor (*sic*) and Ralph Simpson and maybe by other potters as well. Most of these large dishes were decorated in a similar manner with a trellis border with a name or inscription, and an elaborately drawn design of trailed and dotted slip, on a coating of white slip in black, brown, orange or white. The whole under a yellow lead glaze.

The illustrated subjects include the Royal Arms with the lion and unicorn, King Charles II hiding in an oak, or accompanied by his wife Catherine of Braganza, or Bishop Juxon; William III, George I and cavaliers and heraldic designs. Apart from these large and handsome dishes, which were obviously made more for decoration than use, many other slip-decorated pieces were made in Staffordshire including tygs and teapots, cradles and baking-dishes.

To see slipware at its best, one should visit the City Art Gallery and Museum at Stoke-on-Trent. In the superb ceramic department there is a fine display of slipware, brilliantly lit.

The so-called 'Metropolitan' slipware has always been something of a puzzle, because although quantities of tygs and other pieces had been found in London, no kiln site with sherds and wasters has ever come to light. This Metropolitan ware was made of a light brown clay which

Two-handled posset pot of buff coloured clay with feathered slip decoration in dark red. Round the top is the name Thomas Heath and the date 1698. Covered with a yellow lead glaze. Made in Staffordshire. 121mm high. *Fitzwilliam Museum, Cambridge.*

27

A trailed slip-decorated jug of the 'Metropolitan' type. It bears the pious inscription 'FAST AND PRAY AND PRAY / AND PITTY THE POOR AMEND THY / LIFE AND SENNE NO MOR 1656. 279mm high. *Museum of London.*

fired to quite a bright red, or to a darker brownish red. Unlike much of the Staffordshire slipware, the ware was not first coated with white slip, but the pattern was trailed directly on to the body of the piece. The patterns were not very imaginative, consisting of rather crudely drawn zigzags or herringbone designs and many are inscribed with pious mottos or exhortations.

Some years ago, when the site was being cleared for the building of the new town at Harlow in Essex, about twenty-six miles from London, five kiln sites were discovered with literally tons of sherds, many of them with religious inscriptions and with similar designs to those on the Metropolitan ware. These kilns were discovered in the neighbourhood of Potter Street (which had been called Potter Street since the early fifteenth century).

Early in the seventeenth century a new road was built from London to Newmarket, by way of Harlow and Epping and this must have provided a very convenient way of transport for the products of the potteries that were established in this area, and which flourished throughout the seventeenth century. The shortage of specimens with dates before 1666 is no doubt due to the wholesale destruction of the Great Fire in that year.

The chief productions of these potteries were flat plates from about 150mm to 380mm in diameter and rather crude tygs and jugs. They do not compare favourably either in technique or in originality of design with the work of the Staffordshire potters.

The *sgraffito* type of decoration was largely practised at the Devon potteries of Bideford, Fremington and Barnstaple, which date from the beginning of the seventeenth century. Here many large and elaborate 'Harvest' jugs were made, as well as dishes and posset pots (see pages 274 and 276). The jugs often bear a date and sometimes a poem or an inscription. The designs included ships in full sail, the royal arms and bold floral patterns. From Devon, much of this pottery was exported to America, the ships returning with cargoes of tobacco; this slipware trade lasted until the middle of the eighteenth century, when the Dutch put the Devon exporters out of business, by exporting large quantities of their Delft ware to America.

For further reading

L.M. Solon. *The Art of the Old English Potter.* New York 1886. Reprinted by E.P. Publishing Ltd 1976.
Reginald G. Haggar. *English Country Pottery.* Phoenix House, London 1950.
Ronald G. Cooper. *The Pottery of Thomas Toft.* Leeds City Art Gallery 1952.
Ronald G. Cooper. *English Slipware Dishes.* Tiranti 1968.

Plate 3. Slip-decorated dish with the royal coat of arms.
Made by Thomas Toft in Staffordshire. *c.* 1660. 534mm
diameter. *City Museum and Art Gallery, Stoke-on-Trent.*

So far thirty-five dishes have been found with Thomas
Toft's name on them. Of these seven are decorated with the
royal coat of arms, ranging from 508mm to 559mm in
diameter. All but one of these have trellis borders. These
dishes were probably made at the time of Charles II's
Restoration.

Toft's decoration was in coloured slips, trailed over a dish
already covered in a layer of white slip. His signature varied
from dish to dish, sometimes in simple capital letters with
heavy serifs, at other times in an arbitrary mixture of upper
and lower case letters as on this dish, where the Christian
name is in lower case letters and surname has the letters T, F
and T in capitals with a solitary lower case o.

Slip-decorated dish showing Charles II hiding in the Boscobel Oak. Made by William Talor (*sic*) in Staffordshire. *c.* 1660. 445mm diameter. *Fitzwilliam Museum, Cambridge.*

Slip-decorated dish. The Pelican in her Piety, made by Ralph Simpson in Staffordshire. *c.* 1714. (The border of roundels and faces is very similar to a George I dish.) 432mm diameter. *Crown copyright Victoria and Albert Museum.*

Slip-decorated dish with a portrait of William III. Made by
Ralph Simpson in Staffordshire. *c.* 1689. 458mm diameter.
Crown copyright Victoria and Albert Museum.

Plate 4. Slipware harvest jug of red earthenware decorated with white slip. This unique specimen has baffled the authorities who put it down to either Staffordshire or Wrotham, but it is not typical of either locality. Inscribed with the initials IB. Late 17th century. 406mm high. *City Museum and Art Gallery, Stoke-on-Trent.*

Slip-decorated cradle. These were often dated and were made for presentation pieces to newly married couples. Dates are recorded from 1693-1839. Made in Staffordshire. *c.* 1700. 254mm long. *Crown copyright Victoria and Albert Museum.*

Tyg of buff coloured earthenware with brown slip dotted with white and bands of combed slip. Made in Staffordshire 1701. 108mm high. *Crown copyright Victoria and Albert Museum.*

Tyg decorated with trailed slip and bands of feathering. Made in Staffordshire. *c.* 1700. 105mm high. *Crown copyright Victoria and Albert Museum.*

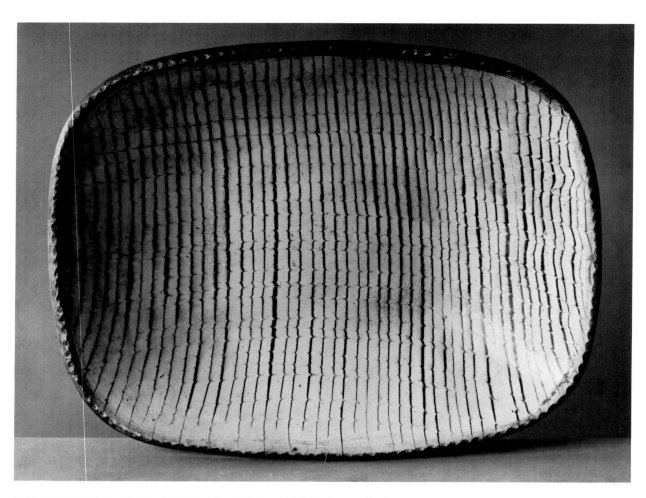

Shallow baking dish with a notched edge, decorated with lines of dark brown slip over a coating of white slip. The lines have then been combed with a sharp point in lines from left to right and vice versa, dragging the brown slip slightly each way. 521mm high. *Crown copyright Victoria and Albert Museum.*

Teapot of buff coloured earthenware with slip-decoration in dark and light reds and white. Made in Staffordshire in the early eighteenth century. 216mm high. *Fitzwilliam Museum, Cambridge.*

Circular earthenware dish with notched edge, decorated with marbled or 'joggled' slip. Made in Staffordshire in the late seventeenth or early eighteenth century. 349 diameter. *Crown copyright Victoria and Albert Museum.*

Slip-decorated owl dish. Made in Staffordshire. *c.* 1720. 425mm diameter. There is a similar dish in existence decorated with a hen and chickens. *City Museum and Art Gallery, Stoke-on-Trent.*

Circular earthenware bowl, with white slip on a red body, *sgraffito* decoration. Made in Staffordshire 1755. 248mm diameter. *Crown copyright Victoria and Albert Museum.*

Circular earthenware dish. The body is an agate ware of red and buff clay coated with white slip, the design cut through it (*sgraffito*), under a straw coloured lead glaze. Made in Staffordshire in the mid-eighteenth century. 324mm diameter. *Fitzwilliam Museum, Cambridge.*

Harvest jug decorated with beautifully balanced *sgraffito* decoration. Just below the neck is the following inscription: 'lo i into your house am sent as a token from a frind (*sic*) when your harvest folks are dry then I will then them attend'. Made in Barnstaple and dated 1708. Height 330mm. *Reproduced by courtesy of the Trustees of the British Museum.*

36

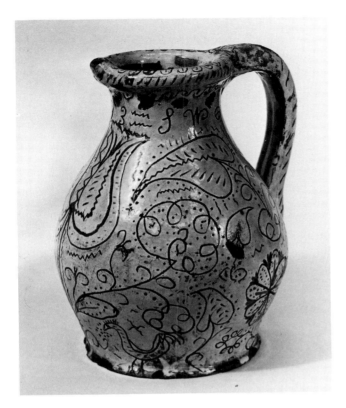

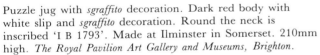

Puzzle jug with *sgraffito* decoration. Dark red body with white slip and *sgraffito* decoration. Round the neck is inscribed 'I B 1793'. Made at Ilminster in Somerset. 210mm high. *The Royal Pavilion Art Gallery and Museums, Brighton.*

Harvest pitcher with *sgraffito* decoration. The royal motto reads 'Hone soet que mal y pense.' The other side is the inscription
   'Harvis is com all bissey
   Now mackin of your
   Barley mow when men do
   Laber hard and swet good
   Ale is better for their meet
   Bideford April 28 1775 M + W'.
Round the base are the words 'Deu et mon drots 1775'. 343mm high. *Royal Albert Memorial Museum, Exeter.*

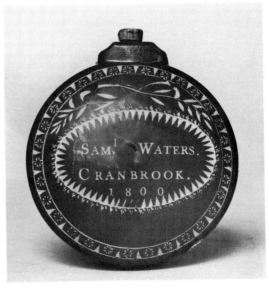

Spirit flask. Made of red clay with incised and impressed decoration partly made up of printers' flowers, inlaid with a white clay and glazed with a yellow lead glaze. On the obverse, within a border is the verse:
   'Wine cheers the heart
   and warms the blood
   and at this season's migh
   ty good.'
Beneath are crossed branches and along the edge the words 'SOUTH CHAILEY POTTREY'. 124mm high. Made in Sussex, 1800. *Fitzwilliam Museum, Cambridge.*

3. Delft ware

We shall now have to go back a little in time to the last decades of the sixteenth century, to see quite another type of English pottery. This was of foreign origin and had nothing to do with our traditional lead-glazed slip-decorated earthenwares.

Tin-enamelled earthenware or delft, as it is usually called, is an earthenware covered with an opaque whitish glaze made from oxide of tin. It was made in Syria, Asia Minor and Egypt as early as the sixth century AD. It was first made in Europe by the Moors in Spain, then by the Italians. This technique finally arrived in England by way of the Netherlands in the middle of the sixteenth century. The main centres of production in this country were London, Bristol and Liverpool, though it was also made in Ireland and Scotland.

Though the Dutch learned their tin-glazing technique from the Italians, their actual manner of decoration was much more frequently derived from oriental porcelain, which was then being imported by the Dutch East India Company, than from the decorations on Italian maiolica. Chinese porcelain was being imported into England by the mid-seventeenth century, but it was extremely expensive and only within reach of the wealthy. The delft ware of the English potters of this period was an attempt to provide the middle classes, who could not afford Chinese porcelain, with the best imitation they were able to make. However, delft ware was often thick, clumsy and easily chipped and it was always completely opaque. It certainly bore a superficial resemblance to Chinese porcelain. The English manufacturers of delft ware never perhaps achieved the high degree of artistic perfection reached by the Dutch, but they added something to the foreign designs which prevented them from being mere slavish copies.

There seems little doubt that London was the first place in England where delft ware was made. The earliest pieces that have been found were jugs with mottled brown or blue glaze and similar in shape to the German stoneware that was being imported into this country at that time. These early jugs are sometimes mounted in silver, which was hallmarked, so the pieces can easily be dated, some as early as 1570. One such jug (1581-2) came from the church at West Malling in Kent and two others have been found in that neighbourhood. No traces of a kiln however, have been found, and in all probability the 'Malling' jugs (as they have come to be called) were made in London.

In 1571, two Flemish potters called Jacob Janson and Jasper Andries sent a petition to Queen Elizabeth, asking for permission to settle by the banks of the Thames. They are said to have produced delft ware at a pottery near Aldgate, where they probably produced apothecaries' jars among other things, though the earliest recorded date on one of these is 1628.

Jug of the Malling type, covered in a rich speckled blue tin glaze. Probably made in London during the last quarter of the sixteenth century. 152mm high. *Museum of London.*

Puzzle jug, painted in blue on a white ground. Inscribed with initials and date. It was the custom to put the initial of the surname first, followed by the Christian name initials of the couple to whom the piece was inscribed. Made in Lambeth 1653. 168mm high. *Fitzwilliam Museum, Cambridge.*

Wine jug, painted in blue, orange and yellow. Made in Lambeth 1660. 178mm high. *Fitzwilliam Museum, Cambridge.*

Mug painted in blue on a white ground. Round the neck are the names JOHN POTTEN & SUSANNA 1633. Made in Lambeth. 136mm high. *Fitzwilliam Museum, Cambridge.*

A delft ware pottery was started in Southwark about 1625 and from there some craftsmen travelled to the west country and settled outside Bristol, where the Brislington pottery was founded about 1650. Other potteries making tin-glazed earthenware soon grew up in the same neighbourhood. And in London, the Lambeth pottery must have been working by the 1630's. This factory became the largest centre for the production of delft ware and continued working until the end of the eighteenth century. Typical Lambeth productions were wine bottles, pill slabs and drug jars, plates and large shallow bowls or chargers decorated with blue brush marks round the rim, and designs of formalized fruit and flowers, also scenes of the Fall and portraits of sovereigns. Arms of Liveried Companies are found on wine cups and dishes. Many other objects were made including fuddling cups, puzzle jugs, mugs, candlesticks, barber surgeons' dishes, bleeding bowls, posset pots and vases and even ornaments and tiles. The choice of decoration was very varied and often the only colour to be used was blue, derived from cobalt. Sometimes this would be combined with a decoration in white on a very pale bluish or greyish ground, a particularly attractive technique known as 'white on white' or *'bianco sopra bianco'* as it was of Italian origin. This type of decoration was used from about the middle of the eighteenth century at Lambeth and also at Bristol. The Lambeth delft glaze often has a warm pinky tinge.

Large dish, moulded in relief copied from an original by Bernard Palissy, who took the subject from a painting by Titian called *La Fécondité*. Painted in blue, green, yellow and manganese purple. Made in Lambeth about 1665. 470mm wide. *Castle Museum, Nottingham.*

Sauce-boat in the form of a recumbent figure of Pomona in a bath. Painted in blue, orange and manganese purple. Copied from a design by Palissy. *c.* 1650. Made in Lambeth. 203mm wide. *Fitzwilliam Museum, Cambridge.*

At Bristol, from about 1650 chargers and plates were made similar to those made at Lambeth. It is difficult to say exactly which pottery produced each piece. Sometimes the comparison of a piece with fragments found on the site will help in identification. The later delft designs were often painted with several colours. Green, brick red, brown, yellow and purple were used to produce rich and varied effects.

English delft drug jars are a study in themselves. Most of them were made at Lambeth though some were made at Liverpool; some of them bear the initials of the druggist or apothecary for whom they were made as well as the date (but dated specimens are rarer in the eighteenth century). They were of several basic shapes; for dry or powdered drugs, the jars were usually cylindrical, tapering slightly towards the base. Jars for syrups and solutions were either much the same sort of shape, only with a spout at the front and a handle at the back, or the body was rounder and the foot more splayed. The eighteenth century syrup pots became more spherical and were mounted on a gracefully splayed base. The spout was placed at the back, so that it did not interfere with the painted label or cartouche with the name of the drug on the front of the pot. The tops of the jars were slightly out-turned to allow for a covering piece of parchment to be tied over the top. The eighteenth century syrup pots were held by the narrow part above the splayed foot which made a handle superfluous. Most of the jars were painted in blue only, polychrome examples being rare.

Not very many drug jars in London survived the Great Fire of 1666, for most of them bear dates later than this. The earliest designs show Italian influence with a grotesque head at each side of the ribbon or label upon which the name of the drug is written. By the 1660's the label appears surmounted by the head and outspread wings of an angel, and this type of decoration remains a common feature until the end of the seventeenth century. It is amusing to note that the coiffure of the angel changed with the fashion in hair styles, the earliest being a thin-haired puritan character. One even resembles Oliver Cromwell, even though it is dated six years after the Restoration. The later angels are drawn wearing more and more luxuriant hair until in 1697 the angel wears a full bottomed William III wig.

In about 1672 designs appeared with birds and flowers and later still a cherub or a pair of cherubs make their appearance. Apollo the Healer is depicted on some of the jars dating from the middle of the seventeenth century, and some of the most important jars are painted with the arms of the Apothecaries' Company, sometimes with polychrome decoration.

Some of the drugs named on the jars sound most extraordinary. For example *O. Vulpin* or oil of foxes, which was an embrocation made

Unguent pot, decorated in blue and manganese purple. Made in Lambeth in the latter part of the seventeenth century. 114mm high. *Museum of London.*

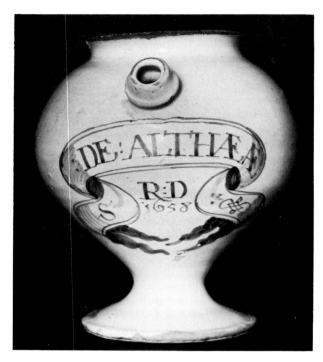

Wet drug jar or syrup pot: *S. de Althaeae*: syrup of marshmallow. Made from an emollient herb with soothing properties. The jar is painted in blue on a white ground. This plain ribbon design was used at the time of the Commonwealth. Made in Lambeth 1658. 191mm high. *Courtesy Pharmaceutical Society, London.*

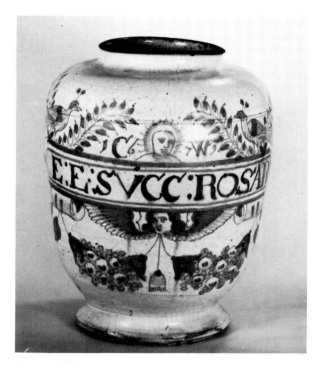

Drug jar: *Electuarium e succo rosarium*, a sweet syrup of roses. Quincy in 1724 scornfully dismisses it as being not particularly beneficial for anything, but adds that it is hardly ever prescribed. A complicated design painted in blue incorporating Apollo the Healer, an angel and peacocks. Dated 1679. 206mm high. *Lothian Collection.*

Drug jar: *V. Opthalnos*: an ointment for the eyes made from calamine, lead oxide and other ingredients. Painted in blue on a white ground, an example of the bird and basket design used in the early eighteenth century. Made in Lambeth. Early eighteenth century. *Courtesy Pharmaceutical Society, London.*

Wet drug jar: *O. Vulpin*: oil of foxes; made by boiling a fox's carcase with various herbs in wine. 'Exceeding good for pains in the joynts' according to Culpeper. The jar is painted in blue on a white ground with an angel design, much used in the late seventeenth century. Made in Lambeth 1684. 191mm. *Collection: Dr. John F. Wilkinson.*

Apothecaries' pill-slab, decorated in blue. Pierced for hanging. Made in Lambeth 1663. 267mm high. *Courtesy Pharmaceutical Society, London.*

Pill-slab painted in blue with the arms of the Apothecaries' company, with the lettering in manganese. A cedar of Lebanon surmounts the arms. Pierced for hanging. Made in Lambeth. *c.* 1700. 298mm high. *Courtesy Pharmaceutical Society, London.*

Wine cup painted in blue, orange and manganese purple with a portrait of King Charles II. Inscribed CR and IK 1677. Made in Lambeth. 86mm high. *Fitzwilliam Museum, Cambridge.*

from the fat of middle aged foxes, and said to be very beneficial for chest complaints.

The drug jars were made in various sizes to hold the apothecaries' stock-in-trade. Some very small delft pots were made to hold such preparations as Singleton's *Golden Eye Ointment* or Jacob Hemet's *Essence of Pearl* dentifrice (this was used by George II). These little pots were inscribed in blue in a cursive hand, and were obviously made in large quantities and supplied to the makers in which to package their medicaments. The delft pill slabs were made in various shapes, some like hearts or shields, others were octagonal or oblong. Often they were decorated with the arms of the Apothecaries' Company, but rarely are they dated. They are always pierced with two little holes at the top, so that they could be hung up. As few of these show signs of having been used, it seems likely that they were made for decoration in a window or shop, or perhaps to show the customers that the apothecary was a genuine member of the Apothecaries' Company. The seventeenth century wine bottles or decanters were often dated and marked with the name of the wine: Claret, Sack, Whit (*sic*) or occasionally Rhenish. They were probably made for the better class taverns or for wine merchants to use as decanters when their customers were tasting wine. It seems unlikely that the wine was actually bottled in them though the neck was grooved or ringed to enable a parchment cover to be tied over the top. Wine cups were also made, often decorated with the arms of liveried companies, a portrait of the king or even a bawdy joke.

Delft ware does not seem to have been made at Liverpool before the

Syrup pot: *S.e Mecon*, syrup of poppies, a cough syrup containing opium. This shape of pot could be conveniently grasped by the narrow waist, which did away with the necessity for a handle. The cherub design is painted in blue. *c.* 1750. Made in Lambeth. 191mm high. *Courtesy Pharmaceutical Society, London.*

eighteenth century, at least the first known dated piece is a large plaque inscribed 'A West Prospect of Great Crosby 1716'. But the first mention of pottery at Liverpool occurs in a list of town dues payable at the port in 1674, which contains the following item:

'For every cartload of mugs (shipped) into foreign ports 6d; for every cartload of mugs along the coast 4d; for every crate of cupps or pipes along the coast 1d.'

In the *Transactions of the Historical Society of Lancashire and Cheshire*, 3 May 1855, there is an interesting account by Dr. Joseph Mayer of a potter, Zachariah Barnes, making delft ware at Liverpool in the latter half of the eighteenth century, when its use had been superseded in most of the country by salt-glazed stoneware and later by cream-coloured earthenware. Dr. Mayer wrote: 'Amongst other articles were very large round dishes, chiefly sent into Wales, where the simple habits of their forefathers remained unchanged long after their alteration in England; and the master of the house and his guests dipped their spoons into the mess and helped themselves from the dish placed in the middle of the table. Quantities of this ware were sent to the great border fairs, held at Chester, whither the inhabitants of the more remote and inaccessible parts of the mountain districts of Wales assembled, to buy their stores for the year. This continued until a very recent time...'

Delft ware was made for a short time at Wincanton in Somerset from 1736 and also in the eighteenth century, in Glasgow, Dublin and Limerick.

For further reading

W.J. Pountney. *Old Bristol Potteries*. Arrowsmith, Bristol 1920. Reprint 1972.

G.E. Howard. *Early English Drug Jars*. Medici, London 1931.

Anthony Ray. *English Delftware Pottery in the Robert Hall Warren Collection Ashmolean Museum, Oxford*. Faber 1968.

F.H. Garner and Michael Archer. *English Delftware*. Faber 1948. Revised edition 1972.

Louis Lipski, Ed. and Augmented by Michael Archer. *Dated English Delftware Tin glazed Earthenware 1600-1800*. Sotheby Publications. 1984.

Plate 5. Circular charger lettered K W and decorated with an equestrian portrait of William of Orange. Chargers of this type were made as a reflection of popular support after his accession. *c.* 1690. 340mm diameter. *Private Collection.*

Barber-surgeons' dish painted in blue with a design that incorporates the tools of both the barbers' and the surgeons' trade. Made in Lambeth. *c.* 1690. 263mm diameter.
Castle Museum, Nottingham.

Circular dish with blue dash border and decoration in blue, olive green, yellow and black. The back of the dish is covered with a transparent greenish glaze. Early eighteenth century. Probably made in Lambeth. 343mm diameter. *Fitzwilliam Museum, Cambridge.*

Circular dish painted in blue and brownish orange. The back of the dish is glazed only with a transparent lead glaze. This was often the case. Made in Lambeth. *c.* 1650. 397mm diameter. *Fitzwilliam Museum, Cambridge.*

Plate 6. Circular dish with tulip decoration, probably made
in Bristol during the first half of the 18th century. 381mm.
Courtesy Earle D. Vandekar. Photograph: Michael Spence.

Circular dish with polychrome decoration in the Italian style. The dashing horseman is probably intended to be Charles II when Prince of Wales. Made in Lambeth *c.* 1645. 324mm diameter. *Fitzwilliam Museum, Cambridge.*

Circular dish painted with a portrait of James II (1685-88) painted in blue on a light greeny blue ground. There are other chargers almost identical to this one (even to the position of the eyes) marked Charles II. They were made in Lambeth between 1660 and 1700. 336mm diameter. *Crown copyright, Victoria and Albert Museum.*

Circular dish with a portrait of Mary II, wife of William III (elder daughter of James II), painted in blue, yellow and manganese purple. Late 17th century. Attributed to Brislington, near Bristol. 336mm diameter. *Crown copyright Victoria and Albert Museum.*

Circular plate with portraits of King William III and Mary II painted in blue and orange. Made in Lambeth. *c.* 1690. 200mm diameter. *Crown copyright Victoria and Albert Museum.*

Plate with a pottery kiln painted on it in blue in the Chinese style. Made in Lambeth in the mid-eighteenth century. 222mm diameter. *Private Collection*.

Plate painted in blue with a formalized spray of flowers within a border. The rather deep plate has no foot rim. Made in Bristol. *c.* 1725-50. 220mm diameter. *Private Collection*.

Plate painted in blue with a very simple pseudo-Oriental landscape. The plate has no foot rim. Probably made in Bristol. *c.* 1725-50. 222mm diameter. *Private Collection*.

Plate painted in blue with a crane or heron in a stylized landscape within a border of simplified floral forms. The shallow plate has no foot rim. Made in either London or Bristol. *c.* 1725-50. 225mm diameter. *Private Collection*.

Punch bowl with the inscription inside 'One bowl more and then'. Painted outside in blue, yellow and purple. Made in Lambeth. *c.* 1760. 267mm diameter. Flower brick, painted in purple, blue, yellow and green. Made in Liverpool. *c.* 1760.

79mm high. Plate painted in blue and manganese purple. Made in Bristol. *c.* 1760. 235mm diameter. *Crown copyright, Victoria and Albert Museum.*

Teapot with attached lid. It would have been filled through a hole in the bottom on the inkwell principle, in the manner of the Cadogan teapots. Probably made at Joseph Flower's pottery at Bristol. *c.* 1750. 143mm high. *Fitzwilliam Museum, Cambridge.*

Mug probably painted by John Bowen at Flower's pottery, Bristol. Blue painting with a red line round the rim, below which is the inscription 'Mary Turner Aged 2 Years 14 Days Sepr 2 1752'. 95mm high. *Fitzwilliam Museum, Cambridge.*

Tile painted in blue with details in green and red. Made in Bristol during the first half of the eighteenth century. 127mm square. *Fitzwilliam Museum, Cambridge.*

Tile of a pale lavender colour painted with blue and opaque white (*bianco sopra bianco*). Made by Joseph Flower in Bristol. *c.* 1760. 127mm square. *Fitzwilliam Museum, Cambridge.*

Polychrome delft tiles with hand-painted decoration in blue, red and green. Made in Bristol in the early 18th century.

Each tile 124mm square. *Crown copyright, Victoria and Albert Museum.*

Punch bowl, painted in blue on a white ground. Probably made in Bristol. *c.* 1715. 267mm diameter. *Fitzwilliam Museum, Cambridge.*

Punch bowl painted in blue, yellow, brownish red, manganese purple and green. Made in Liverpool about 1760. 355mm diameter. *Fitzwilliam Museum, Cambridge.*

Stoneware bust of Prince Rupert by John Dwight of Fulham, made about 1672-80. 610mm high. *Reproduced by courtesy of the Trustees of the British Museum.*

Below left: Jug decorated with marbling and stamped ornaments. Made at the Fulham potteries about 1680. 191mm high. *Crown copyright Victoria and Albert Museum.*

Below: Bellarmine jug of salt-glazed stoneware from Dwight's factory at Fulham. *c.* 1675. 216mm high. *Crown copyright Victoria and Albert Museum.*

4. Stoneware 1672-1900

Light coloured stoneware bust by John Dwight, said to be of Elizabeth, wife of Samuel Pepys. As she had died in 1669, it seems unlikely he could have modelled it from life. Possibly Pepys commissioned Dwight to make it after her death. Late seventeenth century. 175mm high.
Reproduced by courtesy of the Trustees of the British Museum.

Drab coloured stoneware jug, the upper part mottled brown. Made at Fulham in the late seventeenth century. 98mm high.
Fitzwilliam Museum, Cambridge.

Stoneware is made from clay to which a certain amount of sand has been added. It is fired at a somewhat higher temperature than ordinary earthenware, so that it becomes partly vitrified and impervious to liquids. It was sometimes glazed with common salt, which was thrown into the kiln when it was at full heat. The salt volatilized and reacted on the water vapour in the kiln to form a coating of silicate of soda, which gave the ware its characteristic orange peel texture. It was first made in the Middle Ages in Germany on the Lower Rhine and quantities of this ware were imported into England in the sixteenth and seventeenth centuries.

BROWN AND DRAB SALT-GLAZED STONEWARE MADE AT FULHAM BY JOHN DWIGHT

Stoneware was made in this country as early as 1672, when John Dwight MA Oxon. at one time secretary to the Bishop of Chester, founded the Fulham Pottery. In the previous year Dwight had obtained a warrant from Charles II for making 'Transparent earthenware or china and stoneware vulgarly called Cologne ware'.

At Fulham Dwight made copies of the German tavern wine bottles then being imported into this country. Recent excavations on the site show that only a limited number of these were embellished with a bearded mask on the front of the neck and these varied very much in their quality and design. These bottles were commonly known as Greybeards or Bellarmines, after Cardinal Bellarmine, whose most controversial writings had so upset the Reformed Church in the Netherlands. Ten different versions have so far been found.

Most of John Dwight's bottles and globular jugs or 'gorges' were decorated with medallions embossed with emblems or names of taverns or their landlords. Well over a hundred different designs have now been excavated. These include heraldic devices, royal cyphers, allegorical, fanciful and naturalistic animals.

Interesting fragments have also come to light of small vessels made of buff, white and blue material which appear closely to resemble porcelain, probably the ware that Dwight referred to in his notebooks.

Some quite remarkable portrait busts in a hard, drab grey stoneware came from the Dwight pottery. Among these were portraits of King Charles II, Prince Rupert and a charming lady said to be Mrs. Pepys, (though that lady had actually died in 1669) and Dwight's infant daughter lying upon her death bed. Her tiny hand was also cast in stoneware.

In addition to the common ware for use in inns and taverns he made mugs, jugs and other vessels in clays which had been mingled together to resemble agate; and he also made red ware teapots in imitation of the Chinese Yi-Hsing[1] ware that was then being imported into this country in the chests of tea.

In 1693 Dwight put in hand lawsuits against a number of potters for infringing his patent. Among them were three members of the Wedgwood family of Burslem, the brothers Elers of Bradwell and James Morley of Nottingham. The results of the litigation remain obscure but it proves that brown stoneware was being made in Staffordshire and that there was a connection between Dwight and the Elers. Dwight died in 1703, but the pottery at Fulham was carried on by his family.

For further reading

Journal of Ceramic History No 11, John Dwight's Fulham Pottery 1672-1978. (A collection of documentary sources ed. D. Haselgrove and John Murray.) Pub. Stoke-on-Trent Museum 1979.

HARD UNGLAZED RED STONEWARE OF THE ELERS TYPE

The brothers John Philip and David Elers came over to England at about the same time as William of Orange in 1688. Although they were said to be of aristocratic birth, they had learned a good deal about the craft of pottery-making both in Delft and Cologne. However, they must have been very versatile craftsmen for on arrival in England they at first practised as silversmiths. Possibly inspired by the obviously increasing need for teapots, cups and saucers (resulting from the ever growing habit of tea drinking) they decided to set up a pottery to make 'fine red porcelain'. On Dwight's advice they went to Staffordshire and started a pottery in Bradwell Wood, where there was a deposit of red clay. In this project they had the assistance of John Chandler, one of Dwight's former workmen, who had defected to them.

The Elers red ware was not porcelain at all, but a very fine stoneware, with a dense, red, semi-vitrified body. The fine quality was achieved by intensely careful preparation of the clay, and the hardness by the high temperature at which it was fired. The pieces were cast and then turned upon a lathe[2]. Any decoration was applied as a dab of clay which was then pressed with a metal die, made in the form of a leaf or flower, any surplus clay was then very carefully cleared away. Spouts and handles were usually modelled by hand. The Elers must have taken infinite care at every stage of production for the ware was always beautifully finished. They did not actually mark their ware with their names, but many of their pieces bear pseudo-Chinese stamps on

Teapot made of the Elers' type of red stoneware with relief decorations of prunus blossom. Made in Staffordshire in the late seventeenth century. 114mm high. *Crown copyright Victoria and Albert Museum.*

---

1. The red stoneware Yi-Hsing teapots were made in Kiangsu Province in the 16th and 17th centuries. They were decorated with both moulded and applied designs and were seldom glazed.
2. G.W. Elliott on Elers Ware. *Trans. English Ceramic Circle* Vol. 10. Pt. 2 1977.

Pear-shaped coffee pot in the hard red unglazed stoneware of the Elers' type, decorated with sprigged patterns in the Elers' manner. The number 45 appears on the shield. Made in Staffordshire. Mid-eighteenth century. 216mm high. *Fitzwilliam Museum, Cambridge.*

Pear-shaped coffee pot in unglazed red stoneware with engine-turned decoration and a simulated Chinese impressed mark on the base. *c.* 1765. 229mm high. *City Museum and Art Gallery, Stoke-on-Trent.*

Red stoneware teapot with engine turned decoration and marked on the base with an imitation Chinese seal mark (after the manner of the Elers). *c.* 1765. 137mm high. *Crown copyright Victoria and Albert Museum.*

the base. It was certainly not cheap, their red teapots sold for 10s to 25s each in London (no mean sum in those days), where David Elers opened up a warehouse in the Poultry.

The Elers left Staffordshire in 1698/9, by which time they had introduced not only the fine red stoneware but, according to Simeon Shaw, a black ware similar to the later black basalt ware of Josiah Wedgwood. They had also introduced many technical improvements, such as the use of the lathe, metal stamps, alabaster moulds and the refining of clays. They always worked under conditions of great secrecy employing only workmen who appeared to be dull witted. However, two young Staffordshire potters, John Astbury and Josiah Twyford – so the story goes – worked for two years for the Elers, pretending all the time to be half-wits, while absorbing all the Elers' knowledge and skill.

For further reading

Josiah Wedgwood. *Staffordshire Pottery and its History*. Sampson Low, Marston and Co. London 1913.

R. Edwards. 'London Potters circa 1570-1710'. *Journal of Ceramic History.* No.6. 1974.

T.A. Lockett and P.A. Halfpenny (Ed.). *Stonewares and Stone chinas of Northern England to 1851*. City Museum and Art Gallery, Stoke-on-Trent. 1982.

Stephen C. Corn. 'The Elers Enigma'. *Antique Collecting* 1985.

Posset pot of a light yellowish-brown stoneware. The lower part has a pierced out casing. The upper part bears on one side the royal arms in moulded relief and on the other side, divided by the spout, the legend:

Samuel Watkinson   Mayor   of Nottingham
Sarah Watkinson   Mayoress
                      1700
This is the earliest dated piece of Nottingham stoneware. 267mm high. *Castle Museum, Nottingham.*

BROWN SALT-GLAZED STONEWARE FROM NOTTINGHAM

A fine brown salt-glazed stoneware was being made in Nottingham throughout the eighteenth century. The earliest known dated piece is 1700 and the latest is 1799. This salt-glazed ware was covered with a wash of ferruginous clay, which burnt to an iridescent brown sheen. It was made by the Morleys of Mughouse Lane – the same James Morley against whom Dwight took proceedings in 1693, and whose trade card appears opposite.

Nottingham ware was carefully thrown and then turned on the lathe. Any decorations such as scrolls or leaves or inscriptions were scratched on to the unfired clay with a sharp point. The incised decorations were freely drawn floral forms combined with horizontal and vertical bands and herring-bone decoration. Rouletting was also employed where the design was rolled on with a small wheel. The double walled pieces, the outer wall pierced for decoration, were particularly attractive. The handles were usually made by hand. Typical pieces were loving-cups, puzzle-jugs, mugs and punch bowls. Curious jugs in the shape of a bear were also made, the surface of these was covered in shavings of clay to simulate fur. Bear baiting was a popular if revolting sport in the eighteenth century. Later in the early nineteenth century, bear jugs were made with a political significance, the Russian bear hugging Napoleon to his chest.

Few pieces are marked with makers' names, though there were at least ten different potters working in the eighteenth century in the Nottingham area. The ware is always one colour and can vary from light to a dark and even purplish brown, sometimes with a metallic sheen. It is never top-dipped in a darker glaze as was the custom with some of the London potteries. By the end of the eighteenth century the trade was declining, mainly because of competition from the Derbyshire and Staffordshire potteries.

Jug (or perhaps a tobacco jar) in the form of a bear. The surface is covered in small shavings of clay. Made in Nottingham in the eighteenth century. 260mm high. *Castle Museum, Nottingham.*

James Morley's trade card. Engraved about 1690. This was the James Morley against whom John Dwight had taken proceedings in 1693, for infringing his patent. *Bodleian Library, Oxford.*

A Decantor

A Carved Teapot

A Capuchine

A Flower-Pot

A Mogg

A Carved Jug

Such as have Occation for these Sorts of Pots commonly called Stone-Ware, or for such as are of any other Shape not here Represented may be furnished w.ᵗʰ them by the Maker James Morley at y̆ Pot-House i Nottingham

Similar brown salt-glazed stoneware was also made at Chesterfield and Brampton, though the Nottingham ware was superior in quality to any of its rivals. The quality remained of an extraordinarily high standard throughout the entire period of its production.

For further reading

Hugh Turner 'Brown Saltglazed Stoneware of the 19th Century. *Antique Collecting*, March 1980.

Adrian Oswald, R.J.C. Hildyard and R.G. Hughes *English Brown Stoneware 1670-1900*. Faber. 1982.

Left: Mug made of dark brown salt-glazed stoneware incised 'Joseph Boot 1748'. Made in Nottingham. 121mm high. *Castle Museum, Nottingham.*

Right: Mug made of dark brown salt-glazed stoneware with an incised decoration and the date 1720. 108mm high. *Castle Museum, Nottingham.*

Punch bowl with incised decoration made in Nottingham in
1750. 324mm high. *Crown copyright Victoria and Albert Museum.*

Teapot with incised decoration and a twisted handle. Made
in Nottingham about 1750. 140mm high. *Castle Museum,
Nottingham.*

Teapot decorated with bands of incised lines and crumbled
clay particles. Made in Nottingham about 1790. 136mm
high. *Castle Museum, Nottingham.*

Brown salt-glazed stoneware jug showing a toper on one side and a horseman resting on the other. This is identical in shape and design to a Pratt ware jug. Possibly made at Brampton in Derbyshire. *c.* 1810. 145mm high. *Private Collection.*

Brown stoneware coffee pot decorated in relief with a pheasant running through a cornfield on one side and two pointers on the other. Probably made at Brampton. *c.* 1790. 260mm high. *Private Collection.*

Toby jug made at Brampton at the beginning of the nineteenth century. The Brampton stoneware is quite often, understandably, mistaken for Nottingham stoneware. 305mm high. *Castle Museum, Nottingham.*

BROWN SALT-GLAZED STONEWARE FROM DERBYSHIRE

The making of brown salt-glazed stoneware began in Derbyshire at about the same time that James Morley had started his pottery in Nottingham, in fact his name is connected with both areas. There was plenty of indigenous clay and coal in the county and the production of salt-glazed stoneware persisted here until the second world war.

The eighteenth century Derbyshire potters were almost as skilled as those at Nottingham, whose work was very similar, though by comparing the designs on dated and inscribed pieces it is sometimes possible to tell in which county the objects were made.

The first locality where the brown salt-glazed stoneware was made was Crich, but there were potteries in other places including Chesterfield, Belper, Brampton and Denby.

In Brampton in the nineteenth century there were about ten potteries, some of them making quite large and decorative pieces like the fine tavern jugs on page 62. Relief decorations superseded the earlier incised and rouletted designs of the previous century.

The Derbyshire potters made domestic wares of all types and in some quantity, but the bulk of the production, certainly in the early years of the nineteenth century must have been stoneware bottles and flasks. In the 1834 Government Report considering the abolition of duty on bottles, it is clear that the manufacture of these was higher in Derbyshire than anywhere else in the United Kingdom.

It is not very common to find marked pieces, though the Oldfields of Brampton stamped their flasks and Toby jugs.

The old stoneware pottery at Belper was taken over in 1834 by the Bourne's of Denby, whose factory is still in existence today.

Brown stoneware tavern jug of fine quality decorated in relief with roses, thistles, and shamrocks. The portraits in rococo frames are of the young Queen Victoria (on the other side) and here, her mother, the Duchess of Kent wearing a large feathered hat, inspired no doubt by the miniature by William Ross. Made at one of the Brampton factories. *c.* 1838. 254mm high. *Private Collection.*

A similar tavern jug with a lion couchant and a design incorporating thistles, roses and shamrocks. *c.* 1840. 216mm high. *Private Collection.*

Ale mug with three greyhound handles made of buff coloured stoneware and top-dipped in a darker brown glaze. There are two sprigged decorations of a toper and one of St. George and the Dragon between the handles. Made in Derbyshire probably at Bourne's factory at Shipley or Denby. *c.* 1840. *Private Collection.*

Both sides of a brown salt-glazed stoneware mug, top-dipped in a dark brown glaze with relief decorations. Printed mark on the base BOURNE DENBY ENGLAND in three separate lines. 20th century. 89mm high. *Private Collection.*

Top left: Brown stoneware spirit flask, moulded with a bust of Lord Melbourne who was Prime Minister from 1835-41. Impressed OLDFIELD & CO MAKERS. Made at Brampton near Chesterfield. *c.* 1835. 235mm high. *Courtesy James Blewitt Collection.*

Top right: Two brown salt-glazed stoneware spirit flasks. One depicting Queen Adelaide, wife of William IV, impressed 'S. Bedford 94 Fore Street City'. Probably made at Lambeth. *c.* 1830. 264mm high.

The other moulded with a bust of William IV, impressed OLDFIELD & CO MAKERS. Made at Brampton. *c.* 1830. 286mm high. Reference books state the firm was in business 1838-88, but as William IV came to the throne in 1830 and died in 1837, it seems that the pottery may have been established by the early 1830s. *Private Collection.*

Brown salt-glazed stoneware 'Reform' bottle, made to contain 'The true Spirit of Reform', very similar to the Brampton flasks, but made by Doulton and Watts, Lambeth 1832. 357mm high. *Royal Doulton Potteries.*

An enormous salt-glazed stoneware jug made to
commemorate the twenty-first birthday of William Powell's
eldest son. Made at Powell's Temple Gate Pottery, Bristol in
1834. 915mm high. *City of Bristol Museum and Art Gallery.*

A magnificent great salt-glazed stoneware jug, top-dipped in a darker brown and decorated with classical, hunting and rustic scenes in relief, with leaf, vine and beaded borders. Made by John Milsom of 124 Temple Street, Bristol. This firm was taken over some years later by Charles Price and Sons (who subsequently bought up all the Bristol stoneware potteries). 1830. Approximately 915mm high. *City of Bristol Museum and Art Gallery*

An equally large stoneware jug to the one on the opposite page, glazed with the new leadless glaze developed by Powell and Amatt. This was made to commemorate the twenty-first birthday of William Powell's second son, at the Temple Gate Pottery, Bristol in 1844. 915mm high. *City of Bristol Museum and Art Gallery.*

Detail from the commemoration jug for William Powell's second son's twenty-first birthday.

SALT-GLAZED AND OTHER BROWN STONEWARE MADE AT BRISTOL

From the early years of the eighteenth century utilitarian brown salt-glazed stoneware was made in Bristol. Little decorative ware seems to have been made though recent research has shown that some hunting jugs with crisp sprigged decorations were made there[1]. By 1832 there were at least ten Bristol potteries turning out stoneware bottles. There was a duty on these and their payment in that year amounted to nearly a tenth of the revenue collected on bottles in England. One potter, Charles Price, paying over £90, a considerable sum in those days. Price's greatest business rival was William Powell, whose pottery was established about 1816. Though his firm made mainly bottles and mugs two very large jugs were made there to celebrate the twenty-first

1. R.J.C. Hildyard, *A Documentary Piece of 18th Century Bristol Stoneware.* Bristol City Museum Monograph IV 1982.

A collection of 19th century stoneware from Bristol, made for local tradesmen. *Left to right*: Flask stamped T. EVENS Redcliffe Hill BRISTOL. 142mm high; filter with sprigged decoration, 285mm high; barrel stamped JOHN HAZELDINE BRISTOL 1871, 112mm high. These three subjects are unmarked with potter's names. The two large jars on the right are from the Temple Gate Pottery, one made for

T. Brown and Sons, Cirencester is marked POWELL POTTER BRISTOL, 390mm high, and the other for WYLD & CO Bridge BRISTOL is marked POWELL BRISTOL, 378mm high. The jar with the printed transfer design is marked PRICE BRISTOL, 175mm high. Price eventually took over Powell's pottery in 1906 and traded as Price Powell and Co. *City of Bristol Museum and Art Gallery.*

birthdays of his two sons, in 1834 and 1844. The former decorated with sprigged classical figures in salt-glazed stoneware and the other glazed with the new 'Bristol' glaze. It was in 1835 that Powell and Anthony Amatt developed this new leadless glaze, which was to supersede the salt-glaze and which was capable of surviving the high temperature necessary for the firing of stoneware. This new glaze, sometimes used in two forms, colourless and of a yellowish tinge was applied to the unfired pots, obviating the necessity of firing the objects twice. This new ware was glazed both inside and out and was guaranteed to resist acids and not to absorb them. 'Bristol' glaze was soon adopted by potteries in other parts of the country.

The Powell stoneware pottery continued in business until early in the twentieth century and it was bought up by Price, Sons & Co. and demolished. The new firm of Price, Powell & Co. was in its turn finally destroyed by bombs during the second world war.

Brown salt-glazed stoneware harvest jug made to commemorate the wedding of Queen Victoria and Prince Albert whose portraits appear beneath the spout. On the other side is the royal coat of arms in high relief. On the base is a raised cartouche with 'S. Green Lambeth' incised on it. *c.* 1840. 230mm high. *Private Collection.* Stephen Green was working in Lambeth from 1820-58.

Brown salt-glazed stoneware mug in the form of Admiral Nelson's head. Made by Doulton and Watts at Lambeth. *c.* 1820. 203mm high. *Royal Doulton Potteries.*

Salt-glazed stoneware filter. Made by Doulton and Watts. *c.* 1854. 610mm high. *Royal Doulton Potteries.*

LATER BROWN SALT-GLAZED STONEWARE MADE IN LONDON

Apart from the Dwight pottery at Fulham there were many other potters making brown salt-glazed stoneware in the London area in the eighteenth and nineteenth centuries. Among the most interesting were the Kisheres of Mortlake who produced hunting jugs with relief decoration in buff coloured stoneware, top-dipped in a darker colour, in the 1780-1800 period; and Stephen Green of Lambeth who often marked his wares which included handsome relief moulded jugs and spirit flasks commemorating the coronation of Queen Victoria.

But it was John Doulton and his successors who were the most successful of all the London makers of stoneware; production only ceased in 1956, when the firm moved up to Staffordshire.

John Doulton, who was born at Fulham in 1793, was apprenticed to the pottery that John Dwight had founded. At that time the pottery was making strictly utilitarian wares such as ink and blacking bottles[1] and

---

1. It was Doulton and Watts's blacking bottles that Charles Dickens remembered labelling by the hundred, during his childhood when he was working at Warrens' warehouse near Hungerford Stairs.

67

Four brown salt-glazed stoneware jugs, top-dipped in a darker brown glaze. The one on the left is relief moulded in the style of the early nineteenth century Doulton and Watts jugs. It is marked DOULTON & CO LIMITED LAMBETH in an oval frame. The other three are all decorated with applied reliefs of white clay and all bear marks dating them between 1891 and 1922. The highest is 140mm and the smallest is 51mm. *Private Collection*.

This kind of ware was turned out in large quantities by the Doulton factory from the beginning of the firm in 1815 throughout the nineteenth and into the twentieth century.

Brown stoneware jug decorated with pale green applied relief portraits and a dark green relief lettered inscription. The impressed mark on the base DOULTON LAMBETH was the mark used from 1880-91. There is also impressed 'cc' and an 's' with the incised initials E P, the mark of Emily Partington, a Senior Assistant 1880-91. 'cc' was the mark of Annie Cupit. 191mm high. *Private Collection*.

jars for spirits and chemicals, though they also made mugs and jugs decorated in relief with hunting scenes.

After finishing his apprenticeship, John Doulton, who had become a very expert craftsman, went into partnership with Martha Jones and John Watts. Mrs. Jones retired in 1820 and the firm became Doulton and Watts. Due to the extremely hard work of both partners the firm began to expand; by the middle of the nineteenth century it had become the largest and best known manufacturer of chemical stoneware in Europe.

As well as the utilitarian pipes, chimney pots and water filters, the firm made decorative flasks and jugs with the likenesses of Nelson and other famous people. In 1835 Henry (John Doulton's second son) then aged fifteen had joined the family business and proved himself to be not only an extremely good technician but an inventive man as well. It was through his inventiveness that steam was harnessed to drive the potters' wheels. When John Watts retired in 1854 the firm became Doulton and Co.

Up to the mid-1860s the firm had not really concerned itself very much with producing decorative wares, but Henry Doulton became interested in the Lambeth School of Art and many of its students came to work at the Doulton pottery. The enduring effect this had on the production of decorative stoneware will be referred to later in the section on the artist potters of the later nineteenth century.

Brown stoneware jug with a shiny glaze made by Doultons to commemorate the death of Benjamin Disraeli whose portrait in relief decorates the front. There is also a quotation from his maiden speech: 'I will sit down now but the time will come when you will hear me' and 'House of Commons 7 December 1837.' And round the neck of the jug is the inscription 'Benjamin Disraeli Earl of Beaconsfield born December 21 1804 died April 19 1881.' The diamond registration mark on the base indicates that it was made 1 June 1881. In addition to the DOULTON LAMBETH mark in an oval there is a printed oval enclosing 'John Mortlock & Co. Oxford Street London.' This was a dealer who was in business from 1880-1930. 229mm high. *Private Collection.*

Brown stoneware jug with the top and base dipped in a dark brown glaze, made to commemorate the somewhat futile 'Emin Pasha Relief Expedition 1887-1889.' On the front is a portrait of H.M. Stanley and the inscription 'Out of Darkness into Light.' On one side the word 'ENTERPRISE' on a globe supported by two classical figures and the names of three members of the expedition E.M. BARTTELOT, W. BONNY and A.J. MOUNTJOY-JEPHSON. On the other side the word 'VALOUR' between two soldiers and a seated native and the names of three other members of the expedition W.C. STAIRS, R.H. NELSON and T.H. PARKE. Marked on the base 'Doulton Lambeth gg', a small crown and the figure 1. 197mm high. *Private Collection.* Emin Pasha was not at all grateful for the concern shown him and refused to join his 'rescuers'. He was killed by natives three weeks later. 'gg' was the mark of Mary Goode, listed as a Senior Assistant in 1882.

Salt-glazed stoneware cat, designed by Agnete Hoy for the Royal Doulton Company in 1955. 254mm high. *Royal Doulton.*

In 1952 Agnete Hoy became the head of design at the Royal Doulton Pottery, Lambeth. Miss Hoy had trained at the Copenhagen College of Art and had worked in the design studios at Bullers in Stoke-on-Trent. From 1952 for the next four years she produced for Doultons numerous designs both in salt-glaze and in a new type of stoneware decoration, using applied transparent glazes on a fine natural cream coloured body, with flowers etc. painted with free brushwork. With the firing in 1956 of the last batch of Agnete Hoy's designs the production of salt-glazed stonewares at Doulton's Lambeth factory finished.

For further reading

Desmond Eyles. *Royal Doulton 1815-1965.* Hutchinson 1965.
Richard Dennis. *Doulton Stoneware Pottery.* Exhibition catalogue pub. R. Dennis London 1971.
Desmond Eyles. *The Doulton Lambeth Wares.* Hutchinson 1975.
M. Batkin and P. Atterbury. *Art among the Insulators.* Stoke-on-Trent. 1977.

5. Salt-glazed stoneware

DRAB AND WHITE SALT-GLAZED STONEWARE OF THE
EIGHTEENTH CENTURY

In the early years of the eighteenth century, a number of Staffordshire potters were experimenting with various ways of producing a ware comparable to the fine Chinese porcelain that was then being imported into the country. The manufacturers of delft ware had done their best, but the tin-enamelled earthenware chipped and scratched easily. The potters were trying to find a ware that was white and reasonably thin and fragile-looking, while retaining great strength and if possible it had to be translucent. The latter quality the salt-glazed potters never achieved.

Taking a lead from the work of John Dwight of Fulham, they turned their attention to the manufacture of a lighter coloured salt-glazed stoneware. The earliest white salt-glazed ware was made of Staffordshire clay and sand and dipped in a white pipe clay slip.

About 1720, John Astbury according to tradition first introduced the white Devonshire clays into Staffordshire and also perfected a white body by adding ground calcined flints to a light coloured clay mixture. This resulted in a ware that was both hard and strong. Astbury failed to produce the translucency of porcelain, but he had invented a fine stoneware that could be moulded with very great precision. Very soon a number of Staffordshire potters were also making white salt-glazed stoneware, and when the kilns were being fired, the neighbourhood was plunged into smoky darkness, caused by the action of the salt when thrown into the red hot kilns.

In the 1720s and '30s, Aaron Wedgwood and his sons Thomas and John of the Big House, Burslem were known to have made buff-coloured stoneware, which was thrown and turned and decorated with raised designs of white pipe clay. This is known as 'Drab-ware' and is sometimes mistakenly named Crouch ware, which is a brown stoneware.

Until about 1730 pots were either thrown on a wheel or were made by press moulding, that is by taking a 'bat' of clay and pressing it into a mould. There was a limit to the thinness of ware that could be achieved by this method, so when the demand grew for teapots and sauceboats and other complicated shapes, a new method had to be invented, and this was the slip casting of the ware in a mould.

The moulds were first of all made of Derbyshire alabaster, and a highly skilled job it was to make them. Later, about 1745, plaster of Paris moulds were introduced from France.

The original alabaster or plaster mould was kept as a master copy and further plaster copies were made from this as working moulds. The porous mould, in two or more pieces, was assembled, and the clay, mixed with water to form slip was poured into the mould. This was left to stand for a few minutes while the porous mould absorbed water from

Salt-glazed jelly mould, made in
Staffordshire. *c.* 1740. 32mm high.
Crown copyright Victoria and Albert Museum.

Drab-ware teapot with white pipeclay
decoration. Attributed to Dr. Thomas
Wedgwood who died in 1737. *c.* 1720.
114mm high. *Private Collection*.

Almost white salt-glazed bowl with
sprigged-on decoration. Made to
commemorate the taking of Porto Bello
by Admiral Vernon in 1739. Made in
Staffordshire. 1740. 133mm wide. *Royal
Pavilion Art Gallery and Museums, Brighton*.

Pew group of a lady with two suitors made of white salt-glazed stoneware with details picked out in dark brown stained clay. Made in Staffordshire. *c.* 1745. 159mm high. *Reproduced by courtesy of the Trustees of the British Museum.*

Pew group, though damaged, is obviously from the same hand as the one above, with details picked out in dark brown stained clay. The lady has two new suitors and is showing her preference. The loser holds a small box in his hand. Made in Staffordshire. *c.* 1745. 172mm high. *Private Collection.*

72

'Scratch blue' mug. Inscribed IH 1752. Staffordshire. 127mm high. *Crown copyright Victoria and Albert Museum.*

Pew group with two primitively modelled figures in white salt-glazed stoneware with details picked out in dark brown stained clay. Three grotesque masks hang behind them on the back of the pew. Made in Staffordshire. *c.* 1745. 152mm high. *Fitzwilliam Museum, Cambridge.*

the slip, depositing against the sides of the mould a thin layer of solid clay. Then the superfluous slip was poured off and when the clay was sufficiently dry, the mould could be removed from the thin clay casting. This method of slip casting was only applicable to stoneware. It was not until after the first quarter of the nineteenth century that it became possible to slip cast ordinary earthenware.[1]

Tableware of all kinds was made in salt-glazed stoneware, decorated with intricate patterns of raised basket-work or rococo scroll forms, often with pierced borders. The crisp precision of the moulding of these patterns is the most remarkable feature of this ware. Though Aaron Wood is generally written about as being a celebrated block cutter, many more moulds made by his brother Ralph are still in existence. Ralph Wood was employed by Thomas and John Wedgwood of the Big House, Burslem from 1748-1770.

Colour was first introduced by incising a design into the body of the ware, in its leather-hard state, and then rubbing cobalt-stained clay into the indentations. This technique dates from the 1740's and the ware is known as 'scratch blue'.

About 1750 coloured enamelling was used with great success. The colours were painted on over the glaze and the ware was then re-fired in a muffle kiln. These enamel colours have an exceptionally clear and jewel-like quality. Salt-glazed teapots were often made in the most fantastic shapes: houses, camels and even pecten shells. Teapots of a more orthodox shape were painted with enamel colours in many different designs including somewhat naive attempts at oriental landscapes and figures. Patterns were painted incorporating birds, flowers, feathers, portraits of the King of Prussia and the Young Pretender hiding in an oak tree.

Primitive figures were made, either as toys or for ornament. Some of these took the form of a group of figures sitting on a settle or a pew. These were white but picked out here and there with dark brown clay for such details as shoes, eyes and buttons. Other figures, both human and animal, including some very spirited mounted soldiers were also made in white salt-glazed stoneware.

Agate ware was also used with a salt glaze, both for teapots and for figures. The ware was made of white and dark brown clay carefully cut and blended to resemble agate. Sometimes blue was added as well.

Enamel coloured salt-glazed figures are extremely rare and lack the charm of the simpler white and brown ones.

By about 1770, the manufacture of salt-glazed stoneware had almost ceased, cream-coloured earthenware having become firmly established by that date. However, white salt-glazed stoneware was still being

---

1. See *Pratt Ware 1780-1840* pages 27-29.

White salt-glazed horseman with details picked out in dark brown clay. Made in Staffordshire. *c.* 1745. 235mm high.
Crown copyright Victoria and Albert Museum.

Salt-glazed salt cellar, made in Staffordshire and dated 1744. 76mm high.
Reproduced by courtesy of the Trustees of the British Museum.

produced in Wales. There are two examples with 'scratch blue' inscriptions in the Royal Institution of South Wales in Swansea. One of these is dated 1773 and the other is a jar inscribed 'M.E. Swansea Pot Works 1775'. William Coles was then running the pottery and there is documentary evidence that 'M.E.' was Mary Eaton who purchased the piece in 1775 and took it to Stonemill Farm, somewhere in the district, where it remained until 1966.

Salt-glazed stoneware is never marked with the name of a maker, though there are some moulds signed with the maker's name.

For further reading

Arnold Mountford. *The Illustrated Guide to Staffordshire Salt-glazed Stoneware.* Barrie and Jenkins 1971.

R.L. Hobson. *A Guide to the English Pottery and Porcelain in the Department of Ceramics and Ethnography* British Museum 3rd. Ed. 1923.

L.M. Solon. *The Art of the Old English Potter.* New York. 1886. Reprinted E.P. Publishing Ltd. 1976.

T.A. Lockett and P.A. Halfpenny (Ed.) *Stonewares and Stone chinas of Northern England to 1851.* City Museum and Art Gallery, Stoke-on-Trent 1982.

Moulded salt-glazed teapot in the form of a camel, made in Staffordshire about 1745. 259mm high. *Fitzwilliam Museum, Cambridge.*

White salt-glazed teapot moulded in the form of a pecten shell with a crabstock spout and plain looped handle. The lid is surmounted with a dove. *c.* 1740. 110mm high. *Private Collection.*

Teapot in the form of a house with a dolphin spout and scaly handle. Made in Staffordshire. *c.* 1740. 108mm high. *Private Collection.*

75

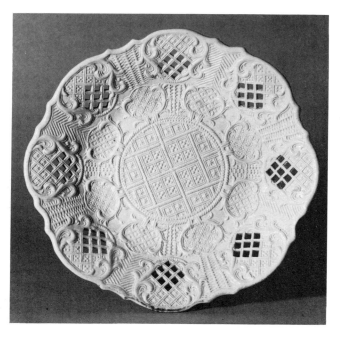

Salt-glazed plate with moulded decoration. Made in Staffordshire by Aaron Wood. *c.* 1760 (an inscription by his son Enoch Wood dated 1836 on the back testifies to this). 432mm diameter. *Crown copyright Victoria and Albert Museum.*

Fine crisp press-moulded plate of white salt-glazed stoneware, with pierced raised scroll decoration and basket work pattern borders in high and low relief. Made in Staffordshire. *c.* 1760. 242mm diameter. *Private Collection.*

Fine crisp press-moulded plate of white salt-glazed stoneware, with pierced raised scroll decoration and basket work pattern borders in high and low relief. Made in Staffordshire. *c.* 1760. 305mm diameter. *Private Collection.*

White salt-glazed plate with an elaborately moulded and pierced design painted with a polychrome pseudo-Chinese design. *c.* 1760. 305mm diameter. *Private Collection.*

Plate 7. A press-moulded white salt-glazed leaf-shaped dish,
decorated with sprays of red currants modelled in high relief
and painted with bright enamel colours. Made in Staffordshire.
c. 1760. 242mm wide. *Courtesy Earle D. Vandekar.*
Photograph Michael Spence.

White salt-glazed moulded teapot painted with a design of oakleaves and Chinese flowers. The figure at the top of the shell is meant to represent Bonnie Prince Charlie. Made in Staffordshire. *c.* 1745. 140mm high.

White salt-glazed teapot painted with Oriental flowers in brilliant enamel colours, green, pink, yellow and turquoise blue. Made in Staffordshire. *c.* 1760. 90mm high. *Private Collection.*

Puzzle jug with incised decoration coloured with cobalt. This technique is known as 'scratch blue'. Made in Staffordshire and dated 1764. 254mm high. *Crown copyright Victoria and Albert Museum.*

Top right: Pear-shaped salt-glazed jug painted with an Arcadian scene of shepherd and shepherdess in bright enamel colours, including a fine Naples yellow. In a cartouche are the initials of the couple for whom it was probably given as a wedding present. Made in Staffordshire 1764. 210mm high. *Crown copyright Victoria and Albert Museum.*

Jug of salt-glazed stoneware with incised and impressed decoration, painted in blue. The initials are those of George III. Made in Staffordshire about 1770. 330mm high. *Crown copyright Victoria and Albert Museum.* 'Scratch blue' tankards and jugs of this type were made for use in taverns.

Plate 8. Tortoiseshell glazed plate of the Whieldon type with a moulded border design. *c.* 1750. 241mm diameter. *City Museum and Art Gallery, Stoke-on-Trent.*

Plate 9. Whieldon type teapot with tortoiseshell coloured glazes of manganese, with a little green and yellow. Made in Staffordshire. *c.* 1755. 90mm high. *Private Collection.*

6. Lead-glazed Red Earthenware

ALSO TORTOISESHELL, AGATE AND MARBLED WARE OF THE
EIGHTEENTH CENTURY

Staffordshire red-ware teapot of the Astbury type with a design in white pipeclay covered with a pale straw coloured glaze. The lid is of a later date. *c.* 1740. 127mm high. *Private Collection.*

Two Astbury/Whieldon type bandsmen purporting to belong to the mid-eighteenth century and now thought to have been made *c.* 1920. 140mm high. *City Museum and Art Gallery, Stoke-on-Trent.*

At the same time that white salt-glazed stoneware was being made, other potters were experimenting with earthenware bodies and coloured glazes. For some time during the eighteenth century the body of the ware remained much the same, whether it was to be glazed with salt or lead, but by about 1740 manufacturers tended to specialize in the use of either one glaze or the other and experiments went on to find the most suitable clay mixture for use with each type of glaze.

The most famous potters concerned with these developments were John Astbury (who had worked with the Elers), his son Thomas, Thomas Whieldon and Enoch Booth.

As we have seen, Astbury was something of an innovator, not only did he introduce ground calcined flints into the body of the stoneware used with salt-glaze, but he is said to have been the first potter to have imported white clay from Devonshire into Staffordshire. (It was all brought from the nearest port on the backs of pack animals).

John Astbury and his son made red, brown and black fine thin earthenware rather like that made by the Elers, but the Astburys ornamented their ware with sprigged decorations made of white pipeclay and they used a fine silky lead glaze, which gave a pleasantly smooth finish to their tablewares. Sometimes the ware was only decorated with a simple band of white slip. They did not mark their wares, but the factory wasters of this red or brown ware have been found on the site of the old Astbury works. The same kind of ware was also made by other potters in the Stoke-on-Trent district, for many other sites have yielded similar pottery. So the term 'Astbury' can only apply loosely to indicate the type of pottery, and not specifically to state the maker.

Figures of musicians and soldiers modelled in different coloured clays have also been attributed to the Astburys. Many of these however have proved to be twentieth century reproductions. Captain Price in his preface to the catalogue of his collection of Astbury, Whieldon and Ralph Wood figures states that his collection which included 101 Astbury figures was started in 1907 and more or less completed in 1917. He goes on to say 'as a matter of fact over eighty figures were bought in the latter year.' Later on he writes about the Astbury figures...'they are very difficult to find. From 1907 to 1917 not a single Astbury figure appeared at auction at Christies.'

This seems highly suspicious. Recently it has come to light that a potter in Vauxhall was making these little figures during the 1914-18 war and up to 1920, and that many of them were sold through the leading London salerooms.

John Astbury died in 1743 and his son later made fine cream coloured earthenware.

A group of Astbury/Whieldon type earthenware of the mid-eighteenth century. The pieces are delicately potted and the sprigged decorations and spouts are of white pipeclay. The lead glaze on the decorations on the covered jugs is mottled with typical Whieldon tortoiseshell colouring. The tallest piece is approximately 175mm high. *Crown copyright, Victoria and Albert Museum.*

Dark red earthenware kettle with a fine brown silky glaze and applied pipeclay ornaments. Attributed to John Astbury. *c.* 1740. It is interesting to compare this piece with that on page 237. 187mm high. *Reproduced by courtesy of the Trustees of the British Museum.*

Diminutive Staffordshire teapot modelled after an Oriental original and decorated with coloured glazes, green, manganese brown and yellow. *c.* 1755. 51mm high. *Crown copyright, Victoria and Albert Museum.*

Lead glazing had always been a dangerous process, as the oxide of lead was used in powder form, causing lead poisoning to the people working with it. However, by about 1740, Enoch Booth had perfected a fluid glaze in which the dangerous lead powder was ground up in water with flint and clay. The ware to be glazed was then dipped into this after it had been fired to the biscuit state. The liquid glaze clung to the porous biscuit in an even coating, and the pieces were then refired.

Some time before 1740, Thomas Whieldon is known to have been making knife handles for the Sheffield cutlers. These were made by blending together different coloured clays to make an agate-like ware. Later he experimented in the use of coloured glazes which he mixed in various ways in imitation of tortoiseshell. The colours he used were yellow, brown, green, blue and grey from the oxides of iron, manganese, copper and cobalt. Most of the so-called Whieldon ware is either brownish or greenish, and the other colours are sometimes added as large blotches.

The block-cutter Aaron Wood had worked for Whieldon for a time from 1746, and a number of young men who worked for him as apprentices afterwards distinguished themselves. Amongst these was Josiah Spode. In one of Thomas Whieldon's hiring books, there is an entry referring to Josiah Spode for 9 April 1749: 'Hired Siah Spode, to give him from this time to Martlemas next 2s 3d, or 2s 6d if he deserves it'[1]. Spode was sixteen at the time.

In 1754, Whieldon took as a partner young Josiah Wedgwood. While working with Whieldon, Wedgwood invented a fine green glaze which was used to decorate wares in all kinds of fanciful shapes such as cauliflowers and pineapples. Together they continued to make agate, marbled and tortoiseshell pieces. The partners continued to refine the earthenware body that they were using under the tortoiseshell glazes, until Wedgwood felt it was good enough to stand on its own merits, without the need for covering up with a dark glaze. In 1759, the partnership came to an end. Wedgwood started up on his own and began to make the cream-coloured earthenware for which he became so famous. He introduced this in 1761.

Whieldon continued to make his variegated wares but the demand for them gradually diminished. He finally retired in 1780. A great many earthenware potteries during the period 1740-80 made tortoiseshell ware and as it is never marked, it is really quite impossible to say who made it. It is only safe to use 'Whieldon ware' as a generic term.

Whieldon's pottery was originally a small thatched building, as

Tortoiseshell ware teapot of the Whieldon type with manganese purple-brown coloured glaze. Made in Staffordshire. *c.* 1755. 114mm high. *Private Collection.*

1. Josiah C. Wedgwood *Staffordshire Pottery and its History.* London 1913.

Horseman modelled in different coloured clays and glazed
with an almost colourless lead glaze. Made in Staffordshire.
c. 1740. 178mm high. *Crown copyright Victoria and Albert
Museum.*

Mounted horseman and lady glazed with brown, green and
grey tortoiseshell glazes. Made in Staffordshire. *c.* 1740.
190mm high. *Crown copyright Victoria and Albert Museum.*

Solid agate ware jug attributed to Thomas Whieldon. *c.* 1745. 235mm high. *Reproduced by courtesy of the Trustees of the British Museum.*

Cat modelled in dark red, buff and white clays to form an agate ware. Glazed with yellowish lead glaze. Made in Staffordshire. *c.* 1750. 172mm high. *Fitzwilliam Museum, Cambridge.*

Agate ware teapot made of white and light red clay and lead glazed. Made in Staffordshire. *c.* 1745. 130mm high. *Fitzwilliam Museum, Cambridge.*

Tea-bowl and saucer and tankard with black chequered borders and 'granite' decoration, made by mingling tiny particles of different coloured clays. Made in Leeds. *c.* 1800. Diameter of saucer 127mm. *Crown copyright, Victoria and Albert Museum.* (See footnote opposite.)

Tortoiseshell glazed plate of the Whieldon type with brown and green colouring. The moulded border design incorporates the words 'Success to the King of Prussia and his Forces'. This popular ally against the French was much commemorated on English pottery. Made in Staffordshire. *c.* 1756. 241mm diameter. *The Royal Pavilion Art Gallery and Museum, Brighton.*

indeed all the potteries were up until the 1760's, for they were all very small, only consisting of a pot oven or kiln and a few sheds. It was not until Wedgwood built Etruria that the potteries became factories in the modern sense of the word. But before going on to consider the achievements of Josiah Wedgwood we must first have a look at the coloured glaze figures of the Woods.

Note to illustration opposite
According to John Smith of Stourbridge this unique type of decoration was made by mingling small segments of agate-type bits of coloured clays, moistening the mixture and adding them to the pot's surface. When sufficiently dry the surface was smoothed by turning on the lathe. This technique originated c.1775.

For further reading

Llewellynn Jewitt. *The Wedgwoods, being a life of Josiah Wedgwood.* London 1865.

L.M. Solon. *The Art of the Old English Pottery.* New York 1886. Reprinted by E.P. Publishing Ltd. 1976.

G. Woolliscroft Rhead. *The Earthenware Collector.* Herbert Jenkins, London 1920.

Figures of a shepherd and shepherdess decorated in coloured glazes. Perhaps from the John Wood factory and made about 1780. 223mm high. *Fitzwilliam Museum, Cambridge.*

7. The Wood family of Burslem

COLOURED GLAZE FIGURES AND TOBY JUGS OF THE LAST HALF OF
THE EIGHTEENTH CENTURY

The first coloured glaze English pottery figures and Toby jugs to be impressed with a maker's name were produced by the Wood family of Burslem in the second half of the eighteenth century.

Ralph Wood the Elder (1715-72), was the brother of Aaron, the mould maker, and they were both sons of a miller of Cheddleton. The miller apprenticed both his sons to potters, Ralph to John Astbury in about 1730 and Aaron to Dr. Thomas Wedgwood.

Ralph Wood, after his apprenticeship was over, went to work with Thomas Whieldon, who was one of the best potters of the time. While he was with Whieldon he made salt-glazed stoneware and then the tortoiseshell glazed ware of the Astbury/Whieldon type.

In a map of Burslem in 1750 (drawn at a later date by Enoch Wood), Ralph Wood I is shown as residing at Ivy House in Shoe Lane (belonging to Thomas and John Wedgwood) almost opposite to the Big House Pottery of these Wedgwood brothers, who were renowned for their salt-glazed productions.

Many of Ralph Wood's blocks from which the moulds for salt-glazed useful wares were taken, made between 1748 and 1770, still survive. So far no moulds for figures or Toby jugs have been found. For the last sixteen years of his life Ralph Wood worked as a block cutter for Thomas and John Wedgwood at the Big House Pottery, Burslem. There seems to be no evidence that he ever ran his own pottery or even that he made any figures or Toby jugs. The early history of the Woods seems somewhat conjectural. Falkner gives tantalising little solid factual information[1] and Simeon Shaw mentions only Enoch Wood.[2]

In 1769 Ralph Wood's two sons John (1746-97) and Ralph II (1748-95) joined their father at the Wedgwoods' Big House Pottery. In 1772 Ralph I died; his two sons left the Wedgwoods' employment and started their own pottery. They soon ran into difficulties. Josiah Wedgwood, writing to his partner Thomas Bentley on 3 April 1773 said:

'I am afraid John & R. Wood must give over Potting in a week or two – They have laid out all their money, & are near £200 in debt! & their fr^{ds}. do not think they are in a way of retrieving. Ralph minds his spiritual affairs too much to do any good with Temporals – He is become a capital Preacher – And poor John for whom we are all very much concern'd, is too mild, & too full of nonexertion to manage a Pottery with any prospect of success'.

After mentioning that he had been prepared to help him financially, he concludes:

---

1. Frank Falkner. *The Wood Family of Burslem.* London 1912.
2. Simeon Shaw. *History of the Staffordshire Potteries.* Hanley 1829.

Apollo decorated in green and yellow coloured glazes. This figure has the rare rebus mark on the base. This group of trees was one of the Wood marks. *c.* 1770-90. 207mm high. *City Museum and Art Gallery, Stoke-on-Trent.*

Figure of Charity, mounted on a square base and decorated with coloured glazes. *c.* 1770-90. *Reproduced by courtesy of the Trustees of the British Museum.*

Back view of a figure of Charity, showing one of the Wood impressed marks. Glazed with a colourless lead china glaze. *c.* 1770-90. 222mm high. *Private Collection.*

Impressed mark on the back of Charity.

A pointer to the dating of the Wood classical figures is that Neo-Classicism did not become fashionable in the English pottery trade until the 1770s and '80s.

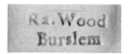

Impressed mark on the base of the Dutch girl.

This mark was probably not set up in type until the 1780s. The use of the short 's' (as in Burslem) had first been introduced by the publisher John Bell in 1775. Benjamin Franklin, writing in 1786, said it was by then in general use. This suggests that Ralph Wood II used this mark after his return to Burslem in 1783.

Dutch boy and girl gardeners. White earthenware with a china glaze. The girl is marked under the base 'Ra.Wood Burslem' impressed. c.1780-90. Height 167mm and 170mm. *Private Collection.*

A similar pair, decorated with coloured glazes is illustrated in *Staffordshire Pottery Figures*, by Herbert Read who suggests that they were probably modelled by John Voyez from French originals. The girl in this pair is impressed 'R. WOOD'.

'...my *feelings* for the Lads carried me farther than prudence could justify for I am fully perswaded they are not made for *Master Potters*.'[3]

In spite of his cousin's gloomy prognostication, John Wedgwood of the Big House Pottery took John Wood into partnership.

When John Wood married Mary Price, the heiress daughter of Nicholas Price of Pont y Pandy, his financial worries were over. He bought the Brownhills estate in Burslem where be built a house and a pottery. Bayley's *Northern Directory* lists John Wood as potting on his own in 1781 and 1783.

Meanwhile Ralph Wood II had moved to Bristol, where he married Sophia Lambert in 1774. He is listed in the local Directory as an earthenware and glass seller and also as a potter, having a shop on the Quay from 1775 to 1781. In that year he was in severe financial difficulties. Overwhelmed by these and other troubles he took himself off to a secret hiding place. However in 1783 he returned to Burslem, where he settled down again with his family.

In the Museum at Stoke-on-Trent there are two ledgers from John Wood's factory covering the periods 1777-1800 and 1783-87 which list numerous figures such as shepherds, gardeners, sailors, Faith and Hope etc., the Man with the Lost Sheep, stags, hinds and many others. In these ledgers both coloured glaze and enamel coloured figures are listed. The enamelled figures were an innovation and were more expensive, involving more work and an extra firing.

There is in existence an invoice from Ralph Wood II to Josiah and Thomas Wedgwood dated 1783 and this lists twenty-seven groups of figures and other ware, in all 288 pieces for £10. 4s 9d, with a discount of £1. 5s. The figures included Apollo, Venus, Neptune, Charity, Man and Boy (is this the group known as Ralph Wood and his son?), the Lost Sheep, an elephant, Satyr cups etc.

In 1784 Ralph Wood II went into partnership with his cousin Enoch. In William Tunnicliffe's *Survey of Staffordshire* (1787), John Wood is listed once again as potting on his own, but Ralph Wood II and Enoch Wood were still in partnership making useful and ornamental wares and figures. By 1789 Ralph Wood II had set up on his own. Money worries continued to beset him. He died in 1795, unreported in the newspapers and leaving no will. He was succeeded by his son Ralph Wood III. In 1801 the youngest of the Ralph Woods died and the pottery was up for sale.[4]

In the *Directory* for 1797, John Wood is still on his own, and in the same year he was murdered by Dr. T.M. Oliver of Burslem, his

Group sometimes known as 'Ralph Wood and his son', said to have been modelled by John Voyez. If this title is correct, it must refer to Ralph Wood II and his son Ralph. *c*. 1780. 210mm high. *City Museum and Art Gallery, Stoke-on-Trent.*

---

3. Keele University Archives E. 18453-25.
4. This chapter has been extensively revised as the result of the recent researches by Mrs. Pat Halfpenny, Keeper of Ceramics, City Museum and Art Gallery, Stoke-on-Trent.

Shepherd and shepherdess with a reclining lamb on a rocky base. The coloured glazes used are green, brown, blue and pale yellow with touches of black. Made by Woods. *c.* 1785. 242mm high. *City Museum and Art Gallery, Stoke-on-Trent.*

daughter Ann Maria's rejected suitor. Dr. Oliver was duly executed.

The Wood figures were well but rather simply modelled in cream-coloured earthenware, and though the Woods used the same oxide stained glazes that Whieldon had developed, they contrived to keep the colours separate by painting them carefully on to the figures with a brush, instead of allowing the colours to mingle together like tortoiseshell. Some of the figures were glazed only with a colourless lead glaze, known as 'china glaze' and a few were marked with the maker's names or mould numbers. Those that are have R. WOOD, Ra WOOD or Ra Wood Burslem impressed. A rebus mark in the form of a group of trees was also used on a figure of Apollo.

The figures vary in subject and complexity, there are some beautifully modelled equestrian figures of such different characters as William III, St. George and Hudibras.

All the human figures have two things in common in their modelling, large hands and well-defined, slightly bulging eyes. The introduction of the Toby jug has been attributed to the Woods, though jugs in human form were known in mediaeval times (see page 20), and some of the Romano-British cinerary urns had faces.

'Fair Hebe' jug, modelled by John Voyez and signed by him with the date 1788. Decorated with coloured glazes and made by R.M. Astbury (name impressed on the base). 241mm high. *Collection Peter Manheim Ltd., London.*

The Toby jug was an immediate success. Hundreds of them must have been made and they were copied by dozens of potters from that day to this. Nobody seems to know exactly when the first one appeared. The inspiration for these jugs may have been Uncle Toby in *Tristram Shandy,* the first volume of which was published in 1760, or a popular song called 'The Little Brown Jug', dedicated to Toby Philpot and written in 1761. The first surviving documentary evidence of a Toby jug is in John Wood's Sales Ledger dated 1785.

The personalities of these jugs are many and varied; apart from the usual stout, bucolic character with the bulbous nose, there were many slightly more refined types: Prince Hal, Lord Howe, the Squire, the Thin Man. Then there were the Welshman with his goat, the Sailor, and the Planter. There is even a formidable female version in the person of Martha Gunn, the Brighton bathing woman.

The modeller John Voyez, brought to Staffordshire by Josiah Wedgwood in 1768, had a somewhat chequered career. There are theories that he modelled some of the Woods' figures for them[5], but there are no signed figures to testify to this. The only model with John Voyez's signature and the Wood type of glazes is a piece known as the 'Fair Hebe' jug, a somewhat uncouth rustic jug in the form of a tree trunk with figures grouped round it. This is actually dated 1788 and the modelling has some affinity with the Wood figures. The same piece occurs with R.M. Astbury's mark and also with the initials R.G. and there are numerous later versions in enamel colours.

The younger Ralph's cousin, Enoch (the son of Aaron) was also a highly skilled modeller and potter, but as his work was more concerned with enamel colours, it is referred to in a later chapter.

---

5. Herbert Read in his *Staffordshire Pottery Figures* puts forward a well-reasoned argument that Voyez was responsible for the facial and other characteristics of the Wood figures and that Voyez in his designs was following French originals by P.L. Cyfflé and others.

For further reading

Cyril Earle. *The Earle Collection of Early Staffordshire Pottery.* A. Brown and Sons, London and New York 1915.

R.K. Price. *Astbury, Whieldon and Ralph Wood Figures and Toby Jugs.* John Lane, London 1922.

Frank Falkner. *The Wood Family of Burslem.* London 1912. Reprinted E.P. Publishing Ltd., Wakefield 1972.

Sir Harold Mackintosh Bt. *Early English Figure Pottery.* Chapman and Hall 1938.

Herbert Read. *Staffordshire Pottery Figures.* Duckworth 1929.

R.G. Haggar. *English Pottery Figures 1660-1860.* Tiranti 1947.

Pat Halfpenny. 'The Wood Family'. *Ceramics* May/June 1986.

Four Toby jugs, all attributed to the younger Ralph Wood
except for the one on the right. They are all decorated in
coloured glazes. Left to right: Admiral Lord Howe, the
Squire, the Sailor (or Planter) and the most typical coarse
featured man. *c.* 1760-90. *Courtesy Sotheby and Co.*

Toby jug in the form of a Sailor (or Planter) seated on a
brass bound chest decorated with coloured glazes, another
version of the figure second from the right above. He wears
a blue coat, black hat and shoes and an ochre waistcoat
above his white trousers. His hands and feet are coloured
pale manganese and a brown kerchief is knotted round his
neck. His sea chest is dark brown and a brown anchor rests
on the green mound at his feet. Impressed mark No. 65 on
the base. Made by Ralph Wood. *c.* 292mm high.
Courtesy Leonard Russell.

94

Toby jug marked Ra Wood Burslem. Decorated in coloured glazes. 1770-90. 248mm high. *Courtesy Sotheby and Co.*

Another version of the Squire Toby jug decorated in coloured glazes and attributed to the younger Ralph Wood. *c.* 1770-80. 292mm high. *Crown copyright, Victoria and Albert Museum.*

Two figures of children decorated with coloured glazes, symbolising Autumn and Winter. Probably made by one of the Woods. Unmarked. *c.* 1770-80. 102mm high. *City Museum and Art Gallery, Stoke-on-Trent.*

Two figures decorated with underglaze colours from a similar set of the Seasons, after models by Ralph Wood. *c.* 1790. 125mm and 123mm high. *Private Collection.* Figures very like these but decorated with enamel colours were produced by Neale and Co. (see page 193.)

Figure of a stag decorated with greyish brown and green coloured glazes. Probably made by the John Wood factory *c.* 1785. 216mm high. *Fitzwilliam Museum, Cambridge.*

Figure of doe decorated with pale grey and green coloured glazes, a pair to the stag above. 114mm high. *Private Collection.*

Plate 10. Figure known as 'The Lost Piece of Silver'. Decorated in green, light brown and yellow coloured glazes. Attributed to the younger Ralph Wood. *c.* 1770. 223mm high. *City Museum and Art Gallery, Stoke-on-Trent.*

Plate 11. St. George killing the Dragon, mounted on a rocky base. *c.* 1775-85. 279mm high. *City Museum and Art Gallery, Stoke-on-Trent.* This figure is sometimes found with the mark RA WOOD Burslem and the mould number 23. It is also to be found with underglaze colouring as well as enamelling over the glaze.

An engraving of the Ivy House Works, Burslem where
Josiah Wedgwood started work on his own account in 1759.

Canal side view of the Etruria works which was built in
1769. Both engravings are from *The Ceramic Art of Great
Britain* by Llewellynn Jewitt 1883.

8. Josiah Wedgwood 1730-95

SOME CONTEMPORARIES AND LATER WARES

Josiah Wedgwood. Blue and white jasper ware portrait medallion, modelled by William Hackwood in 1777.

Thomas Bentley, Wedgwood's partner from 1769-80. Blue and white jasper ware portrait medallion modelled by Joachim Smith in 1774. *Both medallions courtesy of the Trustees of the Wedgwood Museum, Barlaston, Stoke-on-Trent.*

There are so many Wedgwoods in the history of the potteries that it is easy to become confused, even more so as the same Christian names, Thomas, Aaron, John and Josiah occur through various generations. To the general public the name Wedgwood is synonymous with Josiah, the founder of the present Wedgwood empire and with his jasper ware and Queensware.

The other Wedgwoods with whom we are concerned are Thomas, Josiah's eldest brother, to whom he was apprenticed at the Churchyard Works, Burslem; Josiah's older second cousins John and Thomas Wedgwood of the Big House Works, Burslem (who employed Ralph Wood) and Josiah's first cousin 'Useful' Thomas who became his partner in the domestic side of the business; and lastly Ralph Wedgwood, 'Useful' Thomas's inventive son who potted at Burslem and at Ferrybridge in Yorkshire. It is Josiah however who stands head and shoulders above the rest of his family.

The Wedgwoods had for long been established as potters in Staffordshire by the time Josiah, the youngest of a large family, was born in 1730. He was nine when his father died and he went to work at once for his brother Thomas. He was not apprenticed to him until 1744. Sometime during his apprenticeship he had contracted smallpox which left him with the physical handicap of a weak leg. This gave him much discomfort and later in life he had to have it amputated.

In 1754 he became Thomas Whieldon's partner. Whieldon encouraged him to make experiments. Five years later, he started up on his own account in premises known as the Ivy House and Pot Works in Burslem, which he rented from his two cousins John and Thomas Wedgwood of the Big House Works for £15 a year. Wedgwood worked tirelessly reorganizing factory operations as well as continuing with his experiments with different kinds of clay mixtures and glazes.

In 1764 Josiah moved to new premises, the Brick House pot bank, also in Burslem, and took on his cousin 'Useful' Thomas, first as a journeyman and then in 1765 as a partner to look after the production of the domestic ware. In 1767 Josiah Wedgwood took as another partner Thomas Bentley, a merchant in Liverpool. Bentley was a man of cultivated tastes with an excellent head for business. He remained on terms of intimate friendship with Wedgwood until his early death in 1780. He was only fifty. Their actual deed of partnership was signed in 1769, the same year that Wedgwood's newly built works between Hanley and Newcastle-under-Lyme was opened. This was planned for the manufacture of ornamental wares and he named it Etruria. The useful wares continued to be made at the old works. In the same year hand painting was transferred to Chelsea and then to Soho. Meanwhile Bentley was looking after the London Showrooms, supervising the decorating done at the London studios and relieving Wedgwood of many business worries. They made a perfect combination.

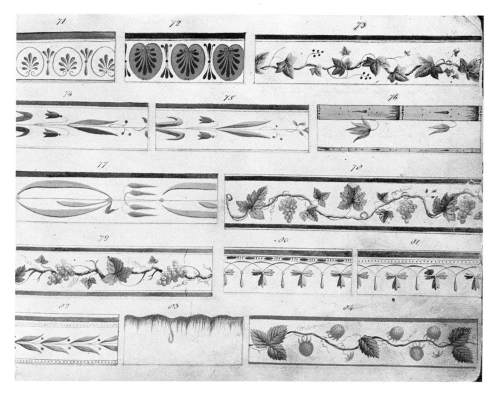

Plate 12. One of the pages from the first Wedgwood pattern book, showing some of the borders that were popular in the 1770s. *Courtesy of the Trustees of the Wedgwood Museum, Barlaston, Stoke-on-Trent.*

Plate 13. A page from a Wedgwood pattern book dated 1810, showing some shapes as well as decorative treatments and borders. *Courtesy of the Trustees of the Wedgwood Museum, Barlaston, Stoke-on-Trent.*

Cauliflower ware teapot. Josiah
Wedgwood invented a particularly
beautiful dark green glaze which he used
on ware of this type. An example of his
early work when he first started up on
his own. *c.* 1760. 114mm high.
Private Collection.

While working for Whieldon Wedgwood had developed a beautiful
rich green glaze, which when he moved to the Ivy House works, he
used to great effect on his cauliflower teapots and other wares of the
same nature.

By about 1760, the dark mottled tortoiseshell glazed ware that
Whieldon and many other potters had been making, was going out of
fashion, and by 1763, Wedgwood had perfected his cream-coloured
earthenware, which was composed of ground flint and pipeclay and
glazed with a silky lead glaze. This body finally superseded both delft
and salt-glazed stoneware, in England as well as on the continent.

Neo-classicism was in the air, and this cream-coloured earthenware
was made into classical shapes inspired by the discoveries at Pompeii
and Herculaneum. Much of the tableware was left undecorated, some
was painted with delightful borders based on geometric or floral
shapes, and some was sent to Liverpool to be decorated by a new
process of transfer printing by the firm of Sadler and Green.

In *Moss's Liverpool Guide* published in 1799, it is written that
'Copper-plate printing upon china and earthenware originated here in
1752 [actually 1756] and remained for sometime a secret with the
inventors Messrs. Sadler and Green' (who used it largely to decorate
tiles). By 1763 this firm was sending regular weekly accounts to
Wedgwood for all the transfer printing that they were doing for him.

In 1765, Josiah Wedgwood was commissioned to make a tea service
for Queen Charlotte. She was so impressed with the result that she
appointed him 'Potter to the Queen' and gave him permission to call
the cream-coloured earthenware 'Queensware' (a name that was to
become a household word, and is still used by the firm of Wedgwood
today).

But the largest creamware dinner service that he ever made was for
the Empress Catherine of Russia. It comprised over 952 pieces with
1,244 scenes and was completed in 1774. The Empress paid about
£3,500 for it.

After perfecting the body for his Queensware, he turned his
attention to 'Egyptian black', or black basalt ware. This was made
from the native clay and ground ironstone with the addition of ochre
and oxide of manganese. This resulted in a fine hard stoneware that
could be polished on a lapidary wheel. In this ware he made many
busts, medallions and vases as well as tea services.[1] The ware was
sometimes decorated in the Etruscan style with red and white encaustic

Tile with a black transfer print signed by
J. Sadler. Made in Liverpool *c.* 1765.
127mm square.
Fitzwilliam Museum, Cambridge.

1. *Among the many makers of black basalt were:*
Richard Barker Lane End 1784-1808. Peter Barker of Mexborough Pottery *c.* 1804. E.J. Birch
of Shelton 1796-1814. Leeds Pottery 1795-1815. Keeling and Toft, Hanley *c.* 1790. S. Hollins
1790-1800. Herculaneum, Liverpool *c.* 1810. S. Greenwood 1780-90. J. Neale 1778-86.
E. Mayer, Hanley 1800-20. J. Glass, Hanley 1822-30. H. Palmer and J. Voyez 1769. Enoch
Wood and Wood and Caldwell 1790-1818. Etruscan ware was also made at Swansea.

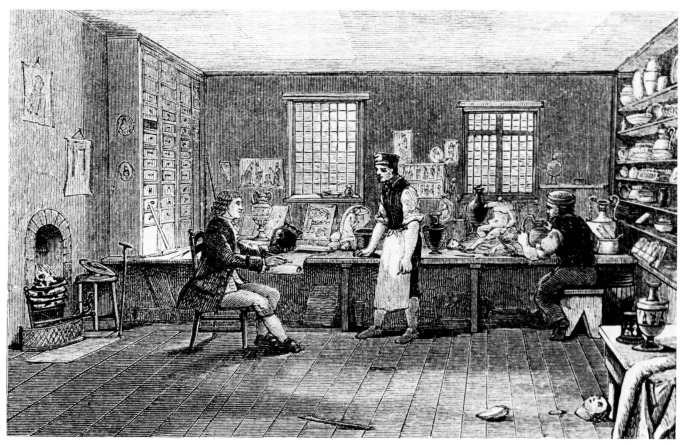

Josiah Wedgwood discusses a vase with one of his modellers
in the Modelling Room at Etruria, as it was in the 1790s.
Courtesy of the Trustees of the Wedgwood Museum, Barlaston, Stoke-on-Trent.

colours. Wedgwood said of the ware: 'The black is sterling and will last
for ever.'

But the ware for which Wedgwood is best known is the dense
vitrified stoneware ornamented with white figures on a coloured
ground, that he called jasper ware. He began experimenting with this
ware about 1774 but it was not until about 1780 that the finest jasper
was produced. Although he had tried to keep it a secret, the ware was
soon imitated by many other potters, sometimes well, but sometimes
with very indifferent results. In particular he distrusted Ralph
Wedgwood the son of his cousin Thomas (see the letter written to Tom
Byerley December 12 1790).[2]

Wedgwood employed many famous artists, including John Voyez,
Flaxman, Stubbs and Hackwood to design the classical reliefs with
which the wares were decorated. Lady Templetown designed some of
the smaller medallions used for buckles and brooches, as well as a tea
service. Although blue and white was the most popular colour combination, other colours were also used including a pretty, soft sage

2. Ed. Finer and Savage. *Selected letters of Josiah Wedgwood*. Cory, Adams and Mackay, London
1965.

Painting by George Stubbs R.A. of the Wedgwood family in the grounds of Etruria Hall in 1780. A black basalt vase similar to the ones below stands on the table on which Josiah Wedgwood is resting his arm. *Courtesy of the Trustees of the Wedgwood Museum, Barlaston, Stoke-on-Trent.*

Wedgwood had thought of asking Joseph Wright of Derby to paint the family picture, but because of his association with Stubbs in the production of enamelled plaques and also recalling a painting that he had seen in the Royal Academy Exhibition of 1779 which he had greatly admired, he wrote to his partner Bentley in that year '....remembering the labourers and cart in the exhibition with paying for the tablets etc., I ultimately determined on Mr. Stubbs...' Stubbs was also anxious to reciprocate Wedgwood's help over the tablets, so maybe there was some quid pro quo arrangement between them.

Wedgwood kept Stubbs's nose to the grindstone, asking for endless alterations to the individual portraits, which Stubbs quite cheerfully agreed to. Wedgwood was clearly a great admirer of Stubbs and not only as an animal painter.

A pair of black basalt vases with applied cameo subjects. The reversible covers were made to convert to candle holders. Marked WEDGWOOD & BENTLEY impressed. Made in 1775. 280mm high. *Courtesy of the Trustees of the Wedgwood Museum, Barlaston, Stoke-on-Trent.*

103

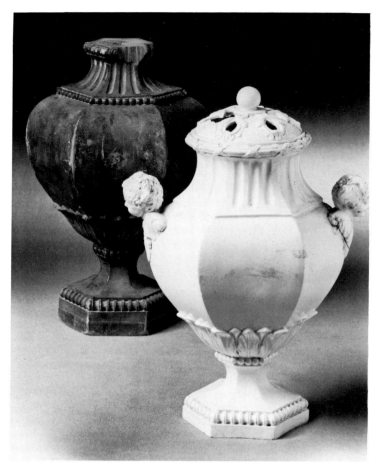

The wooden block mould attributed to John Coward of London, and the cream coloured earthenware vase made from it. The handles are known as the 'Laughing Boy' and the 'Crying Boy'. Coward was employed by Wedgwood from 1768 to repair the old and make new moulds. This vase is unmarked. *c. 1768. 280mm high. Courtesy of the Trustees of the Wedgwood Museum, Barlaston, Stoke-on-Trent.*

This Queensware vase is decorated in relief with Lady Templetown's design 'An Offering to Peace' modelled by William Hackwood in 1783. This same design was used on jasper ware plaques and was borrowed by the makers of Pratt jugs as well. Impressed WEDGWOOD. *c. 1785. 368mm high. Crown copyright, Victoria and Albert Museum.*

Queensware chestnut basket, the design copied from a silverware design. Impressed WEDGWOOD. *c. 1773. 280mm wide.* This shape was shown in the first cream coloured earthenware catalogue (No. 32) issued in 1773. *Courtesy of the Trustees of the Wedgwood Museum, Barlaston, Stoke-on-Trent.*

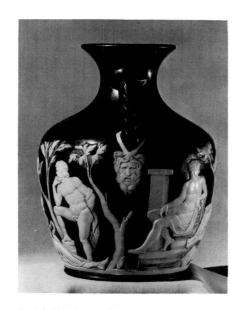

Josiah Wedgwood's copy in black and white jasper of the Portland Vase, 1790. 267mm high. *Courtesy of the Trustees of the Wedgwood Museum, Barlaston, Stoke-on-Trent.*
The original was blown glass in two layers, dark blue and white. The white layer was carved in the manner of a cameo. It was probably made in Alexandria during the reign of Augustus or Tiberius (27BC – 37AD). The scene shows the wooing of Thetis by Peleus. Wedgwood experimented for four years before he produced a satisfactory result. He considered quite rightly, that this was his finest artistic and technical achievement. When the original Portland Vase was smashed by a lunatic in the nineteenth century, the restoration was made possible with the help of Wedgwood's faithful representation.

green, a bamboo yellow, lilac and black. The white relief ornaments were cast in little fired clay moulds and sprigged on to the coloured body of the ware. The inspiration for jasper came from Imperial Roman cameo glass. His most famous piece was the Portland Vase. To begin with Josiah Wedgwood did not mark his ware, but this practice was begun in 1771 and by 1772 most pieces carried an impressed stamp. This was very necessary because many other potters were copying his wares and Wedgwood was jealous of his reputation.[3]

Wedgwood also made seals both in intaglio and cameo and vases in imitation of agate or porphyry.

Just before Bentley's death in 1780, he introduced a white bodied ware, which he called 'Pearl White'. He wrote to Bentley about this in August 1779:

'Your idea of cream-colour having the merit of an original and the pearl white being considered as an imitation of some of the blue and white fabriques, either earthenware or porcelain, is perfectly right, and I should not hesitate a moment in preferring the former if I consulted my own taste and sentiments: but you know what Lady Dartmouth told us, that she and her friends were tired of cream colour, and so they would be of Angels, if they were shown for sale in every chandlers shop through the town. The pearl white must be considered a change rather than an improvement, and I must have something ready to succeed it when the public eye is palled. . .'[4]

Apart from table ware and decorative pieces, Wedgwood was also interested in ceramics for industrial purposes, and after much careful experiment he produced a very hard, dense stoneware which was used for pestles and mortars.

Josiah Wedgwood died in 1795 and was succeeded in the business not by his eldest son, but by his second son Josiah II. In addition to all the experiments in the actual making of pottery, Josiah Wedgwood had been instrumental in getting the roads improved and canals built. With his use of steam power he transformed the Staffordshire pottery manufactory from a semi-rural craft into a well-organized mass-production industry with a large distribution and export service.[5]

3. *Some other makers of jasper ware*
B. Adams *c.* 1800-10. D. Steel, Burslem 1796-1824. John Turner (Lane End) c.1780-90. Neale and Co. 1778. Enoch Wood *c.* 1800 and James Dudson in the 1880s.

4. Ed. Finer and Savage. *Selected letters of Josiah Wedgwood.* Cory, Adams and Mackay, London 1965.

5. Writing to Lord Auckland in 1792 about the relative state of the potteries in 1792 and 80 years before, he said that the worth of the annual output had increased from £10,000 to between £200,000 and £300,000.

A dish from the Empress Catherine of Russia's table service for her palace of *La Grenouillière*. The full service consisted of 952 pieces. It was completed in 1774. 495mm wide.
Crown copyright Victoria and Albert Museum.

Wedgwood Queensware plate, transfer printed in red, the illustration 'The Tiger and the Fox', from *Aesop's Fables*. *c*. 1775. 254mm diameter. Marked WEDGWOOD.
Crown copyright Victoria and Albert Museum.

Cream coloured earthenware dish, printed in black in
Liverpool by Sadler and Green. Marked WEDGWOOD
impressed. Made *c.* 1775. 470mm wide.
Crown copyright Victoria and Albert Museum.

Cream coloured earthenware plate with identical
border to the plate opposite. This one is
unmarked. There are however identically bordered
plates marked LEEDS POTTERY that were made
c. 1780. The ship is a collier brig and from her
general appearance, would give the impression of
belonging to the nineteenth rather than the
eighteenth century. 248mm diameter. *Private
Collection.*

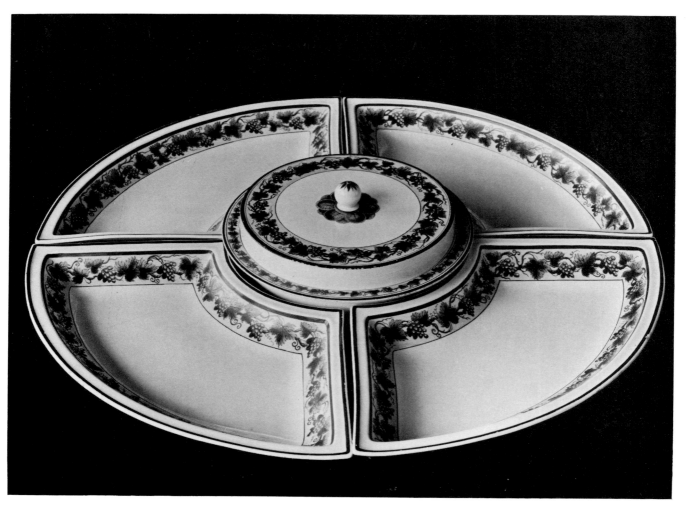

Supper dish in six parts made of cream coloured earthenware
and decorated with a hand painted vine border in green and
mauve. *c.* 1790. 509mm diameter.
Crown copyright, Victoria and Albert Museum.

For further reading
Eliza Meteyard. *The Life of Josiah Wedgwood*. Hurst and Blackett, London
    1865.
Llewellynn Jewitt. *The Wedgwoods, being a life of Josiah Wedgwood*. London
    1865.
Alison Kelly. *The Story of Wedgwood*. Faber 1975
Wolf Mankowitz. *Wedgwood*. Batsford 1953. Reprinted by Spring Books
    1966.
Josiah C. Wedgwood. *A History of the Wedgwood Family*. London 1908.
G. Savage and R. Reilly. *The Dictionary of Wedgwood*. The Antique Collectors'
    Club 1980.
Captain M.H. Grant. *The Makers of Black Basaltes*. William Blackwood,
    Edinburgh 1910. Reprinted Holland Press 1967.
See also
Stonewares and Stone Chinas of Northern England to 1851. Exhibition Catalogue
    published by City Museum and Art Gallery, Stoke-on-Trent 1982.

Cream coloured earthenware dish painted by W.J. Goode 'Oh! What a Charming Cup and Saucer'. This was copied from a design by W. Hogarth 'Taste in High Life' (1742). Impressed WEDGWOOD and A. *c.* 1868. 280mm wide.
Courtesy of the Trustees of the Wedgwood Museum, Barlaston, Stoke-on-Trent.

Cream coloured earthenware plate with a hand painted design by William Wagstaff of 'Sweeps of former times'. Made by Wedgwoods *c.* 1868. 280mm wide.
Courtesy of the Trustees of the Wedgwood Museum, Barlaston, Stoke-on-Trent.
The two dishes, though a century later than the original Queensware are still in the Wedgwood tradition of fine craftsmanship.

Plate 14. Creamware plate with moulded decoration of leaves covered all over front and back with a green glaze. Impressed mark on the base BAKER, BEVANS & IRWIN in a half circle enclosing a large 1. Made at the Glamorgan Pottery, Swansea. This pottery was started in 1813 and continued in production until 1838 when it was acquired by the Dillwyns of the Cambrian Pottery. 210mm diameter. *Private Collection*.

Plate 15. Creamware plate covered all over with a green glaze. Mark BRAMELD + 4 impressed under the base, with two parallel lines that might be the figure 11. Made at Swinton in Yorkshire when the Rockingham factory was being worked by the Bramelds. These impressed marks were used 1815-42. 190mm diameter. *Private Collection*.

Plate 16. Creamware plate covered all over with a green glaze. The back of the rim is ringed with concentric raised lines. Impressed mark BRAMELD + 3. Made at Swinton in Yorkshire when the Rockingham factory was being worked by the Bramelds. These impressed marks were used 1815-42. 205mm diameter. *Private Collection*.

Plate 17. Cream coloured earthenware plate with an all-over green glaze over the sunflower relief design. This was a motif much used in the last quarter of the nineteenth century. Impressed WEDGWOOD on the base and the letters R B and S above, which indicate that it was made in 1890. (After 1891 the word ENGLAND was added to the mark). 220mm diameter. *Private Collection*.

Left: Porphyry vase and cover with applied scroll handles and husk festoons, showing traces of gilding. No. 7 in Josiah Wedgwood's shape book of 1770. Impressed WEDGWOOD & BENTLEY. 1772. 356mm high. *Centre:* Porphyry vase with a fluted body on a black basalt plinth. There are traces of gilding on the swags and leaves round the neck. Impressed WEDGWOOD. 1783. 241mm high. *Right:* A cassolette (vase with a pierced top made to contain some perfumed substance) the cover being reversible to make a candle holder. The body of the cream coloured earthenware vase is covered with a marbled surface slip to represent agate, with white applied decorations, mounted on a white jasper plinth. Impressed WEDGWOOD. 1783. 384mm high. *Courtesy of the Trustees of the Wedgwood Museum, Barlaston, Stoke-on-Trent.*

A pair of Wedgwood and Bentley Porphyry vases on black basalt square bases with gilded decorative handles and floral swags. *c.* 1775. 216mm high. *Courtesy Christie's.*

111

Etruscan vase. Black basalt with encaustic paintings in the Etruscan style. *c.* 1770. 352mm high.
Crown copyright Victoria and Albert Museum.

Both sides of a black basalt vase with encaustic decoration in red slip in the Greek manner. Impressed WEDGWOOD on the base. 1788. 325mm high. *Courtesy Sotheby and Co.*

A *rosso antico* incense burner with black basalt applied decorative motifs mounted on three black dolphins on a concave triangular base with an applied olive leaf border. Mark WEDGWOOD impressed on the base. *c.* 1805. 133mm high. *Courtesy Christie's.*

Below left: Black basalt goblet decorated in relief with a classical figure representing 'Air'. Impressed TURNER on the base. *c.* 1780. 110mm high. *Private Collection.*

Below right: Bust of William Shakespeare made of black basalt, the same model as the enamel coloured version on page 190. Probably by Enoch Wood. *c.* 1790. 245mm high. *Crown copyright Victoria and Albert Museum.*

A collection of jasper ware medallions and plaques, made at Etruria between the years 1775-90. The largest central plaque sometimes called 'A Sacrifice to Peace', is a combination of designs. The left hand group of four figures was designed by Lady Templetown who called it 'Maternal Affection'. It was modelled by William Hackwood in 1783. The figure with the brazier and the girl on the extreme right appear in a plaque entitled 'Sacrifice to Ceres' which was modelled by John Flaxman in 1779. The Wedgwood firm frequently concocted plaques, taking scenes and separate figures from different bas reliefs and even from individual medallions, to make a design of a required width, so it is sometimes very difficult to attribute the design to any one person.
Courtesy of the Trustees of the Wedgwood Museum, Barlaston, Stoke-on-Trent.

A tea-service in blue and white jasper ware. The designs called 'Domestic Employment' were drawn by Lady Templetown and modelled by William Hackwood. 1784. Height of teapot 102mm. *Courtesy of the Trustees of the Wedgwood Museum, Barlaston, Stoke-on-Trent.*

114

Jasper ware vase known as 'The Apotheosis of Homer'. White body, blue dip and white applied decoration modelled by John Flaxman. *c.* 1790. 267mm high. *Courtesy of the Trustees of the Wedgwood Museum, Barlaston, Stoke-on-Trent.*

Tripod vase in white and blue jasper ware. 1789. 203mm high. *Courtesy of the Trustees of the Wedgwood Museum, Barlaston, Stoke-on-Trent.*

Three jasper ware vases. *c.* 1790. *Left:* Classical figures against a blue ground. 220mm high. *Centre:* A tableau 'A Sacrifice to Ceres' against a black dip. Marked WEDGWOOD

impressed. 229mm high. *Right:* Venus in a chariot drawn by swans against a black dip. 304mm high. *Courtesy of the Trustees of the Wedgwood Museum, Barlaston, Stoke-on-Trent.*

Blue and white Wedgwood jasper ware candlesticks in the form of the two goddesses Ceres (with a sheaf of corn) and Cybele (with a lion) holding candle sconces. Designed by Henry Webber, the head of the Ornamental Department at Etruria. *c.* 1790. 312mm and 318mm high.
Courtesy of the Trustees of the Wedgwood Museum, Barlaston, Stoke-on-Trent.

Vase made for music lovers. The design incorporates a *viol da gamba* in blue jasper dip with white relief decorations. Impressed WEDGWOOD. *c.* 1802. 159mm high. *Courtesy of the Trustees of the Wedgwood Museum, Barlaston, Stoke-on-Trent.*

Above right: Jasper ware was revived in 1851 and this vase with a lilac dip background and white relief decoration known as 'Nike and the Warrior' dates from 1871. Impressed WEDGWOOD and S12. 242mm high. The decoration lacks the intense clarity of the earlier work. *Courtesy of the Trustees of the Wedgwood Museum, Barlaston, Stoke-on-Trent.*

Jasper ware pot-pourri vase of a particularly bright hard blue with applied white designs. The circular cover is pierced with round holes. Impressed mark on the base ADAMS. *c.* 1790. 178mm high. *Courtesy Sotheby's.*

117

9. Cream-coloured earthenware

Plaque modelled in cream coloured
earthenware by Enoch Wood at the age
of 11, showing the Wood family coat of
arms. 1771. 241mm square.
Private Collection.

Food warmer and night light of cream
coloured earthenware, the lid is
surmounted by a candlestick. The double
strap handles are twisted and end in leaf
terminals. Made in Leeds or
Staffordshire. *c.* 1770-80. 251mm high.
Crown copyright Victoria and Albert Museum.

Josiah Wedgwood, having perfected his cream coloured earthenware
soon handed over his domestic side of the business to his cousin
'Useful' Thomas Wedgwood,[1] to manage for him, so that he could
concentrate on inventing new bodies and on the decorative wares that
were being made at his new Etruria factory.

Other potters all over the country were soon producing cream
coloured earthenware with varying degrees of success. The Turners of
Lane End shipped much of their cream ware over to Holland to be
decorated there. Enoch Wood (the younger Ralph Wood's cousin)
modelled a plaque of the family coat of arms in cream coloured
earthenware when he was only eleven years old and was responsible
later for the design of many busts and figures. The factory also
produced some good quality useful cream ware.

An excellent cream coloured earthenware was made in Leeds,
possibly from as early as 1765. The earliest of the Leeds cream ware
is of a deep cream colour, very light and silky to the touch. By 1775,
it was lighter in colour. A characteristic of the early ware was the use
of double twisted or rope handle, ending where the handle joined the
body with an embossed leafy terminal. A double reeded flat handle
with floral or leafy terminals was used after about 1775. A curious
knob, made in the form of a double convolvulus seems to be confined
to the Leeds Pottery.

Very elaborate pieces were made in Leeds, with intricate piercing
incorporated in the design. Some of these were *épergnes* or centre pieces
about two feet high. Transfer printing in red, black and purplish
colour was used at Leeds, but not so well or so extensively as in
Liverpool. The enamel coloured painting in a brick red and black was
very typical of Leeds pottery though other colours were used in designs
adapted from Oriental originals as well as from more traditionally
English floral forms. Some of the ware was most effectively decorated
simply in underglaze green stripes.

Although the main production of the Leeds Pottery was useful ware,
figures were also made similar in subject matter to those made in
Staffordshire.

There were other potteries in Yorkshire making cream coloured
earthenware. The Swinton Pottery, under the same management as
the Leeds Pottery made some of the more decorative pieces. The Don
Pottery nearby and also connected through the directors John Green
and the Brameld brothers showed in their catalogue of 1808 examples
of teapots and other ware. David Dunderdale's Castleford Pottery

---

1. Thomas Wedgwood was manager of the Burslem works from 1765 to 1772-3 and then of the
Etruria works until 1788. (K. Niblett. 'A Useful Partner — Thomas Wedgwood 1734-88'. *N.C.S.
Journal.* Vol.5. 1984.).

Plate 18. Creamware teapot with moulded relief decoration painted in enamel colours over the glaze. Marked WOOD in impressed lettering filled in with blue on the base. Presumably from Enoch Wood's factory at Burslem. *c.* 1800. 159mm high. *Private Collection.*
An identical shaped teapot (apart from having a 'widow' knob) is impressed SPODE on the base. It is illustrated in Arthur Hayden's *Spode and his Successors*, London 1925.

pattern book issued in 1796 (and printed in French and Spanish),[2] illustrated many cream ware pieces very similar to some made at the Leeds Pottery, including ware with pierced decoration.

A rather heavy cream coloured earthenware, decorated in the Leeds manner with roses and other flowers, often surrounding bold black lettering, was made at the North Hylton Pottery in Sunderland. This pottery was originally started by William Maling in 1762 and was subsequently taken over, in 1815, by the Phillips, the owners of the Sunderland or Garrison Pottery. The North Hylton was closed down before 1851.

Cream coloured earthenware was certainly made in Liverpool before 1773, for a notice appears in *The Liverpool Advertiser* for 29 October 1773 advertising a pottery for sale on the south side of the town of Liverpool, including a large assortment of cream coloured earthenwares. The Herculaneum Pottery, famous for its cream coloured earthenware was

2. *The Castleford Pottery Pattern Book 1796* with a preface by Peter Walton and an historical note by Heather Lawrence republished by E.P. Publishing Wakefield 1973.

A coffee pot design from *The Castleford Pottery Pattern Book* issued in 1796, showing how similar to the Leeds Pottery creamware the design is.

Top left: Coffee pot with reeded and twisted double handle. Leeds or Staffordshire. *c.* 1790. 305mm high. *Crown copyright Victoria and Albert Museum.*

Coffee pot transfer printed in black. Made in Leeds. *c.* 1800. 267mm high. *Crown copyright Victoria and Albert Museum.*

established in the early 1790s by Richard Abbey. In 1796, over forty pottery workers from Staffordshire went to work there. The Liverpool cream coloured earthenware was not nearly so warm in colour as Wedgwood's Queensware.

Much of the Liverpool ware was made for the American market and is transfer-printed with subjects to suit the American taste, the national Eagle, native scenes and ships. Jugs and punch bowls were made in large quantities. The Herculaneum factory closed down in 1841.

At Swansea a factory was started in the mid 1760s and cream coloured earthenware was produced there that very much resembled that made by Wedgwood, though the earlier productions of the factory were glazed with a softish glaze that was apt to scratch, sometimes the glaze is so thin it almost looks like a salt glaze. The earlier body used at Swansea is perhaps a little unrefined, but some of the later ware is of very good quality. It is not usually quite so light in weight as the Leeds cream coloured earthenware, nor is it quite so creamy a colour.

No transfer printed ware was made at Swansea before about 1787 but in the later years of the Cambrian Pottery it was to become a large part of its output. The most delightful creamware product of the factory was the ware painted by Thomas Pardoe who worked there from 1795-1809. As well as painting simple border patterns, local views and heraldic devices, Pardoe is best known for his charming botanical studies, influenced by Dillwyn (who was a botanist) and the coloured engravings from Curtis's *Botanical Magazine*.

For further reading

Castleford Pottery Pattern Book, The 1796. Reprinted by E.P. Publishing Ltd.
J.R. and F. Kidson. *Historical Notices of the Leeds Old Pottery*. Leeds 1892.
Alan Smith. *Liverpool Herculaneum Pottery 1796-1840*. Barrie and Jenkins 1970.
Donald Towner. *Creamware*. Faber 1978.
Donald Towner. *The Leeds Pottery*. Cory Adams and McKay 1963.
Peter Walton. *Creamware and other English Pottery at Temple Newsam House, Leeds*. Manningham Press 1976.
T.A. Lockett and P.A. Halfpenny (Ed.) *Creamware and Pearlware*. Exhibition Catalogue published by City Museum and Art Gallery, Stoke-on-Trent 1986.

Leech jar with pierced cover. Early nineteenth century, made in Staffordshire or Leeds. Every apothecary's shop would have had its leech jar at that time. 286mm high. *Pharmaceutical Society, London.*

Top left: Two handled food warmer made of cream coloured earthenware in Leeds or Staffordshire. *c.* 1770-80. *Crown copyright, Victoria and Albert Museum.*

Chestnut basket, with intricate pierced decoration. Made in Leeds. Impressed HARTLEY GREENS & CO LEEDS POTTERY. *c.* 1780. 280mm high. *Leeds Art Galleries, Temple Newsam House.*

Pierced and fluted sugar cup, cover and ladle made of
cream coloured earthenware in Leeds. *c.* 1775. 140mm
high.
Crown copyright   Victoria and Albert Museum.

Two engravings of sugar cups from *The Castleford Pottery
Pattern Book* 1796. Also illustrated in the teaware section
of *The Leeds Pottery Pattern Book* (1814 edition).

Teapot decorated with underglaze green stripes, with double twisted handle with floral terminals. Made in Leeds about 1780. 140mm high.
Crown copyright, Victoria and Albert Museum.

Teapot with portrait of King George III and double twisted handle. Made in Leeds in the 1760s. 127mm high.
City Museum and Art Gallery, Stoke-on-Trent.

Teapot with hand painted floral decoration in red, green, purple and black; double twisted handle. Made in Leeds. *c.* 1780. 146mm high.
Private Collection.

Punch bowl with a hand painted scene on the other side showing a figure of Hope leaning on an anchor and a ship in the background. Superficially the style and colouring of this side looks like a production of the Leeds Pottery, but the ware is thick and heavy which perhaps indicates that it might have been made at the North Hylton Pottery near Sunderland. This pottery produced many pieces decorated with verses or inscriptions in fine bold hand lettering with roses and other flowers painted in yellow, green and an Indian red very much in this style. *c.* 1800. 234mm diameter. *Private Collection.*

Loving-cup, painted in enamel colours. Made in Yorkshire or Staffordshire. *c.* 1800. 191mm high. *Leeds Art Gallery, Temple Newsam House.*

Creamware jug decorated with a black transfer printed engraving by William Blake in 1784 after a design by Collins called 'Tythe in Kind or Sow's Revenge'. Probably made in Liverpool. *c.* 1784. 222mm high. *Private Collection.*

Cream coloured earthenware jug, with a black transfer decoration, from a drawing by Hogarth of a cock fight. Made in Liverpool. *c.* 1780. 241mm high.
Crown copyright Victoria and Albert Museum.

Cream coloured earthenware jug commemorating the fall of the Bastille. Black transfer print, probably by Sadler and Green. Made in Liverpool. *c.* 1790. 191mm high. The Liverpool cream coloured earthenware was paler and greyer in colour than that made in Staffordshire or Leeds.
Crown copyright Victoria and Albert Museum.

Creamware jug with free hand painted decoration underglaze coloured in brown, blue, green and yellow. Probably made in Staffordshire. *c.* 1790. 177mm high. *Private Collection.*

Creamware teapot with free hand painted decoration underglaze coloured in dark brown, green and yellow for the butterfly's wings. Probably made in Staffordshire. *c.* 1790. 120mm high. *Private Collection.*

Two creamware mugs, one decorated with a cornstook and agricultural implements. The colours used are the usual underglaze oxide colours of blue, manganese, ochre and black. Probably made in Staffordshire. *c.* 1790. 94mm and 96mm high. *Private Collection.*

Creamware soup plate with no foot rim, feather edged in turquoise blue and decorated with brown transfer designs of shells. Impressed mark NEALE & CO. *c.* 1790. 237mm diameter. *Private Collection.*

Creamware plate with a pierced rim and a hand painted border of pink and yellow flowers with green foliage. The banding is brown. The impressed mark is DAVENPORT with an anchor and 798. This mark with upper case lettering was used after 1805. 200mm diameter. *Private Collection.*

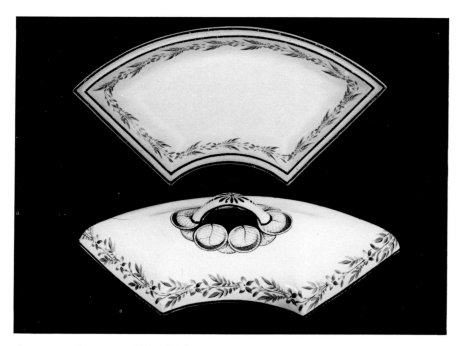

A quarter of a supper dish with its cover made in cream coloured earthenware, painted in green and grey with a border of white jasmine, manganese design round the handle and edging borders. Marked SWANSEA impressed. The glaze is softer and more easily scratched than the Wedgwood Queensware. *c.* 1780. 337mm diameter. *Private Collection.*

Dessert dish with a sepia band round the rim, painted with a striped carnation, probably by Thomas Pardoe. Marked SWANSEA and an impressed spade mark. The originals for these flower paintings were taken from Curtis's *Botanical Magazine*, *c.* 1800. 203mm diameter.
Crown copyright Victoria and Albert Museum.

Dessert plate of pale cream coloured earthenware with a sepia band round the rim, painted with a bladder hibiscus, probably by Thomas Pardoe. Marked SWANSEA and an impressed spade mark. *c.* 1800. 216mm diameter.
Crown copyright, Victoria and Albert Museum.

Dinner plate with a shell edge, painted with armorial bearings. Swansea. *c.* 1810-20. 203mm diameter.
Crown copyright, Victoria and Albert Museum.

Swansea creamware plate, decorated with a black transfer print of a merchant brig of about 1800. Marked DILLWYN impressed. The artist has drawn the pre-Union Jack. Made in the period 1831-50. 226mm diameter. *Private Collection.*

Jug decorated with emblems of the sweep's trade. Made in Staffordshire. *c.* 1800. 260mm high. *The Royal Pavilion Art Gallery and Museum, Brighton.*

Creamware jug decorated mainly in blue and yellow. Inscribed 'John and Lettis Bancroft 1805'. Mr. Bancroft was obviously a tiler and the reverse side of the jug shows all the implements of the tiler's trade. 242mm high. *Courtesy Earle D. Vandekar.*

Creamware jug, black transfer printed, enamel coloured and inscribed 'W.B. No.122' in a wreath under the spout. There is a copper lustre band round the neck and a purple lustre decoration on spout and handle. Inscribed on scrolls is the message 'The Cotton Tree – Success to the Friendly Cotton Spinners Commerce.' *c.* 1810. 152mm high. *Private Collection.* These two jugs were probably made in Staffordshire.

Creamware jug transfer printed with the Arms of the Cordwainers and inscribed in red 'A.P.1810' under the spout. There is also a red hand painted border and a red band round the foot. On three scrolls are lettered 'Unite to maintain our rights inviolate, Prosperity attend the justness of our cause' and 'The Friendly Society of Cordwainers of England'. On the other side of the jug are two enamel coloured Oriental figures. 1810. 152mm high. *Private Collection.*

10. Pearl ware

The 'Pearl white' ware that Josiah Wedgwood had developed in the late 1770s did not particularly please him, he admitted that he much preferred his cream coloured earthenware. The whiteness was obtained by adding more white clay and calcined flint than usual to the clay mixture. The Wedgwood firm went on making pearl ware well into the nineteenth century and from about 1840 the name 'Pearl' was impressed into the body.[1]

Some of the most attractive of the pearl ware designs were made by Wedgwoods in the first decade of the nineteenth century. The 'Waterlily' pattern was a particularly robust transfer design and some of the transfer designs with added enamel colouring such as the 'Japan' patterns were most effective.

Other potters were quick to try to copy this whiter body, some added a certain amount of cobalt or zaffre to the glaze to counteract any creaminess in clay they were using. This can easily be seen in some

1. See Godden *An Illustrated Encyclopedia of British Pottery and Porcelain*.

Pearl ware plate with the Waterlily pattern, sepia transfer design produced by Josiah Wedgwood II in 1806. On his advice, in 1807 a 150-piece service of this ware was ordered by Josiah's sister Susannah. She was married to Dr. Robert Darwin and was later to become the mother of Charles Darwin. 203mm diameter. *Courtesy of the Trustees of the Wedgwood Museum, Barlaston, Stoke-on-Trent.*

Pearl ware soup plate decorated with a blue transfer printed design with enamel colours added, Indian red, blue and green. This is one of the so-called 'Japan' patterns. Made by Wedgwoods. *c.* 1810. 203mm diameter. *Courtesy of the Trustees of the Wedgwood Museum, Barlaston, Stoke-on-Trent.*

Two large pearl ware figures of horses. The top animal is decorated with enamel colours and the other one is spotted with colour under the glaze. Made for display in the shops of harness makers, corn chandlers, horse doctors and chemists specialising in veterinary supplies. Made at the Leeds Pottery between 1800-20. 406mm high. *Leeds Art Gallery, Temple Newsam House and Sotheby and Co.*

Two views of a two-handled pearl ware mug, with yellow frogs and a green lizard, spotted in black. Impressed on the base LEEDS POTTERY. *c.* 1790. 108mm high. *Private Collection.*

relief decorated ware where the glaze has pooled in the indentations.

The Leeds Pottery made some good pearl ware from about 1790, much of it decorated with underglaze blue printing in pseudo-Oriental style. The same pottery made pearl ware figures of a rather naïve and stilted kind. They also made some delightful models of horses (also in cream coloured earthenware) some 381mm-407mm high. These large models were something of a technical triumph for the earthenware potters, for the legs were thin and delicate and quite unsupported. These horses were finished in several ways; some were painted in enamel colours and others were spotted or dappled or sponged with colours under the glaze. They were bought by saddlers and chemists who specialised in veterinary supplies, for the decoration of their shop windows.

These large horses were again made in the late nineteenth and early twentieth centuries by the Seniors of Leeds, but only in cream coloured earthenware.[2]

An even whiter ware with much less cobalt in the glaze was manufactured by Wedgwoods about 1809. This was designated 'White Ware' and indicated 'WW' in the firm's pattern books. It was more expensive than creamware.

2. See Heather Lawrence *Yorkshire Pots and Potteries* 1974.

For further reading
Ann Finer and George Savage (Ed.). *The Selected Letters of Josiah Wedgwood.* Cory, Adams and Mackay, London 1965.
Donald Towner. *The Leeds Pottery.* Cory, Adams and Mackay, London 1963.
T.A. Lockett and P.A. Halfpenny (Ed.) *Creamware and Pearlware.* Exhibition Catalogue published by City Museum and Art Gallery, Stoke-on-Trent 1986.

This pearl ware jug painted in blue and inscribed 'Tidmarsh's Original Staffordshire Warehouse N 1715' was made in Staffordshire, possibly by James Tidmarsh of Cobridge for display in a warehouse in London, owned by one of the Tidmarsh family known to have been dealers in earthenware during the 18th century. 394mm high. *City Museum and Art Gallery, Stoke-on-Trent.*

If the 'N 1715' is a date, quite clearly it cannot refer to the date of manufacture of this jug, which must have been nearer to 1800.

Pearl ware electioneering punch bowl. The reverse side shows the MP entering London with St. Paul's in the background. Inside are the arms of the Tailor's Guild, the name 'J.E. Pepperday' and a scroll bearing the words: 'One bowl more and then'. *c.* 1780. 406mm diameter. *Courtesy Earle D. Vandekar.*

Pearl ware cruet set consisting of a circular stand with a pierced border and circular apertures for holding the individual containers. Each of these is finely painted with sprigs of cornflowers in blue, red and green. The banding is blue and the lettering black. The handle which must have been threaded into the centre is missing. *c.* 1800. Diameter of stand 203mm. *Courtesy Sotheby's.*

Pearl ware diamond shaped teapot with a swan knob on the lid. This is the same shape as other teapots marked HARLEY. (This was Thomas Harley 1778-1832 who was the son-in-law of William Pratt of Lane Delph.) Enamel coloured in pink, green, blue and yellow. *c.* 1805. 165mm high.
Private Collection.

Pearl ware plate with hand painted border design in green, mauve, sepia, yellow and red with a blue band round the edge. Impressed WEDGWOOD and an upper case 'G' on its side above. *c.* 1812-14. 205mm diameter. *Private Collection.* This design is entry 1141 in the second of the early pattern books. Although the body of this plate with its bluish glaze looks very like pearl ware, the pattern is listed under White Ware designs in one of the Wedgwood catalogues.

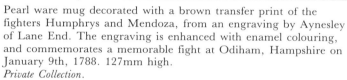

Pearl ware mug decorated with a brown transfer print of the fighters Humphrys and Mendoza, from an engraving by Aynesley of Lane End. The engraving is enhanced with enamel colouring, and commemorates a memorable fight at Odiham, Hampshire on January 9th, 1788. 127mm high.
Private Collection.

Pearl ware mug transfer printed in black with additional enamel colouring made to commemorate the death of Lord Viscount Nelson in 1805. Marked Newcastle Pottery. This was Addison, Falconer and Co. Newcastle Pottery Skinnerburn. 127mm high.
Private Collection.

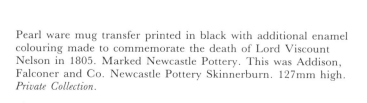

Plate 19. Stone china plate decorated with a hand painted design of flowers in a Chinese landscape, within a pseudo-Oriental border. The predominating colour being Indian red, with two greens, two blues, pink and a little gilding. Under the base is a bluish green transfer of the royal coat of arms with 'Imperial Stone China' above in a copper plate script and the initials J R on a ribbon below the shield and the pattern number 5822, a W pencilled in green and an impressed X. Made by John Ridgway, Hanley. *c.* 1830.
260mm diameter. *Private Collection*.

Plate 20. Soup plate with a blue underglaze transfer pattern of an Oriental landscape enamelled over the glaze in pink, Indian red, yellow and two greens. On the back of the plate is a large blue transfer printed mark of the royal coat of arms (with the inner escutcheon) and with Prince of Wales' Feathers draped over the top. Below in large capital letters in a straight line are the words IMPROVED IRONSTONE CHINA. Similar to No 4454 in Godden's encyclopedia of marks. *c.* 1820.
245mm diameter. *Private Collection*.

According to Mr. Godden, this unidentified mark 'occurs on good quality ironstone wares of the period 1815-25.'

11. Stone China

Ironstone mug. The royal blue ground is ornamented with gilt stars. Reserve panels in polychrome enamels. The rim painted with a diaper pattern border in red and gilt with reserve panels in puce. Marked 'Turner's Patent' in red. *c.* 1805. 153mm high. *City Museum and Art Gallery, Stoke-on-Trent.*

Cream-coloured earthenware had been superseded by earthenware with a much whiter body. The 'pearl white' ware with its rather dull greyish tinge that Wedgwood in 1779 had considered a change rather than an improvement, though made by the Leeds pottery and by other potters in Staffordshire, never really caught the public fancy. However a development that did capture the public imagination was 'stone china'. This was usually a white, clear body, very like porcelain in fact, but it was not translucent. It was harder and more durable than the creamware bodies of the previous century.

The Turners of Lane End were the first potters to experiment with this new body; they added a new ground stone to the clay, and patented their invention in 1800. This 'patent' stone was called 'Tabberner's Mine Rock' or 'Little Mine Rock' and they first obtained it from some land belonging to the Marquis of Stafford. If he had not stopped them using the stone, the Turners might never have gone bankrupt (as they did in 1806).

Spode and Adams bought up some of the Turners' moulds. Josiah Spode II had also been making 'stone china' since 1805; this was decorated with designs of a mainly Oriental character, for the Neo-classicism of the mid-eighteenth century had given way to a fashion for Chinoiserie, the culminating triumph of which can be seen in the Royal Pavilion at Brighton. Many other potters experimented with this body, including the Ridgways and Knight, Elkin & Co.

But the most famous of all the stone china was made by the Masons of Lane Delph. In 1813, Charles James Mason (whose father had first imported and then made porcelain), patented a strong, hard earthenware very like that produced by Spode and he called it 'Mason's Patent Ironstone China'. This was a brilliantly successful name as it sounded not only strong and reliable, but superior as well, and it at once appealed to the public. Mason's designs were robust in the extreme, cribbed or adapted from Oriental originals, with strong bright colours, often with gilding. In addition to table ware he made large vases and other decorative pieces including four-poster beds and fireplace surrounds, the latter sometimes in a heavy rococo style. For some time the business prospered and great fortunes were made for the Mason family. Eventually labour troubles broke out and in 1848 the whole concern was sold up. He had been declared bankrupt. However, by 1849, he was at work again, this time in a small factory at Longton. He exhibited some specimens of his Patent Ironstone China at the Crystal Palace, but in spite of this, he never really recovered from his financial failure. He gave up work in 1853 and died two years later. The history of the Masons makes fascinating reading.[1] The Mason

1. Reginald G. Haggar *The Masons of Lane Delph.* Privately published 1952.

Plate printed with the Willis pattern on glaze in light sepia brilliantly enamelled by hand with bead below shoulder in gold. Marked 2147 in red and SPODE STONE CHINA. *c.* 1813-16. 242mm diameter. *Spode Museum.*

Plate printed with the Peacock pattern on glaze in light sepia brilliantly enamelled by hand, bead at edge and shoulders in gold. Marked 2083 in red and SPODE STONE CHINA. *c.* 1813-16. 242mm diameter. *Spode Museum.*

Stone china plate with a markedly grey-blue body, simulating Chinese export porcelain. The decoration is hand painted in Indian red, yellow, green, turquoise and blue over a blue transfer outline. This bears the earliest of the SPODE stone china marks printed in blue and the pattern number pencilled in red (2117). *c.* 1813. 210mm diameter. *Private Collection.*

moulds and patterns were acquired by Francis Morley (a distant descendant of the Morley who had made stoneware in Nottingham and whose trade card is shown on page 59), and some of them have been in use ever since. Francis Morley had married a Ridgway (another famous potting family) and when his father-in-law retired he took on his business. It was Morley, who, in 1840 had introduced the use of lithographic printing into the ceramic industry. He took into partnership a young man called Taylor Ashworth, who became his partner three years later. Upon Morley's retirement the name of the firm was changed to Geo. L. Ashworth and Brothers and was so called until 1968, although in 1883 the business had been bought by Mr J.H. Goddard for his son John Shaw Goddard, whose son and later grandson remained in control. In 1968 the name of the firm was changed to Mason's Ironstone China Limited. In 1973 the firm joined the Wedgwood group.

For further reading

R.G. Haggar. *The Masons of Lane Delph*. Printed for Geo. L. Ashworth by Percy Lund Humphries 1952.

Bevis Hillier. *The Turners of Lane End*. Cory, Adams and Mackay, London 1965.

R.G. Haggar and E. Adams. *Mason Porcelain and Ironstone 1796-1853*. Faber 1977.

G.A. Godden. *Mason's China and the Ironstone Wares*. Antique Collectors' Club 1984.

Plate with a Japanese waterlily pattern hand painted in a dark, rich blue, two greens, pink and orange with gilding added. Impressed mark on base MASON'S PATENT IRONSTONE CHINA. *c.* 1813-25. 241mm diameter. *Private Collection*.

Ironstone plate decorated with a border of Oriental animals transfer printed in brown and filled in with bright enamel colours against a dark blue background. Printed mark 'Mason's' in brown on the back then a crown and 'Patent Ironstone China' in a ribbon below. *c.* 1830-40. 238mm diameter. *Private Collection*.

Jug decorated with a similar pattern to the plate above, but with a blue printed Crown mark and IRONSTONE WARRANTED. Probably made later to match. 165mm high. *Private Collection*.

Elaborately painted and gilded vase made by C.M. and C.J. Mason. Impressed mark on base MASON'S PATENT IRONSTONE CHINA. *c.* 1820. 368mm high. *Private Collection* .

Small jug with a handle in the form of some grotesque animal, decorated in a rich royal blue with gilding. Unmarked, but probably made by Mason's. *c.* 1813-25. 95mm high. *Private Collection*.

Small jug with a serpent handle, decorated in a rich royal blue with gilding. Marked MASON'S PATENT IRONSTONE CHINA impressed. *c.* 1813-25. 114mm high. *Private Collection*.

Small jug with serpent handle decorated in bright enamel colours of blue, red and green with additional gilding. Mark MASON'S PATENT IRONSTONE CHINA impressed. *c.* 1813-25. 95mm high. *Private Collection*.

Small plate transfer printed in blue under the glaze with the scene of a heron in an Oriental landscape with waterbirds and peonies in the border. Enamel coloured over the glaze in pink and Indian red with much added gilding. Impressed on the back a crown encircled with CLEWS STONE CHINA WARRANTED. *c.* 1825. 155mm diameter. *Private Collection*. James and Ralph Clews were potting at Cobridge, Staffordshire from 1818 to 1834.

Plate with a brown outline transfer design, hand coloured in dark blue, Indian red and pale green with a little outline gilding. Under the base is a brown transfer printed coat of arms with the lettering KNIGHT, ELKIN & CO IRONSTONE CHINA and No 48 pencilled in red. Also there is an impressed oblong mark with the same wording with the addition of WARRANTED. *c.* 1830. 223mm diameter. *Private Collection.*

An octagonal shaped jug, sparely painted with enamel colours and little gilding; uncoloured reliefs of Britannia, Clio and Apollo and vegetable forms separate the coloured decorations. The handle terminates in a serpent's head. Under the base is a blue transfer printed urn, backed with vegetation and a drape with the words IRONSTONE CHINA. This mark was used by the Hackwoods, a family of potters who worked both in Shelton and Hanley. *c.* 1830-40. 192mm high. *Private Collection.*

Meat dish, transfer printed in blue, made by Thomas Dimmock and Co., Shelton and Hanley. The name of the pattern 'Morea' is in a cartouche with STONE CHINA, there is also an impressed mark of two interlaced cursive capital Ds. *c.* 1828-59. 426mm wide. *Private Collection.*

12. Josiah Spode and early transfer printing

Miniature of Josiah Spode the first (1733-1797). *Spode Museum.*

The taste of Josiah Wedgwood had been influenced almost entirely by the Neo-classical movement. He was not attracted by Oriental art or influenced by the Chinese inspired designs then being painted in underglaze blue at the porcelain factories of Worcester and Caughley.

Josiah Spode, who had been apprenticed to Whieldon and was three years younger than Wedgwood, was certainly influenced by Oriental designs. Also it was he who introduced underglaze blue printing into Staffordshire. He employed two men from the Caughley factory, Thomas Lucas, an engraver, and James Richards, a printer. Spode no doubt saw (as Wedgwood had remarked in 1779) that the public was always demanding a change and the intricately engraved transfer-printed blue patterns in the Oriental taste which he introduced to Staffordshire in 1781 were certainly a change from the plain or sparsely decorated Queensware of the preceding period. Mintons (Spode's great rivals) and many other Staffordshire potters as well as potters in other districts, were quick to follow Spode's lead and the production of blue transfer-printed earthenware continued throughout the nineteenth century. In fact until the present day, versions of the famous 'Willow' pattern are still being made.

From 1781-1833 literally dozens of patterns were produced by the Spode engravers, and altogether hundreds of designs must have been made by the English potters. Many were copied from Chinese designs, others from Indian and Italian originals (though on the whole very few of them were Neo-classical). A large series of designs was taken by the Spode factory from a book of anonymous engravings published in 1803.[1] It became common practice for the potters to borrow their designs wholesale from books of this sort, and the whole surface of the ware was covered in the resulting prints.

The body of Spode's earthenware varied in colour from very pale cream to pure white and it had a silky-feeling glaze. It is very light in weight compared to modern earthenware. The stone china and pearl ware bodies also used by the firm were of equally good quality.

Although the blue-and-white transfer-printed ware was mainly bought by the professional classes, when mass production really got under way it became less and less expensive, until it was within the reach of everybody.

---

1. *Views in the Ottoman Empire chiefly in Caramania, a port of Asia Minor, hitherto unexplored with some curious selections from the Island of Rhodes and Cyprus, and the celebrated cities of Corinth, Carthage and Tripoli, from the original drawings in possession of Sir R. Ainslie, taken during his Embassy to Constantinople by* Luigi Mayer.

Small scale pottery model of the Spode
factory at Stoke as it was in about 1820.
Each oven measures 70mm in height.
Many of the parts of the model were
recognisable with old buildings still
standing in the 1950s. *Spode Museum.*

An engraved bill-head used at the Spode
factory in the late eighteenth century.
The signature is of W. Copeland who
was closely associated with Josiah Spode
the first, and whose son eventually
became sole owner of the Spode factory
in 1847. *Spode Museum.*

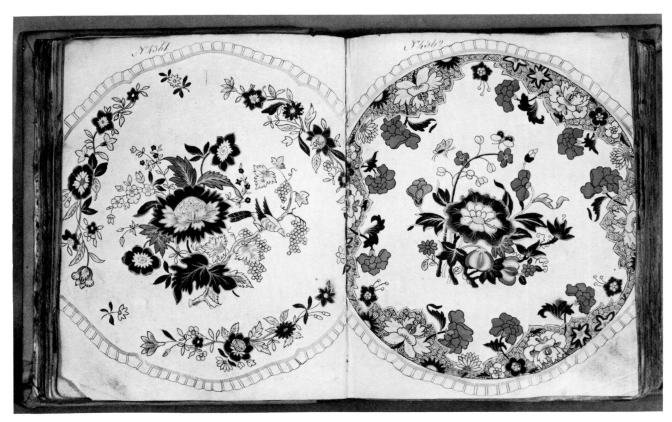

A double spread from the fourth of the old pattern books of Josiah Spode. The first of these books was begun in 1770. *Spode Museum.*

The 'Ship' border drawn on this page of the pattern book can be seen on Plate 22 opposite.

Print taken from a copper engraving for the centre of a dinner plate of a Willow Pattern service produced by Spode. *c.* 1790. The design was developed from a Chinese pattern called 'Mandarin'. The foreground is line and not stipple. *Courtesy Robert Copeland.*

Print taken from the engraving for a dinner plate from a Willow Pattern service. It was said to have been engraved by Thomas Minton. *c.* 1790-93, but as stipple engraving did not come in until 1800, the dates do not tally.

Plate 21. Pearl ware plate with the 'Bowpot' design in the centre. This design (1816) was copied from the Chinese and first introduced in 1813. The pattern number for this particular version is 3995, and was introduced in 1824. It is set within the so-called 'Ship' border. The design has been printed in black outline and beautifully hand coloured with green predominating over the pinks, blues, Indian reds and yellows. Impressed SPODE and SPODE printed in black, also a painter's mark of a green circle and three dots. *c.* 1824. 223mm diameter.
Private Collection.

Plate 22. Creamware plate decorated in the centre with a spray of English flowers, pattern No B 171. Outline transfer in green and hand painted in underglaze colours. The 'Ship' border (actually a Kakiemon design with peonies) is transfer printed in red and filled in with underglaze colours. On the back of the plate is the impressed mark SPODE and a transfer printed mark in red of a cartouche enclosing the words 'Spode's New Faience'. *c.* 1827-33. 212mm diameter. *Private Collection.*

The Ship border is so-called because it was first used on a plate decorated with a scene incorporating an Oriental version of an East Indiaman. The border was used from 1816 to 1833.

Plate 23. Creamware dessert plate with a green all-over transfer printed design painted in enamel colours with mauve, blue, green and primrose yellow predominating. The pattern is number No B 163 and appeared in 1826. Impressed SPODE and marked SPODE printed in black on the base. *c.* 1829-33. 267mm diameter. *Private Collection.*

This dessert plate is exactly as illustrated in the Spode pattern book No B 163.

Oblong tray with a pearl ware body decorated with the blue transfer print of the pattern known as 'Bridge 1'. This was copied from a Chinese original. *c.* 1800. Mark SPODE impressed

42

in rather small capital letters. *c.* 1800-30. 243mm long. *Private Collection*.

Earthenware plate with the 'Greek' pattern transfer printed in blue under the glaze. The quality of the engraving in this series is of the highest standard. These Greek patterns were based on drawings in a large work giving details of the collection of Sir William Hamilton.[1] *c.* 1806. 248mm diameter. *Private Collection*.

[1]*Etruscan, Greek and Roman Antiquities* by Pierre François Hugues with engravings by F.A. David. Paris 1785.

Earthenware plate: 'Caramanian' pattern, printed in cobalt blue under the glaze. A very fine production where Spode used old prints as a basis for the centre decoration. The scene depicts 'Sarcophagi and Sepulchres at the head of the harbour at Cacamo'. The border of animals, figures, etc. is not quite in keeping with the centre, and an attempt has been made by the artist to tie in the two by including palm trees in the centre, which do not appear in the original print. The engraving technique is mainly stipple and punch-work, very finely executed. *c.* 1809. 254mm diameter. Impressed SPODE. *Private Collection*.

Shell-shaped dish printed in blue with a transfer design copied from a Chinese original of the K'ang Hsi period (1700-22). The design is known as 'Long Eliza' or 'Lange Lijsen' after a Dutch version of the design meaning 'slender damsel'. Marked SPODE impressed and also SPODE in blue on the base. There is also a capital A pencilled in blue. *c.* 1812-33. 235mm wide. *Private Collection.*

White earthenware plate with a border of 'Blue Italian' pattern printed under the glaze with an odd centre print in sepia. After firing the border has been enamelled in red and traced in gold. The centre design is coloured with pink, red, yellow and green enamel with a little gilding. Impressed SPODE and 2635 pencilled in red on the base. *c.* 1818. 205mm diameter. *Private Collection.*

Earthenware plate: 'Floral' pattern. Blue printed floral cartouche on the back with the word 'Floral' in script, also impressed SPODE in small capitals. Printed in cobalt blue under the glaze. A delightful pattern quite distinct in style from other Spode blue decorations. Practically the whole of this pattern is engraved using line work. Each piece has a different botanical floral centre and all are remarkably good. This pattern was one of the later productions of the Spode period and reflects great credit on the craftsmen of the time. In the centre of this plate is a passion flower. *c.* 1830-33. 254mm diameter. *Private Collection.*

149

Pearl ware dish decorated with a dark chocolate outline transfer design of peonies and other flowers and enamelled in pink, Indian red, blue and two greens. The border is the familiar 'Ship' design and there is a chocolate coloured line round the edge of the dish. This is probably pattern No 3831, introduced in 1824. Impressed mark SPODE in capitals and SPODE printed in brown on the back. *c*. 1824-33. 267mm wide. *Private Collection*.

Creamware plate with hand painted decoration of freely painted lotus, other flowers and two golden ducks in orange, pink, blue, two greens, red and gilding. The red outlined gilt border, pattern No 3684 is also freely drawn. This pattern was first introduced in 1823. There is no foot rim to this plate which is very light in weight. It is impressed SPODE on the base. *c*. 1823. 212mm diameter.

16

Private Collection.

This plate is almost certainly a 'matching', that is a piece that has been specially made to replace a broken plate from a Chinese service.

Cream coloured earthenware plate with hand painted Chinese style pattern, the outline faintly traced in sepia and red. The flowers and leaves are delicately shaded and filled in with bright enamel on glaze colours. Impressed SPODE and 3730 pencilled in red on the base. *c*. 1820. 212mm wide. *Private Collection*.

For further reading

A.W. Coysh and R.K. Henrywood. *The Dictionary of Blue and White Printed Pottery 1780-1880*. Antique Collectors' Club 1982.
David Drakard and Paul Holdway. *Spode Printed Ware*. Longman 1983.
Arthur Hayden. *Spode and his Successors*. Longman 1925.
Leonard Whiter. *Spode*. Barrie and Jenkins 1970.
S.B. Williams. *Antique Blue and White Spode*. Batsford 1943.

13. Nineteenth century transfer printed wares

INCLUDING RAILWAY COMMEMORATIVE POTTERY

A large export trade with America grew up, Enoch Wood's factory exporting ship loads of printed ware, much specially designed for that market. Blue and other colours were used on the transfer-printed tablewares of the nineteenth century. Many of the more expensive designs were transfer-printed in a basic outline of either grey or purple and enamel colours were filled in by hand on top of the glaze when it had been fired. Other transfers were printed in black or red.

For the cheaper side of the trade, dozens of small potteries were turning out transfer printed wares of all kinds to suit the new mass market created by the industrial revolution. Some of these wares were very primitive, but none the less have a certain charm.

Rather more sophisticated pieces were made by such firms as those of Enoch Wood and Minton. The Wood factory produced some beautiful dark blue transfer-decorated plates with American railway scenes (the Baltimore and Ohio railroad being one of them), sometimes bordered by the same shell design as on page 152, which they exported in large shipments to the New World.

A number of small factories in Staffordshire produced railway commemorative pieces, though they by no means always marked their ware. It was also made in potteries in Sunderland and Stockton-on-Tees and Newcastle upon Tyne. The greatest quantity of railway ware was produced between 1830 (the opening of the Liverpool and Manchester Railway) and 1850, though other pieces were made right through the nineteenth century and as late as the 1950s.

The nineteenth century was the great age of steam – the Railway Age – the age of cheap and popular travel. The potteries cashed in on this by making railway souvenirs in great quantities for the travelling public to buy. The opening of a new line, the introduction of a new

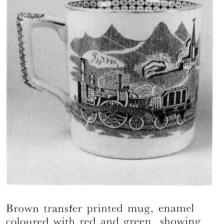

Brown transfer printed mug, enamel coloured with red and green, showing the locomotive 'Express' drawing two carriages and an empty horsedrawn carriage mounted on a wagon base. Made in Staffordshire and with the mark RAILWAY W. ADAMS & CO ENGLAND printed on the base in brown transfer. Made after 1891. 102mm high. A later version of a much earlier design. *Private Collection.*

An engraving of the east front of the Fountain Place Works, the manufactory of Enoch Wood and Sons at Burslem in 1833.

White earthenware plate, transfer printed in a rich dark blue under the glaze. Made by Enoch Wood and Sons (printed in blue on the back) specially for the American market. *c.* 1830. 252mm diameter. *Crown copyright Victoria and Albert Museum.*

Plate transfer printed in red and green with a view of the Moorish Arch of the Liverpool and Manchester Railway. Marked E.W. & S. in a shield with a lion crest (Enoch Wood and Sons, Burslem). *c.* 1830. 227mm diameter. *Private Collection.*

This jug was presented to Joseph Bailey by Joseph Wood 'for the great attention and humanity rendered to him after his providential escape from the wreck of the Earl Moira on the 9 August 1821' Joseph Wood (born 1795) was the brother of Enoch Wood II. *The Earl of Moira* was the Liverpool-Dublin packet; she went down on the Burbo Banks

near Liverpool with the loss of forty lives. She was a cutter of 89 tons and built in 1808. This jug must have been made at Enoch Wood's factory in 1821. There are two views of the factory on the sides of the jug and the inscription under the spout. Transfer printed in black with hand painted lettering. 367mm high. *Private Collection.*

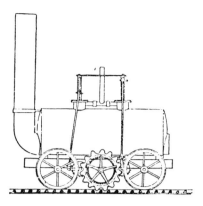

Locomotive *Blenkinsop* 1812, from *The Development of the Locomotive 1803-1896*. Clement E. Stretton.

Large jug transfer printed in blue with an engraving showing John Blenkinsop's locomotive and train of coal wagons on the viaduct at Leeds. Christ Church, Leeds, on the other side. Possibly made in Leeds or at the Don Pottery. *c.* 1812. 214mm high. *Private Collection*

Mug transfer printed in dark red showing the *William the Fourth* locomotive built by Braithwaite and Ericsson in 1830 on the Liverpool and Manchester Railway. Unmarked but probably Leeds. 1830. 95mm high.

locomotive, the building of a new bridge were all seized upon by the designers of transfers. The opening of the Liverpool and Manchester Railway was the most commemorated event of all.

The railway pottery was nearly all of a fairly crude quality, but as always there were exceptions. However, today, even the crudest of these pieces are of interest to the collector, not only of nineteenth century pottery, but of railway relics as well.

These railway pieces were made to be used: mugs, jugs, bowls and plates are most often found; they are seldom in good condition being chipped, cracked and discoloured as though they had been subject to hard wear. As they must have been made very cheaply and in large quantities, obviously they were little valued at the time.[1]

The manufacture of this railway commemoration pottery began before Queen Victoria came to the throne. The first railway was bringing coal to Leeds from the Middleton Colliery by about 1812 (incidentally passing the site of the Leeds Pottery), and Blenkinsop's engine with its train of coal trucks is the first locomotive to be illustrated on pottery.[2] The *William the Fourth, Novelty, Rocket, Fury, Express* and many more followed.

1. A few of the main producers of railway pottery: Ellis, Unwin and Mountford, Unwin Mountford and Taylor *c.* 1864-65. Edge Malkin and Co. 1871. Ford Challinor and Co. 1855. Jackson and Gosling, Wood Challinor, and W. Smith and Co. of Stockton-upon-Tees 1825-55. Enoch Wood and Sons 1830s.
2. John Blenkinsop, the Manager of the Middleton Collieries, paid the Leeds Pottery £7 per annum for allowing the line to cross their land. He also allowed them a discount on the price of coal supplied to the pottery.

Jug transfer printed in lilac. Entrance to the Liverpool and Manchester Railway. The shape of this jug, though not uncommon, is rarely found with railway transfer decoration. Probably made in Staffordshire. *c.* 1830. Unmarked. Base 80mm diameter. *Private Collection.*

Frog mug transfer printed in black with a design showing the *Rocket* and *Northumberland* and the Liverpool Exchange Buildings. Inside the *Novelty* and carriages for passengers as well as a portrait of Queen Adelaide. The transfers are copied from prints by W. Crane *Eight Views illustrating the Liverpool and Manchester Railway* (Chester) 1830. Unmarked. *c.* 1830. 118mm high. *Private Collection.*

Bowl transfer printed in sepia. The *Fury* locomotive on the L. & M.R. The *Fury* was built by Fenton Murray in August 1831. Bowls of this type are very rare, though mugs are common enough. Marked on base 'Railway' on a scroll and J. & R.G. (John and Robert Godwin, Cobridge, Staffs. 1834-66). Base 85mm diameter. *Private Collection.*

Quart mug transfer printed in black with a design showing the entrance to the Liverpool and Manchester Railway. This view of the Moorish Arch is taken from Henry Booth's *An Account of the Liverpool and Manchester Railway* 1st Edition 1830. The *Novelty* was built by Braithwaite and Ericsson and took part in the famous Rainhill Trials. Unmarked. 1830. Base 130mm diameter.

Blue transfer printed mug showing the *London* locomotive L. & M.R.. The three coaches the other side called *Victoria, Coronation* and *London Royal Mail Liverpool*. 1837, the year of Queen Victoria's Coronation and the partial opening of the main lines from London to Liverpool. Unmarked. 124mm high. *Private Collection*.

Both sides of an earthenware mug with black transfer designs enriched with pink and green enamel colouring. The engine named 'Wooda' is drawing a tender, two carriages and a

horse-drawn carriage with a party of holiday makers mounted on a wagon base. Made in Staffordshire probably by John and Robert Godwin. *c.* 1840. 102mm high.

White deep earthenware dish. Transfer printed in black under the glaze. On the back a cartouche with the word 'Tourist' and W.S. & Co. and impressed WEDGEWOOD. Made by W. Smith and Co. of Stockton-on-Tees some time before 1848. 337mm wide. *Private Collection*.

White earthenware perforated fish drainer, transfer printed in black under the glaze with a design from the 'Tourist' pattern. Made by W. Smith and Co. of Stockton-on-Tees before 1848. 305mm wide. *Private Collection*.

A good white earthenware with black transfer printed designs was made by W. Smith and Co. of Stockton-on-Tees from about 1825-55. William Smith produced a blue 'Willow' pattern which he marked 'Queensware'; other patterns printed in black like his 'Tourist' pattern he shamelessly stamped WEDGEWOOD (with an 'E' in the middle) until the Wedgwood firm prevented him from doing this by taking out an injunction in 1848.

White earthenware loving cup decorated with a black underglaze transfer design of exotic birds. The other side bears the following verse:

'A friend that is social, good natured and free
To a pot of my liquor right welcome shall be;
But he that is proud and ill natured may pass
By my door to an alehouse and pay for his glass.'

Probably made at one of the Sunderland potteries. *c.* 1840-50. 162mm high. *Private Collection.*

Cream coloured earthenware jug with a black transfer design under the glaze, composed of the tools of the farmer's trade with a long doggerel verse and various pious mottoes including INDUSTRY PRODUCETH WEALTH. *c.* 1850. 130mm high. *Private Collection.*

Coarse white earthenware commemoration mug with black transfer designs. On one side a verse describing the rescue of the crew of the *Forfarshire* in 1838 in the Farne Islands, on the front and inscription 'Grace Darling the Northumbrian Heroine Born 1815 Died Oct 20 1842' and on the other side a portrait of the lady rowing her boat through tempestuous seas, enamel coloured in blue, pink, green and ochre. Probably made at one of the Tyneside potteries. *c.* 1842. 102mm high. *Private Collection.*

White earthenware jug, transfer printed in brown under the glaze and enamel coloured over the glaze in blue, green, pink and yellow. On the other side is a somewhat bizarre floral arrangement. Impressed under the base TWIGG'S in capital letters. Made by J. Twigg and Co either at the Newhill Pottery or the Kilnhurst Old Pottery *c.*1850. 233mm high. *Private Collection.*

Brown earthenware coffee pot, dish and two tiles in 'Paisley', 'Mosaic' and 'Plaited cane' designs, transfer printed in yellow slip and made at the Scott Brothers Southwick Pottery, Sunderland. Dish impressed SCOTT BROTHERS. *c.* 1850. Width of dish 317mm. *Sunderland Museum Collection*.

Below:
Two brown earthenware jugs and a coffee pot all with the 'Paisley' transfer design in yellow slip made at the Scott Brothers Southwick Pottery, Sunderland. *c.* 1850. Coffee pot 214mm high. *c.* 1850. *Sunderland Museum Collection*.

Brown earthenware jug transfer printed in yellow slip with a pseudo-Oriental design. Though similar in technique to the Scott's productions the design is much more sophisticated and the inside of the jug has been washed with white slip. Probably made in Staffordshire (or possibly Swansea). *c.* 1810. 145mm high. *Private Collection.*

Right: Brown earthenware jug transfer printed in yellow slip with an Oriental design including figures and peonies. The inside of the jug has been washed with white slip. Probably made in Staffordshire. *c.* 1810. 148mm high. *Private Collection.*

Note:
Rodney Hampson suggests that the Scotts' ware was printed in a white slip covered in a yellow glaze. The yellow transfer ware made in Staffordshire was printed in a yellow slip under a colourless glaze.

YELLOW TRANSFER WARE

Among transfer printed wares was a distinctive type of pottery covered with a shiny brown (or sometimes olive grey) glaze, with yellow designs giving a curious but pleasing 'negative' effect. Cane-weave, Mosaic and Paisley patterns were all used. This ware was made at the Southwick Pottery in Sunderland, owned from 1800-1890 by a family called Scott. Some pieces were marked A. Scott and Sons or Scott Brothers and Co. and other variations. These marks have been frequently confused with the Scott Brothers who were at one time thought to have had a pottery at Portobello near Edinburgh *c.* 1786-96. Patrick McVeigh in his book *Scottish East Coast Potteries 1750-1830* has done much to dispel the Scott-Portobello myth and also suggests that the ware might have been made in Staffordshire. The rather bold, even crude patterns on the marked Scott pieces bear little relation to the pseudo-Chinese, rather delicately engraved designs with pagodas, junks and peonies found on other brown earthenware. These pieces are usually coated inside with white slip, unlike the identified Scott pieces. There is now proof that this type of ware was made in Staffordshire. Rodney Hampson found a description by W.H. Goss, written in 1879, of a similar jug which had been hidden by Thomas Wedgwood in 1810, with other specimens of local manufacture, in Burslem.

Similar ware with Chinoiserie designs also seems to have been made in Swansea in the early nineteenth century. Unmarked specimens attributed to the Cambrian Pottery can be seen at the Glynn Vivian Art Gallery, Swansea and at the National Museum of Wales at Cardiff. The Cardiff example is coated inside with white slip and is reputed to have been used as a beer jug at the Pontypool Japan Works (no proof, however that it was made in Wales). Similar jugs and mugs decorated with yellow transfers commemorating Admirals Nelson and Collingwood are also to be found. These are white inside and may have been made at either Swansea or in Staffordshire.

Shell decorated with splashed pink lustre of the type known as 'Moonlight'. Made by Wedgwood. *c.* 1805. 254mm wide. *Crown copyright Victoria and Albert Museum.*

Splashed pink lustre so-called 'Moonlight' plate in the form of a pecten shell. Impressed WEDGWOOD. *c.* 1810. 210mm diameter. *Courtesy of the Trustees of the Wedgwood Museum, Barlaston, Stoke-on-Trent.*

Fine white earthenware figure of a Hussar, coated with silver lustre. Probably made by Richard Wilson at Hanley. *c.* 1810. 261mm high. *Reproduced by courtesy of the Trustees of the British Museum.*

14. Lustre decorated earthenware

Although lustre decoration had long been used on Spanish pottery, and pottery of this type was imported in quite large quantities into England during the eighteenth century, it was not until nearly the end of that century that the technique was used over here, and it was not until the early nineteenth century that lustre decorated pottery was made on a commercial scale. It is unfortunate both for the collector and the student, that very little lustre decorated pottery is marked.

There were three basic types of lustred pottery, silver (derived from platinum), bronze, copper or gold lustre (all derived from gold) and pink or purple lustre made from a gold powdered compound called Purple of Cassius.

The lustre decoration was used in different ways, over the whole surface of an object, in imitation of metal; it was used with a 'resist' where the pattern was painted on to the surface with sugar dissolved in the painting medium. Wherever the painting occurred the lustre was prevented from adhering and when the painting was washed off after the lustre coating had been applied, the pattern showed white (or whatever was the colour of the ground) against the metallic surface. Sometimes the lustre was used in bands in conjunction with other forms of decoration painted, transferred or embossed.

Jug decorated with a resist pattern of silver lustre on a yellow ground. *c.* 1810. 158mm high. *City Museum and Art Gallery, Stoke-on-Trent.*

Platinum was not discovered until 1750 and it was not used in the decoration of ceramics until nearly fifty years later, though John Hancock (who was apprenticed to Duesbury of Derby, who also worked with the Swansea factory and with the Turners at Lane End before settling down at Spode's factory) claimed in a letter that he wrote in 1846, to have discovered the lustre technique, which he put into practice while he was working at Spode's. The Spode factory in actual fact, seems to have produced very little lustre ware. There are a few jugs with gold lustre banded necks marked Spode, but no marked silver lustre pieces.

Josiah Wedgwood had experimented with lustre, but it was not until after his death that the firm started to make the pink 'moonlight' lustre (using Purple of Cassius). This was about 1805-15. About the same time the firm was making a small amount of copper lustre.

Also in Staffordshire, the firm of Wood and Caldwell produced some solid gold lustre figures and Batkin and Bailey made silver lustred ware including some curious wigstands. Riddle and Bryan of Longton also made copper lustre. Ridgways made teapots and candlesticks in shapes copied from those of the silversmith in about 1820, and there are in the Victoria and Albert Museum a particularly beautiful silver lustre coffee pot of this type, marked with the anchor mark of the Davenport factory, and some pieces marked WEDGWOOD. The earliest silver lustre ware was made on a brown earthenware body, coated with a

Creamware jug with a slightly blue tinged glaze, decorated with bands of silver lustre and black transfer printed medallions hand painted with enamel colours, pink, yellow, blue and green. Staffordshire. *c.* 1810. 140mm wide.
Private Collection.

Silver lustre jug decorated with a resist pattern. Made in Staffordshire. *c.* 1810-20. 125mm high.
Crown copyright Victoria and Albert Museum.

Jug decorated with a resist pattern of silver lustre on a white ground. Made in Staffordshire. *c.* 1810. 115mm high.
Private Collection.

double layer of platinum which gave it a particularly lustrous finish. The later ware was on a cream or white body and the single silver coating did not have the same metallic richness, though when decorated with resist patterns was effective enough. 'Poor man's silver' as it has come to be known was also made in Leeds and Sunderland from about 1810-30. After this the newly introduced technique of electro-plating metal made the silver lustred ware obsolete.

Silver and copper lustre Communion cups were widely used in the Baptist Chapels of Wales and probably elsewhere. These sometimes had two handles or were of a simple goblet shape based on contemporary silver or pewter designs. Examples of these can be seen at the Welsh Folk Museum, St. Fagans near Cardiff.

Some fine silver 'resist' pieces were made in Staffordshire and at Leeds, with elaborate patterns that incorporated birds and vines. The lustre decoration was not referred to in any of the Leeds pattern books until 1819 (a year before the pottery became bankrupt) though it may well have been made there earlier.

Ford and Patterson's pottery at Newcastle upon Tyne made some pink lustre ware decorated with free-hand painted landscapes. Sewell of Newcastle also made pink lustre decorated pottery.

The firms of Dixon, Austin, Dixon Phillips and Co., Dawson and Co. of the Low Ford Pottery and Scott and Sons of the Southwick Pottery all made lustred wares in Sunderland in the 1800-50 period, most of them decorated with black transfer prints.

The most popular subject depicted in many forms was the famous Iron Bridge over the river Wear that was opened in 1796; but many other subjects, particularly those with a nautical flavour are to be found. In addition to a picture, a verse was often included in the design and bands of pink lustre completed the decoration. Sometimes the whole background was covered in 'splashed' pink lustre.

Commemorative pieces were often produced both here and in Staffordshire; historical events, famous people and even the railways came in for their share of attention.

The body of the Sunderland ware (though the early specimens are light in weight) was usually rather heavy and thick and it was very white. It was aimed at a popular market and was bought largely by the unsophisticated seafarers that traded along the East coast.

Many different types of objects were manufactured, but the biggest trade of all must have been in bowls and jugs, mugs and basins. A macabre joke, copied from earlier ware, consisted of placing a large three dimensional frog or toad near the bottom of the mug, perhaps intended to have a sobering effect on hard drinkers. Frogs were also to be found in chamber pots.

Copper lustre goblet with a central white band decorated with a lilac transfer on either side showing figures of Faith and Hope (with her anchor). Probably made in Staffordshire. *c.* 1810. 115mm high. *Private Collection.*

Copper lustre mug with a white band decorated with purple transfers. Exactly the same transfer as on the Staffordshire goblet in same copper lustre. *c.* 1820. 80mm high. *Private Collection.*

Copper lustre jug banded in green with a resist pattern of leaves. Probably made in Staffordshire. *c.* 1820. 139mm high. *Private Collection.*

A collection of copper lustred ware showing different treatments of decoration. Made in Sunderland in the early nineteenth century. Height of largest jug 159mm.
Tyne and Wear County Council Museums.

Plaques were made inscribed with religious texts or lettered with solemn warnings 'Prepare to meet thy God' or 'The Eye of God see'st all'. These had also been made in Staffordshire, a wave of religious fervour sweeping through the country after John Wesley's tour of the potteries in 1781.

There are many twentieth century reproductions of this type of ware to be found today.

For further reading

W.D. John and W. Baker. *Old English Lustre Pottery*. The Ceramic Book Company 1951.

A. Thorne. *Pink Lustre Pottery*. B.T. Batsford 1926.

John C. Baker. *Sunderland Pottery*. Tyne and Wear County Council Museums 1984.

Tom Graham. '19th Century Lustre Pottery' *Antique Collecting* January and February 1985.

Plate 24. A collection of 'Poor man's silver' made in Staffordshire or Sunderland though the two-handled chalice might have been made at the Leeds Pottery as it resembles pieces known to have been made there. None of these pieces is marked. *c.* 1820. Teapot 165mm high.
Private Collection.

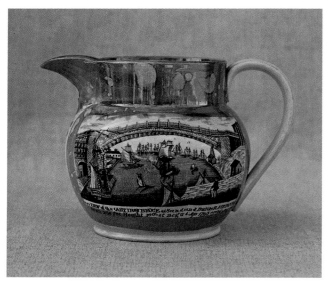

Plate 25. White pottery jug decorated with 'splashed pink' lustre and black engraved transfer design showing the west side of the Bridge over the Wear, which was opened in 1796 and was then the largest single span cast iron bridge in the world. There are many versions of this engraved subject.

The first transfer printed subjects appeared towards the end of the eighteenth century soon after the bridge was opened. The legend beneath the engraving was invariably in a copper plate script until some time after 1820. On the other side of the jug is an eight line verse entitled *The Sailor's Tear*.

Some features of the engraving on this jug, including the brig in the left foreground, have been taken from an engraving published by Reed and Son of Sunderland and dated 1837.

This jug was probably made by the Garrison Pottery at Sunderland about 1850. 135mm high.
Private Collection.

Two jugs decorated in pink lustre. The one on the left
painted in the style typical of the Patterson Pottery (formerly
Ford and Patterson 1820-30), Sherriff Hill, Newcastle.
Pottery in existence 1830-1904. This is probably about 1850.
The other jug very similar in shape, decorated with black
hand painted transfers, time of the Crimean War. *c.* 1854.
Smallest jug 114mm high. *Private Collection.*

Two silver lustre cream jugs, based on
silverware shapes. Both jugs have brown
earthenware bodies and therefore have
been covered with two coatings of
platinum lustre. Probably made in
Staffordshire. *c.* 1820. *Private Collection.*

A collection of Sunderland jugs. The top row are all from the Garrison Pottery, the second from the right is marked Dixon & Co Sunderland 1813. The jug on the bottom row on the left is from Dawson's Pottery, the centre probably Garrison Pottery and the 'Crimea' jug on the right hand bottom is from Scott's Pottery. Early to mid-nineteenth century. The height of largest jug 273mm. *Tyne and Wear County Council Museums.*

A mug decorated with bands of pink lustre and a black transfer print hand coloured with enamels. There is a brown frog inside the mug. Made in Sunderland. *c.* 1810. 133mm high. *Tyne and Wear County Council Museums.*

A small cream jug banded with purple lustre and decorated with yellow, green and brown enamel colours with cherubs in relief against a grey background. Impressed mark on the base ENOCH WOOD & SONS. *c.* 1820. 79mm high. *Private Collection.*

Plaque transfer printed in black and decorated with
pink and copper lustre. Made in Sunderland.
c. 1830. 203mm high.
Crown copyright Victoria and Albert Museum.

Plaque decorated in pink lustre and with an engraved
transfer portrait of Sir Robert Peel, Bart. Probably
made commemorating his death in 1850 when he was
thrown from his horse in Hyde Park, London.
Marked Dixon Phillips & Co (impressed on the
back). Made in Sunderland. *c.* 1850. 194mm high.
Private Collection.

Jug with a pearl ware body, moulded in relief and coloured under the glaze with scenes of the Sailor's Return and Farewell. Impressed PRATT on the base. Made by William Pratt at Lane Delph. *c.* 1790. 155mm high. *Private Collection.*

Jug with a pearl ware body, moulded in relief and coloured under the glaze with scenes of men drinking and smoking. Impressed WEDGWOOD on the base. *c.* 1795. 157mm high. The firm of Josiah Wedgwood has no record of ever having made this type of ware. It might have been made by other potters on contract to the Etruria firm or possibly by Ralph Wedgwood at Burslem or Ferrybridge.

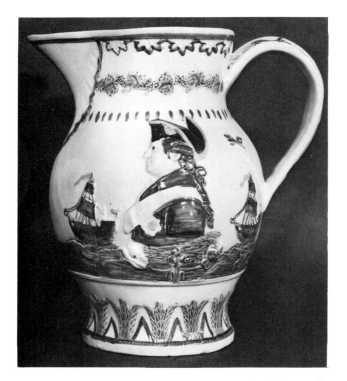

Jug made of cream coloured earthenware moulded in relief and coloured under the glaze with portraits of Admiral Duncan and Captain Trollope. Impressed W. DANIEL on the base. Made in Staffordshire. *c.* 1797. 195mm high. *Private Collection.*

Jug decorated with relief modelling and underglaze colours. One side shows a rustic scene of smokers and drinkers, the other a band of musicians. Impressed on the rim of the foot HERCULANEUM 13. Made in Liverpool. *c.* 1790. 165mm high. *Private Collection.*

15. Pratt ware c.1780-1840

UNDERGLAZE COLOURED RELIEF DECORATED EARTHENWARE AND
FIGURES, ANIMALS AND PLAQUES

Relief moulded plaque decorated in
underglaze colours with a portrait of
Admiral Jervis, Earl St. Vincent, made
after the defeat of the Spaniards off Cape
St. Vincent in 1797. 89mm high.
Private Collection.
This portrait is after the Wedgwood
jasper ware medallion, modelled by John
de Vaere in 1798.

Creamware jug decorated in relief and
coloured under the glaze with portraits of
Admiral Jervis and naval vessels.
c. 1798. 153mm high. *Private Collection.*

Pratt ware is a convenient name for the underglaze coloured, relief
decorated earthenware made between 1780 and 1840. The ware is
most widely known for jugs with designs moulded in relief of sporting
and bucolic scenes or commemorative subjects, including naval and
military heroes. These jugs are often decorated with borders of either
acanthus or stiff pointed leaves.

The term Pratt for this kind of ware has been in common use for the
last three-quarters of a century, based solely on the evidence of two
jugs impressed PRATT. William Pratt (who died in 1799) worked at
Lane Delph and his sons carried on both there and at Fenton. It was
at Fenton in the middle of the nineteenth century that F. and R. Pratt
produced the multi-coloured transfer decorated pot lids and dinner
services which are sometimes referred to as Pratt ware.

The body of the earlier Pratt ware was usually white, but sometimes
of a pale cream colour, the lead glaze was often tinged slightly with
blue. The colours used were limited to the oxide colours that could
withstand the heat necessary to fuse the glaze; blue, yellows, oranges,
greens, browns and black (a typical maiolica palette in fact). Very
occasionally a dark raspberry colour was introduced.

Other objects besides jugs were also made including plaques, tea
caddies, flasks, teapots, mugs, dishes, cornucopias, vases, cottages,
watchstands, moneyboxes, candlesticks and figures. Pratt ware varies
very much in the quality of the body and also in the painted relief
decoration. The crispness of the modelling varies too, depending on
the condition of the moulds from which the subject was pressed. Old
worn moulds give a blurred impression.

Though the majority of Pratt jugs are unmarked, there are jugs and
other pieces marked with the names of other potters and potteries.
These include Astbury, Barker, Bourne, Daniel, Davenport, Harley,
Marsh, Tittensor, Warburton and Wedgwood in Staffordshire;
Bradley in Shropshire; Emery, Ferrybridge, Hawley, Leeds and
Wedgwood and Co. in Yorkshire; Herculaneum in Liverpool; Dixon
Austin in Sunderland; and Fell, St. Anthony, Sewell and Taylor on
Tyneside. This ware was also made in East and West Coast potteries
in Scotland and at Bovey Tracey in Devonshire.[1]

Some Pratt type jugs and tea caddies were reproduced by J.W. Senior
and his sons George and James, who were working from about 1888 at
a pottery at Hunslet in Leeds. Using old moulds (presumably from the
old Leeds Pottery) they marked their wares LEEDS * POTTERY. The
Seniors continued in business until 1957. Their relief moulded jugs were

---

1. These potteries are discussed at length in *Pratt Ware: English and Scottish Relief Decorated
Underglaze Coloured Earthenware 1780-1840*. John and Griselda Lewis. Antique Collectors' Club
1984.

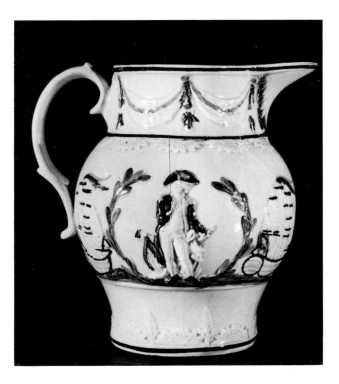

The Duke of York and Prince Coburg jug, showing the two
army commanders on horseback in a wooded landscape,
coloured in blue, orange, green, yellow and black with blue
bands and feather edging. *c.* 1793. 146mm high.
Private Collection.

Admiral Nelson jug with ships of the line. The same design
on both sides. The jug is coloured in green, blue, brown,
orange, yellow and black. *c.* 1800. 130mm high.
Private Collection.

A jug with a relief portrait of Sir Francis Burdett, Bart
(name impressed on scroll) sparingly coloured in burnt
orange, yellow, brown and green. On the other side is a
seated figure of 'Liberty'. The M.P. was imprisoned in the
Tower for sedition in 1810, the probable date of the jug.
140mm high. *Private Collection.*

usually decorated in enamel colours over the glaze and are easily distinguished from the earlier underglaze coloured ware.

The commemorative subjects to be found on this kind of underglaze coloured pottery include royalty, sailors, soldiers and politicians. Admiral Nelson, quite naturally, appears more frequently than any of his contemporaries. Among the admirals are Rodney, Howe, Duncan and Jervis; among the military commanders, the Duke of Cumberland, the Duke of York and the Duke of Wellington and Prince Coburg. Louis XVI, Marie Antoinette and the young Dauphin are found on jugs, mugs and plaques, sometimes titled 'The Royal Sufferers'. This subject and the various Nelson portraits are the easiest to come by.

Many underglaze coloured figures were made, ranging from simple little figures of children haphazardly spotted with dabs of brown, ochre or orange, to quite large figures, Toby jugs and animals, including large bull baiting groups and cow creamers.

Some underglaze figures were taken from the same moulds as the earlier coloured glaze figures of Ralph Wood. It is very rare to find marked figures. There are sets of Seasons in underglaze colouring copied from Ralph Wood's classical figures of Spring, Summer, Autumn and Winter that were made at the Garrison Pottery, Sunderland. These are sometimes found with the impressed mark of Dixon, Austin and Co.

Toby, Bacchus and the Fair Hebe jugs (the two latter designed by John Voyez) were also made with underglaze colouring. Some of the Toby jugs are marked with a large impressed crown, and there are some disproportionately large sheep and cows and also tall clock moneyboxes and watchstands with small attendant figures and sponged bases made at the same elusive pottery.

Jacob Marsh (whose pottery is located on the 1800 map of Burslem) made charming little underglaze coloured figures very much in the Wood manner; they are to be found with his name in a cursive hand pencilled in blue on the underneath of the base.

Girl with a basket of fish. The figure is decorated with underglaze colours. The square base is marbled with blue lines and marked underneath 'Jacob Marsh' in a cursive hand in blue. *c.* 1790. 127mm high. *Private Collection.*

For further reading

John and Griselda Lewis. *Pratt Ware: English and Scottish Relief Decorated and Underglaze Coloured Earthenware 1780-1840.* Antique Collectors' Club 1984.

G. Woolliscroft Rhead. *The Earthenware Collector.* Herbert Jenkins, London 1920.

G. Woolliscroft Rhead. 'Pratt Ware'. *The Connoisseur*, Vol.XXV September 1909.

Arthur Hayden 'Colonel Herbert Brock's Collection of Earthenware Jugs'. *The Connoisseur*, Vol. XXVI 1910.

A plaque showing Paris presenting Venus with the Apple of Discord after the Judgement. Underglaze coloured in blue, green and ochre. *c.* 1800. 216mm high. *Yorkshire Museum.*

A creamware jug modelled in relief with scenes of a smoker resting beside his horse and on the other side a befuddled toper pouring out a glass of ale. Coloured under the glaze with yellow, ochre, green and brown. Unmarked. *c.* 1795. 190mm high. *Private Collection.*

A smaller brown stoneware jug of the same shape with the same scenes is shown on page 61.

An ovoid shaped jug with groups of peacocks on each side, set in a leaf bordered 'sun-burst' medallion. This is the largest of a series of four jugs. *c.* 1800. 230mm high. *Private Collection.*

A jug with a hunting scene, unusually small in scale. On the other side is another similar scene much larger in scale. The handle is in the form of a serpent and the painted chevron pattern round the top of the neck is an unusual feature. *c.* 1800. 150mm high. *Private Collection.*

Plate 26. Two creamware versions of the Loyal Volunteers jug; the one on the left showing the three soldiers wearing fur-crested helmets is decorated in underglaze colours, green, blue, brown, orange and black. Unmarked but probably made in Leeds *c.* 1803. 155mm high. The jug on the right is a later version with a very pale cream body and overglaze enamel colouring. Made by the Seniors in Leeds and impressed LEEDS POTTERY on the base. *c.* 1913. 148mm high.
This was No.574 in Slee's Catalogue, where it was priced at 3s. 6d. (17½p).
Private Collection.

Plate 27. Jug moulded in relief and coloured under the glaze with scenes of a man with a gun and dogs on one side and two gardeners on the side shown above. Possibly made at the Leeds Pottery, as it is one of the designs made later by the Seniors in Leeds. *c.* 1800-10. 155mm high.
Private Collection.

Toby jug obviously made at the same factory as the figures with large rams and cow. Note the treatment of eyebrows, bases and the model of the dog. Marked on the base with a large impressed crown. *c.* 1800-20. 250mm high. *Private Collection.*

Cow with a farmer's wife, decorated in underglaze colours. Impressed WESLEY on the base. *c.* 1820. 153mm high. *Private Collection.*

A pair of rams with attendant figures, coloured under the glaze. The bases are sponged or mottled in blue, black and orange. *c.* 1800-20. 150mm high. *Private Collection.*

SPRING   SUMMER   AUTUMN   WINTER

A set of the Seasons, after Ralph Wood models. Decorated in underglaze colouring. The same figures also occur with pink lustre decoration, and similar figures are mounted on high square bases ornamented with stiff leaves. Marked DIXON, AUSTIN & CO. Made in Sunderland. *c.* 1820-26. Height of tallest 267mm. *Private Collection*.

A standing figure of a horse, decorated under the glaze with manganese sponging and wearing a blue saddle cloth. Mounted on a green washed base. Impressed ST. ANTHONY on the base. Made at the St. Anthony Pottery, Newcastle upon Tyne. *c.* 1810. 146mm high. *City Museum and Art Gallery, Stoke-on-Trent*.

177

Plate 28. Teapot in fine white felspathic stoneware with a smear glaze decorated in
relief with classical acanthus borders, enamelled blue lines and a small
naturalistically painted landscape. An identically shaped teapot in the Bulwer
Collection in the Castle Museum, Norwich is marked with an impressed S. & Co.
and 22. This was probably made by Sowter and Co. of Mexborough. The sliding
lid is similar to that on the American Eagle teapot. *c.* 1800. 140mm high.
Private Collection.

16. White felspathic stoneware of the late 18th and early 19th centuries

Almost white stoneware mug with a hunting scene in relief against a blue enamelled background. The same scene 'The Kill' appears on pieces marked TURNER and SPODE. c. 1790. 83mm high. *Private Collection.*

Sugar box in fine white felspathic stoneware decorated with blue enamelled lines and a naturalistically painted landscape within a medallion. Marked TURNER and impressed on the base. c. 1780-90. 114mm high. *Private Collection.*

A hard, fine, white stoneware was developed about 1780 and was made by many factories. The body contained a high felspar content and was almost translucent when fired. The moulded ware made of this body had an extremely crisp and precise quality and the relief moulded decoration showed up to advantage.

The composition of the body enabled it to be slip-cast, unlike the cream coloured earthenware bodies that preceded it. Some of this stoneware was left unglazed and some was not dipped in glaze in the usual way, but a certain amount of glaze that had previously been applied to the saggar flashed on to the ware during firing, imparting a satiny sheen referred to as 'smear-glaze'.

The Turners of Lane End used a fine felspathic stoneware body from about 1790 until the firm ceased to operate in 1806. Much of the ware was decorated in relief and occasionally enamel colouring was added as either blue or green banding or simple little painted landscapes. Many of the Turner's jugs were top-dipped in a dark brown glaze and decorated with hunting scenes in relief. This kind of ware was also made by other Staffordshire potters including Adams and Lakin and Poole. The Herculaneum Pottery in Liverpool also made some very finely moulded examples of white felspathic stoneware.

In Staffordshire many potters produced teapots and other ware in this body and among them are Clulow of Fenton, Elijah Mayer of Hanley and Heath and Sons of Burslem; but the pottery that has come to be most associated with this particular kind of stoneware is the Castleford Pottery near Leeds in Yorkshire, although this pottery produced other kinds of ware as well. The Castleford Pottery was started about 1790 by David Dunderdale and there are some fine white stoneware teapots bearing his mark

D D & Co

CASTLEFORD

These are moulded in relief with acanthus and other classical borders and incorporate panels of classical figures. Some of these are enhanced with blue enamel banding. It is interesting to note that similar designs were also made in a black basalt body. Many moulds that were used in the production of relief decorated underglaze coloured cream and pearl ware jugs were also used to produce exact counterparts in the white felspathic stoneware body (see pages 174 and 180).

Some teapots are marked S. & Co, probably the mark of Sowter and Co. of Mexborough. These have acanthus borders and a chain and daisy motif surrounding the gallery and sliding lid. An unmarked teapot of this description is ornamented in relief with the American eagle. The sliding lid, with its knob made of a flower with reflexed petals, is not a very ingenious device, as it easily slides off if the pot is tipped the wrong way.

Jug in white felspathic stoneware moulded in relief with scenes of men smoking and drinking, identical to the pearlware underglaze coloured jug on page 170 marked WEDGWOOD impressed. The jug is banded in blue enamel with the additional colours of green, yellow and puce round the neck. *c.* 1795-1800. 157mm high. *Private Collection.*

Jug in fine white felspathic stoneware moulded in relief with a portrait of Lord Garvis (sic) and ships of the line. Banded in blue enamel with green leaf borders. Similar to the underglaze coloured earthenware jug on page 171. *c.* 1798. 114mm high. *Geoffrey A. Godden Collection.*

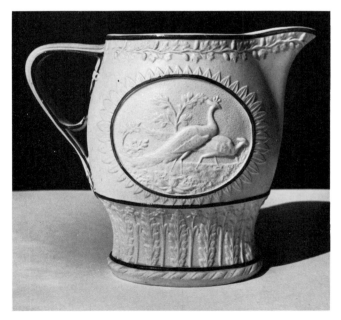

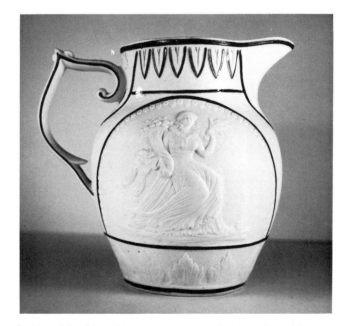

Jug, slip cast in fine white smear-glazed stoneware, painted with blue enamel bands and relief scenes of peacocks, identical in design to the underglaze coloured jug on page 174. *c.* 1800. 153mm high. The handle is similar to some used by the Herculaneum Pottery at Liverpool. *c.* 1800. 153mm high. *Private Collection.*

Jug in white felspathic stoneware moulded in relief with the figures of Peace on one side and Plenty on the other, with classical leaf borders. It is banded in blue enamel with touches of green, brown and puce on the leaves round the neck. *c.* 1800. 185mm high. *Private Collection.*

Teapot in fine white felspathic stoneware with a smear glaze, moulded in relief and decorated with blue enamel lines. Marked

D D & Co

CASTLEFORD

impressed on the base. *c.* 1805.
Crown Copyright Victoria and Albert Museum.

Teapot in fine white felspathic stoneware with a smear glaze decorated in relief with acanthus and other classical borders. The sliding lid has a chain and daisy gallery round it and a reflexed flower finial. On the central panel is the American Eagle with a ribbon in its beak impressed 'E PLURIBUS UNUM'. On the other side of the pot is a head of Liberty wearing a Phrygian cap. Impressed 36 on the base. Similar in design, but not identical to a black basalt teapot attributed to S. & Co. (probably Sowter and Co. of Mexborough) in the possession of Newark Museum, New Jersey. *c.* 1800. 160mm high.
Private Collection.

For further reading

Oxley Grabham. *Yorkshire Potteries, Pots and Potters*. York 1916. Reprinted S.R. Publications, Wakefield 1971.

Heather Lawrence. *Yorkshire Pots and Potteries*. David and Charles, Newton Abbott 1974.

Diana Edwards Roussel. *The Castleford Pottery 1790-1821*. Wakefield Historical Publications 1982.

Light buff stoneware covered jug with an entwined serpent
forming both spout and handle. Scenes of a stag hunt in
white stoneware are sprigged on to the body of the pot. A
jug with similar serpent spout and handle is impressed
TURNER (*c.* 1785-95).[1] On the base of this specimen is a
small daisy like pad of white clay impressed with the number
15. This is the way some pieces of similar stoneware were
marked by the Bramelds of the old Swinton Pottery.
c. 1806-25. 140mm high. *Private Collection.*
A tisanière somewhat similar to this jug, with serpent spout
and handle, is in the Musée des Beaux Arts at Agen, Lot-et-
Garonne. Unmarked, it is known to have been made by
Pierre Honoré Boudon de Saint-Amans when he was
working at Sèvres (1827-9).

Opposite:
Relief moulded lilac parian ware jug with white cherubs
against a lilac background with fruiting vines. The inside of
the jug is covered with a shiny white glaze. Marked on the
base with the black printed lion and unicorn mark used by
Samuel Alcock and Co. of Burslem and Cobridge (1828-53).
Also the word PATENT below the coat of arms and S.A. &
Co. in cursive letters. *c.* 1850. 140mm high. *Private Collection.*

1. See page 114 in *Stonewares and Stone Chinas of Northern England to 1851.*

17. Nineteenth century white and coloured stoneware jugs c.1835-70

Grey stoneware jug decorated with sprigged-on scenes and elaborate plant forms in white clay. The snake handle terminates in a lion's head. No mark but the word ORIENTAL and 66 in a circle impressed underneath the base. This is a shape of jug used by many makers including Spode and Masons. *c.* 1840. 134mm high. *Private Collection.*

Two jugs of this octagonal shape in creamware with similar moulded relief decoration on the necks are in the Musée des Arts Decoratifs, Bordeaux. They were made in Bordeaux in the factory of David Johnston 1835-44, who called the shape 'Algérien'.

After the Castleford type of ware ceased to be made, fine stoneware was used for a different purpose and this was for the making of decorative jugs. These, until recently, have been dismissed as Victorian monstrosities but at last they are really beginning to be appreciated.

In these stoneware jugs of the 1835-70 period it is possible to see all the vulgarity and verve and gusto of the nineteenth century as well as the piety and sentimentality. They were moulded in high relief and the patterns were richly and flamboyantly embossed with subjects ranging from gothic settings of biblical scenes to Bacchanalian revels and classical tableaux, while others were encrusted with plant forms of every description from vines to bulrushes.

The basic shapes of the jugs themselves were varied and range from angular, octagonal, straight-sided jugs on feet, to bulging-bellied and decanter-shaped jugs and even jugs tapering slightly towards the top and resembling plant-encrusted logs of wood. Almost every square inch of these jugs was thick with decoration, while elaborate handles and lips added to the richness of the design. They present a wonderful challenge to the collector, for they are still comparatively easy to find. They must have been made in very large quantities.

Many of these jugs are marked with the name of the maker; some of them can be precisely dated for they were registered at the Patent Office Design Registry and are marked with the appropriate mark. This mark is a diamond shaped device with Class IV at the top (for ceramics) and from the years 1847-67 the year of registration is signified by a letter in the top corner of the diamond; the month by another letter to the left of the diamond and the precise day of the month is indicated in the right hand corner. The parcel number appears at the bottom. These date tables can be found in various reference books including Wakefield's *Victorian Pottery* and G.A. Godden's *Encyclopaedia of British Pottery and Porcelain Marks*.

These jugs were made by many different makers including William Ridgway and Co. of Hanley, and Ridgway and Abington. Edward John Ridgway was the son of William Ridgway who went into partnership with Leonard Abington, who was the modeller responsible for the design of the jugs. T. and R. Boote of Burslem made straight-sided jugs tapering very slightly towards the top – the forerunner of the plain tankard shaped jugs in common use today. Charles Meigh in the 1840s was probably the most accomplished of the 'gothic' designers and his jugs have a balance and symmetry lacking in many of the later designs. Cork and Edge, Samuel Alcock, T.J. and J. Mayer, Holland and Green, J. and M.P. Bell, Mintons and Copelands are among the many names that are to be found upon these stoneware jugs.

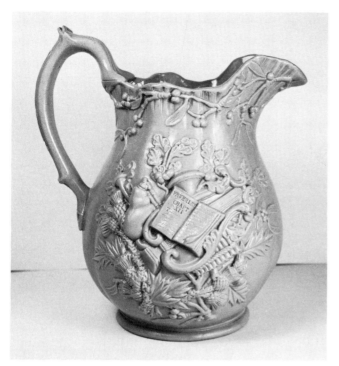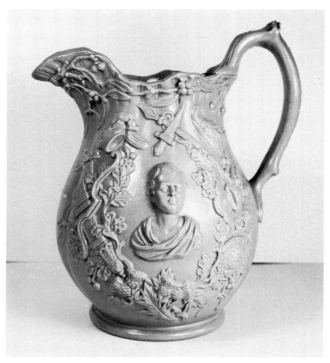

Pale grey-green stoneware jug with elaborate relief moulding commemorating Sir Walter Scott and the Waverley novels. Made by Minton and judging by the style of the model number (91) in a raised decorative scroll, about 1836, a few

years after the death of the author in 1832. 172mm high. *Private Collection.*
This jug was also made in a darker green (model No 95) and in several sizes.

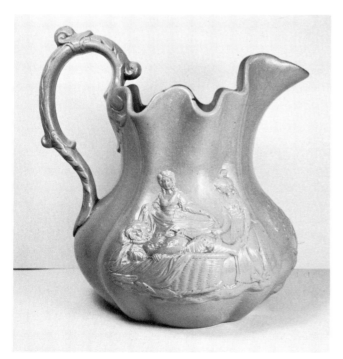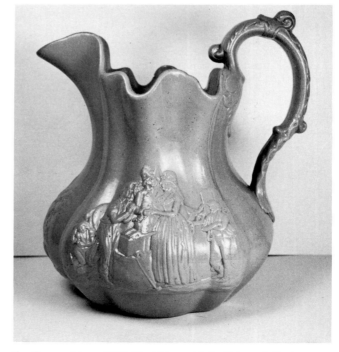

Grey-green stoneware jug with relief decoration on one side of the Marriage at Gretna Green and on the other Falstaff in the linen basket. Under the spout is a greyhound in relief. Marked on the base 'Copeland and Garrett late Spode' and

the figures 31. *c.* 1833-47. 191mm high. *Private Collection*
In the Spode Museum there are Turner moulds of both these subjects.

Buff coloured stoneware jug decorated with a scene in high relief depicting Admiral Sir Sidney Smith at the Siege of Acre. This jug is unmarked but was probably made by Samuel Alcock at Cobridge or Burslem. *c.* 1840. 238mm high. *Private Collection.*

The jug was presumably made after the death of Admiral Sir Sidney Smith in 1840, to commemorate the Siege of St. Jean d'Acre on the coast of Palestine in 1809, when the Admiral, with a small force of British seamen assisted the Turks in defeating the French and so preventing them overrunning Syria.

Lilac stoneware jug modelled in high relief with the same scenes of Admiral Sir Sidney Smith at the Siege of Acre. The interior of the jug is covered with a shiny white glaze. Marked on the base with the black printed lion and unicorn mark used by Samuel Alcock and Co., the word PATENT and also the number 116 (denoting the design and colour combination). *c.* 1840. 128mm high. *Private Collection.*

John Gilpin jug moulded in relief in blue stoneware, unmarked, but presumably made by William Ridgway at the Church Works in Hanley. *c.* 1838-48. 240mm high. *Private Collection.*

This jug was illustrated in William Ridgway's first pattern book. The side shown here has the words 'Stop, stop John Gilpin! Here's the house,' impressed. On the reverse side the scene illustrates the lines 'Six gentlemen upon the road, Thus seeing Gilpin fly...' Gilpin's horse's head acts as a thumb rest on the handle.

A copy of the John Gilpin jug, made in blue faience from a similar mould in the factory of David Johnston in Bordeaux (1835-44), is in the Musée des Arts Decoratifs in that city. It is marked on the base with a printed transfer of a knotted ribbon and the words DAVID JOHNSTON & CIE.

White stoneware jug decorated in high relief with Bacchanalian scenes. On the base is the moulded mark CHARLES MEIGH, Newcastle-under-Lyme. 30 September 1844 and the registration diamond. 235mm high. *Private Collection.*

White stoneware mug moulded in relief with a pattern of vines and dancing figures. The design was adapted by Charles Meigh from the picture *Bacchanalian Dance* by Nicholas Poussin. 1847. 184mm high. *Private Collection.*

Pale blue earthenware jug with a shiny glaze decorated in relief with portraits of the Distin family, their musical instruments picked out with gilding. This jug was originally made by Samuel Alcock at Burslem but also copied by Cork and Edge, also of Burslem. *c.* 1843-8. 178mm high. *Private Collection.*

Jug of cream coloured earthenware showing members of the Distin family as white sprigged-on decorations. Round the neck of the jug and on the top of the handle is a trickled brown glaze. *c.* 1845. 178mm high. *Private Collection.*

Cork and Edge illustrated the jug on the left in the catalogue of the British section of the Paris Universal Exhibition of 1855.
John Distin was the man who played the bugle at the Victory Parade in Paris after Waterloo. He had made the acquaintance of Adolf Saxe, the inventor of the Saxehorn and later the Saxophone, and became the agent for his musical instruments. The Distins formed a musical ensemble with the four sons playing the Saxehorns and Mrs. Distin the piano; they often performed in the Potteries where they were very popular. The Distin family business ultimately became the firm of Boosey and Hawkes.

Octagonal white stoneware jug, moulded in relief with eight
figures of religious significance in gothic niches, known as
the 'Apostle' jug. Designed by Charles Meigh of Hanley and
registered at the Patent Office Design Registry on March 17
1842. 159mm high. *Crown copyright Victoria and Albert Museum.*

Top left: 'The Two Drivers' jug moulded in relief in white stoneware. The design by Henry Townsend shows the old fashioned coach driver with cape and whip on one side and the modern engine driver with his locomotive on the other side. Made originally for Sir Henry Cole's Summerley's Art Manufacturers. Made by Mintons, inscribed underneath No 335 M. *c.* 1847. 178mm high.
Crown copyright Victoria and Albert Museum.

Another and larger version of 'The Two Drivers' jug with a brown glazed background and the figures in white relief. Marked Minton 295 & 6. *c.* 1847. 216mm high.
Private Collection.

Crimean War commemoration jug moulded in relief in pale green stoneware made by E. Ridgway and Abington, Hanley August 1 1855. Also impressed on the base is the letter J and the figure 12. 241mm high. *Private Collection.*
The soldiers are trampling the Russian Imperial Eagle underfoot. On the other side is a kilted Highlander.

Pale grey-green stoneware jug moulded with stylized acanthus and vine. This is unmarked except for four square dots in the form of a square impressed on the base. Very similar jugs were made by Dudson in a buff coloured stoneware about 1875. 159mm high. *Private Collection*.

White stoneware jug with a rich plum coloured enamelled background behind the moulded relief decorations showing figures symbolising America, Africa, Europe and Asia and a map of the Western Hemisphere beneath the spout. Marked in relief with the initials W.B. inside a Staffordshire Knot and the numeral 12, surmounted by the word UNIVERSE on a ribbon. Made by William Brownfield at Cobridge. *c.* 1851-70. 254mm high. *Private Collection*.

Creamware and stoneware jugs, closely following some of the designs of Ridgway, Turner and Wedgwood were made in France by an eccentric French nobleman, Pierre Honoré Boudon de Saint-Amans, at Sèvres and later at Bordeaux, where he worked in association with Lahens and Rateau (1828-31) and David Johnston (1835-44).

On exploring a disused warehouse in their Portmeirion Pottery at Stoke-on-Trent fairly recently, Susan Williams-Ellis discovered a whole lot of old moulds of these relief moulded jugs, made by various potteries in the last century. Some of the best of these they are now issuing in a fine white parian body.

For further reading

Hugh Wakefield. *Victorian Pottery*. Herbert Jenkins, London 1962.

T.A. Lockett and P.A. Halfpenny (Ed.). *Stoneware and Stone Chinas of Northern England to 1851*. City Museum and Art Gallery, Stoke-on-Trent 1982.

R.K. Henrywood. *Relief Moulded Jugs 1820-1900*. Antique Collectors' Club 1984.

Bust of Sir Isaac Newton (1642-1727) the natural philosopher. Made by Enoch Wood and impressed NEWTON on the back of the waisted socle. Painted in enamel colours, his shoulders are draped with emerald and cerise and the socle is painted to simulate marble. There is a companion bust of Matthew Prior the poet and contemporary of Newton. *c.* 1790. 240mm high. *Private Collection.*

Top left: Bust of William Shakespeare, enamel coloured in mauve, orange and turquoise mounted on a buff coloured waisted socle, by Enoch Wood. Made *c.* 1790. 254mm high. *Private Collection.*

Bust of Voltaire, decorated in enamel colours and mounted on a waisted white socle, banded in brown. Probably by Enoch Wood. *c.* 1790. 254mm high. *Fitzwilliam Museum, Cambridge.*

18. Enamel coloured figures

Figure of Diana decorated with enamel colours, made by Ralph Wood the younger. *c.* 1780-90. John Walton made a later version of this figure. 280mm high. *Fitzwilliam Museum, Cambridge.*

Towards the end of the eighteenth century, the coloured glaze and the underglaze coloured figures were followed by figures decorated with enamel colours. These colours were painted on after the piece had been glazed and then the figures were re-fired at a much lower temperature to fix the enamels, thereby allowing for a wider range of colours.

Among the first potters to take advantage of this new technique were Ralph Wood the younger (1748-95), his brother John Wood (1746-97) and their cousin Enoch Wood (1759-1840). Some of these enamel coloured figures, including a well modelled group of *Elijah and the Raven,* were marked 'Ra Wood'. These enamel coloured models included busts of Milton, Shakespeare and other personages both respectable and famous. According to ledgers dated 1777-1800 and 1783-87 from John Wood's Brownhills factory both coloured glaze and enamel coloured figures were being produced during those years. The latter being more expensive to produce were intended to compete with contemporary porcelain figures.

Enoch Wood (1759-1840) had begun modelling at a very early age. At the age of eighteen, he modelled a very complicated jasper ware plaque based on the Rubens' painting *The Descent from the Cross.* A little later he made busts of both Wesley and Whitfield and many other pieces of a pious nature, as well as some allegorical figures such as *Prudence* and *Fortitude. Charity* occurs with the Wedgwood mark.

After being apprenticed to Humphrey Palmer of Hanley, Enoch Wood had at first worked with his cousins Ralph and John and they made enamel coloured figures and Toby jugs. They were well modelled and attractive in colouring. About 1790 he went into partnership with James Caldwell and the firm used the mark WOOD & CALDWELL. In 1819, he bought Caldwell out and took some of his own sons into partnership (he had twelve children) and the firm became Enoch Wood and Sons. He lived to be over eighty and was known as the 'Father of the Potteries.'

Enoch Wood had made a large collection of pottery telling the story of the industry up to 1830. At his death this was dispersed, but in 1835 he had already presented the King of Saxony with 182 pieces. These were lodged at the Royal Museum at Dresden.[1] Fully documented, such a collection would have been of inestimable value to collectors.[2] Enoch Wood also had a habit of interring examples of his factory's productions in the foundations of churches and other new buildings. During the demolition of St. Paul's Church, Burslem in 1974 a large cache of his work was found including busts of Washington, Wellington

---

1. They are now in the Museum für Kunsthandwerk, Dresden.
2. John Ward writing in *The History of the Borough of Stoke-on-Trent* in 1843, said 'Enoch Wood collected early and later specimens of the fictile art, from the rude butter pots of Charles II's time to the highly adorned vase of modern days.'

'The Lost Sheep' figure after a design by Ralph Wood. The shepherd wears a green coat, red waistcoat, pale blue breeches and black hat and shoes. The mound on which he and his dog are standing is coloured brown and green and is decorated with shreds of clay to simulate tufts of grass. The green and brown enamels have flaked badly, something that could not happen with underglaze colouring. There is an impressed 4 under the hollow base. In the list of mould or subject numbers in Frank Falkner's book, this group is listed as No.9, but there is no subject given for 4, 5, 6 or 7.

and Wesley. His works were marked E. WOOD or ENOCH WOOD SCULPSIT.[3]

Among other enamel coloured figure makers were Neale & Co. This firm consisted of James Neale (1740-1814), Humphrey Palmer and later Robert Wilson. Palmer and Wilson were practical potters, Neale was the businessman. The mark NEALE & CO was used from 1776 to 1795. From 1794, when Robert Wilson had become a partner, the wares were sometimes marked NEALE & WILSON.

Neale's firm made a number of enamel coloured figures and Toby jugs after Ralph Wood designs. The set of Seasons illustrated on page 193 is typical of their work. These are also based on Ralph Wood models, but perhaps because of their very precise and sophisticated painting, they are more like porcelain figures than those made by later potters such as Walton or Salt. A distinguishing feature of Neale's colouring was a soft turquoise blue.

The firm of Lakin and Poole made good quality figures, though marked examples are rare. Thomas Lakin, who had specialised in the making of colours and of clay bodies, worked in partnership with John Ellison Poole for a relatively short time from 1791 to about 1795. Their figures were well modelled and delicately painted. There is a very pretty figure of Hygeia[4] marked LAKIN & POOLE, but their most celebrated group was The Assassination of Marat. Lakin later worked for Davenport and ended up as a manager at the Leeds Pottery where he died in 1821.[5]

The Leeds Pottery made some creamware figures decorated in enamel colours, as well as pearlware figures. They date from about 1790-1800. It is a little difficult to generalize, but on the whole the Leeds figures are lighter in weight and are also slightly more naïve than their Staffordshire counterparts. If they are mounted on square bases, these generally are a little higher than the Staffordshire bases.

Figures were made in Liverpool at the Herculaneum pottery, but as many of the employees of this pottery had migrated there from Staffordshire, the Liverpool figures are very similar to those made in Staffordshire, though again, marked examples are extremely rare.

A slightly different type of figure made its appearance about the beginning of the nineteenth century, inspired by the porcelain figures from the continent and from Chelsea and Bow. This consisted of a figure backed by an elaborate tree with formalized greenery and flowers. The name that occurs most frequently on this type of figure

3. See 'Enoch Wood Potter and Antiquary' by Gordon W. Elliott in *The Northern Ceramic Society Journal* Vol. 2, 1975-6.
4. Illustrated in John Hall's *Staffordshire Portrait Figures*.
5. Lakin's widow published posthumously *The Valuable Receipts of the Late Mr. Thomas Lakin*, Leeds, 1824.

Set of the *Seasons* marked Neale and Co impressed. Made in Staffordshire. *c.* 1780. 136mm high. On first sight, these figures are more like porcelain than earthenware. The enamel colours are very precisely painted. *Fitzwilliam Museum, Cambridge.*

The Assassination of Marat. A group made by Lakin and Poole (impressed mark on base). *c.* 1794. 343mm high. This well modelled and carefully painted group is historically somewhat inaccurate as Charlotte Corday actually plunged a knife into Marat's side as he sat in his bath. *Fitzwilliam Museum, Cambridge.*

Sheep with reddish brown markings
standing on a green rocky base with a
lamb below her, in front of a stylised
bocage. Impressed WALTON on a scroll
at the back of the base. *c.*1820. Height
190mm. *Private Collection.*
Similar animals were made by the Kents
later in the century and one is listed in
their catalogue of 1955 (No 107).

Rustic group of a shepherd and
shepherdess, the girl fondling a sheep
and the man with a dog, coloured in
green, blue, ochre and brown. Impressed
TITTENSOR on the back. *c.* 1820.
165mm high. *Courtesy Sotheby's.*

is that of John Walton, who signed his name in either impressed or
embossed roman capitals on a scroll at the back of the base.

Walton was making pottery figures at a factory in Navigation Road,
Burslem from about 1815 until 1835. He was one of the most prolific
of the Staffordshire figure makers. Many of his figures are of religious
subjects such as *Flight into Egypt*, the *Widow of Zarephath* and *Elijah and
the Raven*, as well as saints and apostles, though he also modelled
classical goddesses and pretty Arcadian figures of shepherds and
shepherdesses, gardeners and putti, lions and unicorns, sheep and
rams all with a bocage background.

The leaves that formed the bocage were stamped out of a bat of thin
clay as five lobed serrated units, then pressed together in pairs, the
centre of the front then being finished with the addition of a small
flower. These units were grouped together and mounted on the stem
and branches of the tree that backed the figures.

The names of other potters including John Dale, Ralph Salt and
Charles Tittensor are sometimes found impressed on the back of
similar figures, though most examples are unmarked. Dozens of
potters were engaged on the production of these charming little figures,
which they made by the hundred and sold very cheaply.

John Dale's name occurs on four figures representing the Elements
(in the Victoria and Albert Museum), on various rustic groups and
also on a bust of John Wesley. Dale was working in Burslem in the first
quarter of the nineteenth century. Ralph Salt (1782-1846) first of all
established himself as a painter of china toys on Miles Bank, Hanley.
In 1828 he set up as a manufacturer of figures at a pottery in Marsh
Street, Hanley. He impressed his name, sometimes on a scroll, on the
back of the wares. A pair of rather crude figures impressed GARDNERS
on the front and a group of a sheep and a lamb, very similar to
Walton's sheep are typical of Salt's work. Charles Tittensor (born
1764) was one of a number of Staffordshire Tittensors. From 1803 he
was working in partnership with his brother John at Hanley. From
1818 to 1823 he was working on his own at Shelton. He made both
underglaze coloured and enamelled figures with bocages impressed on
the back TITTENSOR

Potters were always going out of business and sales of potteries were
frequently advertised in the newspapers, showing the whole stock-in-
trade of a factory including moulds. This would account for the fact
that it is quite possible to come across identical figures with entirely
different painting. It seems unlikely that a well-finished and beautifully
decorated piece would have come from the same factory as a poorly
finished specimen.

The Staffordshire potters also made cottages, churches and castles.
These were sometimes purely ornamental, but others were made in the

Plate 29. Courting couple. Unmarked, but almost certainly made in Staffordshire. *c.* 1810. 180mm high. *Private Collection*.

Plate 30. The Tithe Pig Group. There are many versions of this well-known piece. The man on the left is dressed in a pink coat and carries a piglet; his wife holds the baby and the vicar clasps his hands in expectation. The group stands on a green mound strewn with sheaves of corn, two piglets and a basket of eggs. *c.* 1820. 162mm high. *Private Collection*.

Plate 31. Pair of gardeners. Impressed SALT on a scroll on the back of the rocky base. Made by Ralph Salt in Staffordshire. *c.* 1830. 155mm high. *Private Collection*.

A group of three classical figures on square bases. On the left: Hygeia standing beside a flaming altar, water jug in one hand, serpent in the other. Marked with an impressed 'D'. Similar to a Wood figure of the later period. *c.* 1790. 241mm high. The centre figure Charity is stamped with the WEDGWOOD mark. *c.* 1800. 223mm high. On the right: Andromache in a pink robe with crimson flowers. Probably by Ralph Wood the younger or Enoch Wood. *c.* 1790. 235mm high. *Fitzwilliam Museum, Cambridge.*

Faith, Hope and Charity. Three enamel coloured figures on unusual bases, strongly coloured but delicately painted with a certain amount of Indian red in the floral decorations on their robes. The bases are similar to some used by Obadiah Sherratt. *c.* 1810. 215mm high. *Courtesy Leonard Russell.*

St. George and the Dragon. An enamel coloured group. St. George wearing a raspberry red tunic with blue trimmings. Mounted on a rectangular plinth. After the Wood model. *c.* 1820. 330mm high. *Courtesy Leonard Russell.*

Right: Britannia. A handsome seated figure, possibly by Enoch Wood. She wears a yellow flowered dress, edged with gold and a crimson underskirt, a grey helmet with crimson plumes. She has a red and blue shield and is flanked by a dark brown lion. The group is mounted on a mottled green mound, set upon a stone coloured base. *c.* 1800. 355mm high. *Private Collection.*

form of a money box with a slit in the roof or a pastille burner with an arched opening at the back and pierced windows.

Obadiah Sherratt, who is recorded as being a Master Potter at Hot Lane, Sneyd Green, Burslem in 1822, and later at Waterloo Road, by tradition is said to have made very distinctive figures or groups of figures, but so far as I know not one of them is marked. The only known marked pieces by Sherratt are two tankards, in the City Museum, Stoke-on-Trent. Some of these figures had a crudeness and barbarity lacking in the prettier Walton type of figure. Bull baiting, cock and dog fighting were popular sports among the hard working potters in the early years of the nineteenth century. They were a rough lot and drunkenness was a common vice. The pieces attributed to Sherratt caricatured such things in broad earthy groups which have an attractive fairground quality in spite of the subject matter. Many of these groups are mounted on rococo stands with swags of flowers on the front. Until such time as further research proves otherwise, 'Obadiah Sherratt' should only be taken as a generic term like Whieldon or Pratt.

For further reading

G. Woolliscroft Rhead. *The Earthenware Collector.* Herbert Jenkins, London 1920.

John Hall. *Staffordshire Portrait Figures.* Charles Letts and Co., London 1972.

Harold Blakey. 'Thomas Lakin: Staffordshire Potter 1769-1821'. *Northern Ceramic Journal* Vol. 5, 1984.

Plate 32. The Widow of Zarephath. A carefully modelled
and prettily painted figure, with her cask of meal and flagon
of oil, mounted on a rocky green mound set on a square
base, with a brown line running round three sides of it. The
glaze is heavily tinted with blue and the bocage is missing.
c. 1820. 240mm high. *Private Collection.*
A similar figure, but with quite different treatment for the
painting is in the Victoria and Albert Museum and is also
illustrated in Herbert Read's *Staffordshire Pottery Figures.*

Plate 33. The Widow of Zarephath. A quite different version
of this well known figure. There is a child accompanying her
and the rocky base is ornamented with shreds of clay to
simulate tufts of grass. The brown line runs round all sides
of the square base. The glaze is slightly tinted with cobalt.
The bocage is missing. *c.* 1820. 260mm high.
Private Collection. These figures are none the worse for the loss
of their bocage.

Vase flanked by two figures after designs by Ralph Wood and mounted on a
rocky mound with reclining sheep. Subdued enamel colouring with a distinctive
turquoise blue. Impressed NEALE & CO. *c.* 1790. 280mm high.
Courtesy Leonard Russell.

Spill vase decorated with a pair of disconsolate lovers very much in the Walton manner. The neck of the vase is enamelled a pretty lilac colour. Made in Staffordshire. *c.* 1800. 152mm high. *Private Collection*.

Rualers. An early nineteenth century group, inspired by an earlier Wood model (see page 93). After the style of John Walton but unmarked. The lettering is impressed from printers' types; an ampersand has been used for an S. *c.* 1815. 165mm high. *Private Collection*.

Impressed mark on back of square base of 'Girl with a lamb'.

Girl with a lamb in a box of hay. Creamware figure enamel coloured in turquoise, blue, brown, green and pink. The square base has an encircling brown line and is impressed WEDGWOOD on the back. 190mm high. *Private Collection*.

A similar figure (with coloured glazes) was illustrated in *Staffordshire Pottery Figures* by Herbert Read and was said to have been made by the younger Ralph Wood after a model by Voyez, in turn copied from a biscuit figure by Paul Louis Cyfflé. The figure here may have been made under contract for Wedgwoods, possibly by John or Enoch Wood *c.*1800.

200

Two groups depicting the flight of the Holy Family into Egypt and their return therefrom, with black lettering impressed on a white scroll. The figures are mounted on a green rococo base with a green bocage behind them. Marked WALTON on a scroll on the back of the base. *c.* 1820. 190mm high. *Private Collection.*

A group of putti made by different Staffordshire potters in the early years of the nineteenth century. The central figure is possibly by Neale, but none of them is marked. Height of tallest 178mm. *Private Collection.*

A pair of rather crudely modelled wistful figures in arbour settings very comparable to Chelsea-Derby figures. The green mounds are mounted on brown banded square bases. Staffordshire *c.* 1800. 178mm high.
The Royal Pavilion Art Gallery and Museums, Brighton.

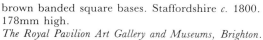

Figure of a shepherd dressed in mottled grey jacket, pink and brown striped waistcoat and yellow breeches standing on a green and ochre rocky base, with a dog at his feet. *c.* 1830. 140mm high. *Private Collection.*

Bird's Nesting. A boy wearing a light blue jacket and brown breeches and standing on a green-washed mound in front of a green bocage holds a bird in one hand and its nest in the other. Marked WALTON in raised letters on a scroll on the back of the base. *c.* 1820. 145mm high. *Private Collection.*

Perswaition. Sometimes inscribed thus, and sometimes mounted on a Sherratt type stand. This is more in the Walton style generally. *c.* 1815-20. No mark.

A group of shepherds and gardeners inspired by the porcelain figures of Chelsea and Meissen. All made by John Walton and marked WALTON impressed on a scroll behind the base. *c.* 1820. 127mm high. *Private Collection*.

A pair of figures at an alfresco teaparty in front of a turreted house and mounted on a swagged rococo stand. Only the baby seems to be enjoying the proceedings. This moral group has been attributed to Obadiah Sherratt. *c.* 1820. 197mm high.
The Royal Pavilion Art Gallery and Museums, Brighton.

Lieutenant Monroe being carried off by a tiger. This gruesome occurence took place somewhere near Calcutta on 2 December 1792. This may have been one of Sherratt's earliest groups, but cannot have been as early as this. Possibly *c.* 1815. 280mm high.
The Royal Pavilion Art Gallery and Museums, Brighton.

Land Lord and Land Lady. A pair of enamel coloured figures mounted on square bases, possibly made by Obadiah Sherratt. *c.* 1820-30. 184mm high.
The Royal Pavilion Art Gallery and Museums, Brighton.

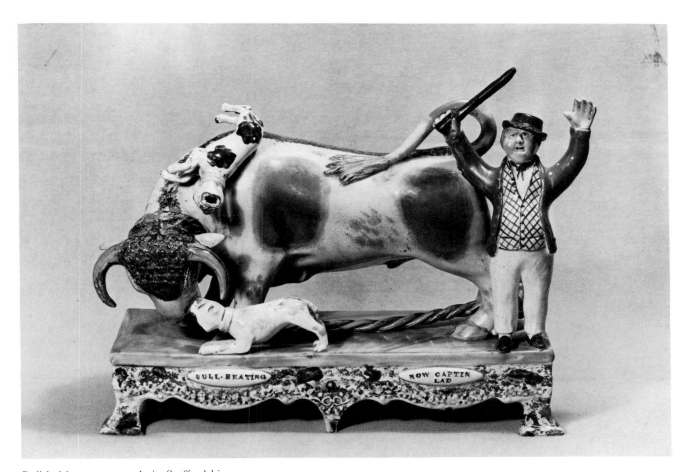

Bull-baiting group made in Staffordshire and attributed to Obadiah Sherratt. This form of stand was typical of those supporting the so-called Sherratt groups. *c.* 1830. 280mm high.
The Royal Pavilion Art Gallery and Museums, Brighton.

Mantelpiece ornament with a solemn warning in a fat faced type (*c.* 1808). The flanking figures are dressed in turquoise coats and yellow breeches. The sun and moon are ringed in orange, the clockface is surrounded in crimson, orange and blue. Mounted on a green base embossed with oak branches and a central rococo decoration in several colours. Staffordshire. *c.* 1810. 235mm high. *Private Collection.*
This piece is somewhat damaged, with various pieces missing from the top. An undamaged version of this mantel ornament was exhibited in a collection of Masonic Pottery at the Freemason's Hall in York in 1951. Above the clockface there was a pyramidal shape formed by a set-square and compasses, enclosing the 'all-seeing eye'. The Masonic connection explains the aprons worn by the flanking figures.

Venus with a cherub and a dolphin, attributed to Obadiah Sherratt. This figure is also found mounted on stands similar to the Bull-baiting group and Polito's Menagerie. Impressed VENUS from printer's type. *c.* 1820. 203mm high.
Crown copyright Victoria and Albert Museum.

The Marriage Ceremony of John Macdonald aged 79 at Gretna Green. An amusing group decorated in strong enamel colours. The elderly bridegroom wears a black coat and yellow breeches, his apprehensive bride wears a turquoise coat and a pink feathered hat. The burly blacksmith is coloured in red, brown, fawn and turquoise. The table and the brick arch over the figures is painted Indian red. The whole group is mounted on a yellow, grey and white marbled plinth set on a black, blue and yellow marbled base, *c.* 1830. 153mm high.
Courtesy Leonard Russell.
John Hall illustrates two comparable groups in his *Staffordshire Portrait Figures*. One is decorated in blue only. Both are entitled 'The New Marriage Act' and the wording underneath is quite different to the one shown here.

Polito's Menagerie. A large naïve group decorated in enamel colours. The background is yellow ochre with naturalistically coloured animals and birds in relief. The three bandsmen on the right are dressed in Indian red with brown hats, except the drummer who has a pink head-dress and ochre trousers. The two musicians on the other side are coloured in blue, pink and yellow and the whole group is mounted on a flat base plate supported on brown rococo legs swagged with coloured flowers. This is the largest version of this subject as there are extra figures mounted on either side.
Attributed to Obadiah Sherratt at Burslem. *c.* 1830. 330mm high.
Courtesy Leonard Russell.

Polito's Menagerie. A smaller version. 280mm high.
City Museum and Art Gallery, Stoke-on-Trent.

Queen Victoria and Prince Albert, made soon after their marriage. *c.* 1840. 216mm high. *Private Collection.*

A pair of equestrian figures probably intended to represent Queen Victoria and Prince Albert. *c.* 1840. 165mm high. *Private Collection.*

19. Victorian cottage pots and portrait figures

WHITE EARTHENWARE MANTLEPIECE ORNAMENTS DECORATED
WITH ENAMEL COLOURS

'Aesthetics'. A drawing by Charles
Keene showing a pair of equestrian
Staffordshire figures on a mantelpiece
with an aesthetic gentleman begging his
lodging-house landlady to 'Remove those
fictile abominations'.

Napoleon, decorated only in black and
pale pink with some gilding. *c.* 1840.
140mm high. *Private Collection.*

At about the time of Queen Victoria's marriage, in 1840, some new
and quite distinctive kinds of pottery figures were manufactured.
These were unlike any kind of ornament that had been made before,
both in form and style and in the actual body of the ware itself.

These mantelpiece ornaments were made in great numbers, largely
for an unsophisticated market, for the parlours of cottages and lodging
houses and the nurseries, school rooms and kitchens of the well-to-do.
They were made in Staffordshire and also at some of the Scottish
potteries, but they are very rarely marked with a maker's name.

They were very simply but ingeniously moulded, most of them
having an almost flat back with little modelling or colouring on the
back. They were usually mounted on a simple oval base that was much
more part of the figure than were the rocky or square bases of the
preceding period. In fact, these Victorian figures owed nothing to the
porcelain figures of the eighteenth century or to the Walton type of
earthenware figures of the beginning of the nineteenth.

The most distinctive colour used on these figures was a rich, dark
glossy blue. This cobalt oxide was applied before glazing. Other
colours including pink, green, yellow, orange and an Indian red were
all painted on top of the glaze. Black was sometimes used under the
glaze, but was more frequently applied at the same time as the other
enamel colours. Gold was occasionally used for lettering and for high-
lighting drapery etc. Some of the later figures (after about 1860) were
decorated only with black, gold and a pale flesh pink. As well as the
human figures, models of animals were much in demand and every
Victorian kitchen must have had its pair of spaniels flanking the
kitchen clock. Greyhounds, poodles, dalmatians and more rarely cats
were made, as well as more exotic creatures like zebras. Particularly
spirited large spaniels were made in Sunderland, often with copper
lustre patches on their bodies, or lustred chains round their necks.
Churches, cottages and castles were also made in a profusion of
designs. Even railway engines were made in this type of pottery.

The most interesting figures, though, were the naïve portrait figures
many of which are actually named, and through them one can trace
much of the social and military history of the Victorian era. The names
on these figures were usually in relief on the front of the base, or
written on in a cursive hand in gold letters, or very occasionally
impressed from printers' type.

Amongst some of the earliest of this type of white earthenware figure
were portraits of Queen Victoria and Prince Albert, though other
members of the Royal family are also found, standing, sitting and even
mounted on horseback. Likenesses of various politicians including Sir
Robert Peel and the Duke of Wellington also appeared. The Crimean

Queen Victoria and Abdul Medjid, Sultan of Turkey and the Emperor Napoleon III. This commemorates the alliance made between the three countries at the time of the Crimean War. 1854. 273mm high. *Private Collection*.

This group is after an illustration in the *Illustrated London News* of a medal struck at the Paris Mint in the same year.

Top left: Prince Albert with Napoleon III standing under each other's national flags. 1854. 337mm high. *Collection: John Hall*.

Omah Pasha (1806-71) was the Commander in Chief of the Turkish forces throughout the Crimean War. 1854. 273mm high. *Collection: Mrs. F. Cashmore*.

This figure was later made from similar moulds by William Kent Ltd.

Admiral Sir Charles Napier (1786-1860). He wears a blue coat with ochre epaulettes and sword and stands on a green washed base with his name in relief on a scroll. *c.* 1850-60. 241mm high. *The Royal Pavilion Art Gallery and Museums, Brighton.*

After a distinguished career in the navy, Napier was ennobled by the Portuguese for his part in the battle of Cape St. Vincent in 1833. He was sent out to the Mediterranean as Commodore in 1839 and in the following year was given command of the land forces at Beyrout where he disobeyed orders to retreat but won a victory, thus causing some dissatisfaction among the establishment. However, in 1846 he was commanding the Channel Fleet, though only as a rear-admiral, and in 1854 the Baltic Fleet. He was not made admiral until 1858.

War (1854) created a demand for portrait figures of many of the personalities involved in that disastrous and incompetent campaign. The Queen with the Sultan of Turkey and Napolean III, the King of Sardinia with Prince Albert, British and French admirals, Turkish and British generals and Miss Nightingale standing stiffly beside a wounded soldier. The Indian Mutiny inspired figures of Sir Colin Campbell, General Sir Henry Havelock and Highland Jessie; the American Civil War — figures of John Brown and Abraham Lincoln. Garibaldi visited England in 1864 and this visit inspired about a dozen different portrait models of the great man, with and without a horse. The Franco-Prussian War of 1870 inspired portraits of various German personalities, but by then the characteristic Staffordshire blue had almost ceased to be used and the figures were less colourful. The wars in Egypt and South Africa were commemorated by portrait figures of General Gordon, Lord Kitchener and General Buller.

Apart from royal, naval and military characters, evangelists such as Moody and Sankey were represented showing another facet of Victorian life; while the shadier side of society was shown by portraits of criminals and their victims. Well known poets, prize fighters, singers, actors, lion-tamers and jockeys all found their way on to the Victorian mantelpiece. Many of the portrait figures were made in different sizes from about eight inches to fourteen or fifteen inches high.

Fictitious characters such as Uncle Tom and Little Eva and Romeo and Juliet were also represented and religious and historical subjects were also popular. Apostles and saints jostled with a crowd of anonymous country people, goatherds, gipsies, fishermen, shepherds, lovers in arbours.

After the death of Queen Victoria, the last of these types of portrait figures were made in the likenesses of Edward VII and Queen Alexandra and Princess May (Queen Mary).

Practically none of these Victorian figures is marked with the maker's name but a figure of Robert Burns has been found with S. Smith Longton on it, Lord Roberts with Hanley/Lancasters Limited/England, and Edward VII and Queen Alexandra with I.H. Sandland.

Mr. Balston has isolated two factories, which he calls the 'Alpha' and the 'Tallis' factories, where two distinct and definite types of figure were made.[1] The Alpha factory mostly used printer's type for impressing the name on to the stand, and the Tallis factory were responsible for the Shakespearean characters modelled from the

---

1. *Staffordshire Portrait Figures of the Victorian Age*: T. Balston, Faber 1958 and John Hall's supplement to this book, 1963.

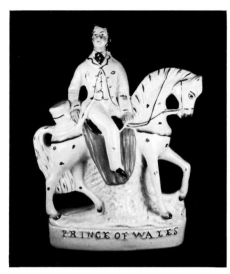

A handsome pair of equestrian figures, one entitled *Prince of Wales* (eldest son of Queen Victoria and Prince Albert) in gilt relief lettering. The saddle cloth is bright orange and he is wearing mauve gloves. Presumably made about the time of his marriage in 1863. 254mm high.
The companion *Princess* (Alexandra, eldest daughter of King Christian IX of Denmark) is wearing a coat with pink facings and a hat trimmed with green feathers. *c.* 1863. 235mm high.
Private Collection. Versions of this pair were made by the Kents.

engravings in the Tallis Shakespeare Gallery (1852-3) and some other figures in the same style. These are made of a hard and heavy body and are modelled and painted on the back as well as on the front, some having indented titles in capital letters or transfer titles. None have raised lettering or gilt script.

Sampson Smith, who must have been the most prolific of the makers of flat-backed figures was working from about 1850 to 1878. There is a cow group spill vase in the City Museum and Art Gallery, Stoke-on-Trent with a back-stamp of 'Sampson Smith, 1851, Longton' on it. This same mark is also found on pieces of a much later date and his factory continued making flat-backed figures for many years after his death. In 1948 a number of his original moulds were found in a disused part of the factory. Among these were figures, dogs and cottages. Using these moulds the trade was revived, though the colouring was not so pleasing as that on the earlier pieces.

Up until 1968 Lancaster and Sandland of Stoke-on-Trent were still making some of the old models. They took great pains to match the old Staffordshire blue. The factory turned out honest reproductions; one only hopes that the dealers into whose hands they fall are as honest in their transactions, for the reproductions are quite good enough to fool the embryo collector.

The Kents of Burslem made 'Old Staffordshire Pottery' including a number of flat backs. Among these were the Prince and Princess mounted on horseback, fruit sellers, fortune tellers, sailors and Scottish dancers as well as many animals, busts and cottages. They started up in business in 1878 and production of these wares finally ceased in 1962. At the time of writing, the Blakeney Art Pottery in Stoke-on-Trent was using the same moulds under licence from Mr. J.S. Kent and making the most skilful reproductions.

For further reading

Gordon P.D. Pugh. *Staffordshire Portrait Figures of the Victorian Era*. Barrie and Jenkins 1970. Antique Collectors' Club 1987.
Thomas Balston. *Staffordshire Portrait Figures of the Victorian Age* with a supplement by John Hall (1963). Faber and Faber 1958.
Reginald G. Haggar. *Staffordshire Chimney Ornaments*. Phoenix House, London 1955.
John Hall. *Staffordshire Portrait Figures*. Charles Letts and Co. 1972.
Kathleen Woolliscroft. *Sampson Smith Manufacturer of all kinds of Figures in great variety*. Gladstone Pottery Museum 1976.
R.G. Haggar. 'Sampson Smith of Garfield Pottery, Longton'. *Apollo* Vol. 54, 1954.
R.G. Haggar. 'Chimney Ornaments, Sampson Smith'. *Apollo* Vol. 51, 1950.
Anthony Oliver. *Victorian Staffordshire Figures*. Heinemann 1971.

Sir John and Lady Franklin. Sir John died while trying to discover the North West Passage in 1847. The impressed names and general style show that these figures were made at what T. Balston called the 'Alpha' factory. *c.* 1847. 286mm high.
The Royal Pavilion Art Gallery and Museum, Brighton.

Above right:
Highland Jessie. An almost legendary figure. The wife of Corporal Brown (no doubt standing beside her) who inspired the garrison at Lucknow to hold out by screaming that she could hear pipes playing 'The Campbells are coming'. The garrison was relieved. 1857. 368mm high.
Collection: Mrs. F. Cashmore.

The Death of Nelson, with the title in gilt script. The uniform jackets are the characteristic underglaze dark shiny blue. *c.* 1845. 216mm high. *Private Collection.*

George Washington (1732-99) from the same model as Benjamin Franklin. 1846-53 period. 394mm high. *Collection: John Hall.*
Though from the same model, the Washington figure is nearly 40mm taller.

Top left: The Empress Eugenie and the Prince Imperial. The Empress (1826-1920) was wife of Napoleon III. Colourless except for pink, black and gilt. 1856. 197mm high. *The Royal Pavilion Art Gallery and Museums, Brighton.*

Jenny Lind wearing a green and red dress with a yellow hat, in the part of Maria in *The Daughter of the Regiment. c.* 1847. 203mm high. *Private Collection.*
Johanna Maria Lind 'the Swedish Nightingale' (1820-87) first appeared in London in 1847. She became a naturalised British subject in 1859. After a long and successful career as an opera singer she was appointed Professor of Singing at the Royal College of Music in 1883.

Plate 34. Benjamin Franklin (1706-90), American Statesman, sent to England on a political mission in 1757. He failed to reconcile the colonies with Great Britain and later negotiated an alliance with France. The figure is taken from the same model as George Washington, but Washington is usually larger. Enoch Wood is said to have made a standing figure of Franklin. These may well be copied from that. (The Wood firm certainly had a large export trade to America.) 1846-53 period. 356mm high.
Crown copyright Victoria and Albert Museum.

Plate 35. Bottom left: David Garrick as Richard III seated in a tent. This is based on Hogarth's painting of the actor (1745). *c.* 1850. 248mm high.
Private Collection.

Plate 36. Florentia Lady Sale mounted on a black and white horse and wearing an ermine trimmed cloak. Coloured with a deep underglaze cobalt and yellow and pink enamels. *c.* 1843. 178mm high.
Private Collection.
Lady Sale, the wife of Sir Robert Sale who was in command of the British forces at Kabul, led the women in retreat and was taken captive, but was rescued by Sir Richmond Shakespeare. She published her journal in 1843. This equestrian figure has also been named as both Queen Victoria and Lady Hester Stanhope, the eccentric and redoubtable traveller in the Middle East.

Death of the Lion Queen (Ellen Bright 1832-50). Ellen was the niece of George Wombwell the circus proprietor. She became the 'Lion Queen' at the age of 16 and was mauled to death at Chatham by a tiger a year later. 1850. 381mm high.
Collection: Mrs. F. Cashmore.

Top left: Heenan and Sayers, the prize fighters. Probably made after their famous fight at Farnborough in 1860. 241mm high.
The Royal Pavilion Art Gallery and Museums, Brighton.
Heenan, an American, was taller and heavier than the British ex-bricklayer, Tom Sayers. After thirty-seven rounds, the police stopped the fight, which was declared a draw.

Garibaldi (1807-82), The Liberator of Italy. After his visit to England in 1864, he became extremely popular and many portrait figures were made of him, both with and without his horse. *c.* 1864. 356mm high.
Collection: John Hall.

Dick Turpin and Tom King, a pair of mounted
equestrian figures made by Sampson Smith. *c.* 1855.
305mm high.
The Royal Pavilion Art Gallery and Museums, Brighton.
Richard Turpin (1706-1739) was the son of an Essex
innkeeper. He took to a life of crime, joining a gang of
robbers. In 1735 he went into partnership with another
highwayman Tom King, whom he shot by accident. He
was finally hanged for horse stealing at York.

Emily Sandford, Potash Farm and James Rush. *c.* 1850.
Height of figures 260mm.
The Royal Pavilion Art Gallery and Museums, Brighton.
James Blomfield Rush was a tenant of Potash Farm,
owned by Isaac Jermy, the Recorder of Norwich of
Stanfield Hall. The day before the mortgage on the
property was about to foreclose Rush went over to
Stanfield Hall and shot Jermy and his son. His mistress
Emily Sandford gave evidence at his trial which helped
to convict him. He was the last man to be hanged
outside Norwich Castle in 1849.

Flower holder. Lovers beneath a tree; the jealous rival eavesdrops. *c.* 1850-60. 254mm high.

Arbour group. The jealous rival about to attack the unsuspecting lovers. *c.* 1850-60. 254mm high.

Flower holder. A rustic couple beneath a tree. *c.* 1850-60. 292mm high.

Watch-stand. The fortune teller and her two clients. *c.* 1850. 280mm high. *All from Private Collections.*

A group of figures with flowers and fruit. Both figures are wearing richly coloured underglaze blue jackets. *c.* 1850. 235mm high.

A loving couple of fruit gatherers, wearing blue coats and yellow hats. The girl is resting her arm on a churn and the pair are mounted on an unusual rococo base ornamented with gilding. *c.* 1840-50. 235mm high.

A woman holding a child, both dressed in blue coats, standing on a boat flying the French flag and with a barrel at her feet. *c.* 1850. 225mm high.

A pair of figures standing in a boat with a tub of oysters, both are wearing blue jackets. *c.* 1850. 225mm high. *All from Private Collections.*

The Sailor's Return. A popular subject in Victorian England. *c.* 1850. 318mm high. *Private Collection.*

The Sheepshearer. A large and very well-modelled figure. The sheep are covered with a sprinkling of granules of clay to simulate wool. *c.* 1850. 356mm high. *Private Collection.* This is after the Baxter print *News from Home.*

A pair of children seated on goats, wearing blue jackets and carefully painted patterned skirts. The goats' horns are bedecked with flowers. *c.* 1850. 152 and 134mm high. *Private Collection.*

A pair of dancers and an archer dressed in
green, probably intended to represent Robin
Hood. *c.* 1850-60. 254mm high. *Private Collection.*

Four unnamed figures, the one on the left
obviously intended for Admiral Lord Nelson; a
Scottish shepherd and shepherdess and a man
with bunches of grapes, probably intended to be
an Italian. All of the 1840-50 period, all approx.
267mm high. *Private Collection.*

The Flight into Egypt, so inscribed with a gilt script on the base. Colourless group except for touches of black, pink and gilt. *c.* 1860-70. 200mm high. *Private Collection.*

The Sand Gatherer. An unusual group of a brown haired girl in a blue, red and green patterned dress with a white donkey spotted with black and laden with yellow sacks of sand. The word SAND in raised lettering on the base. *c.* 1870. 197mm high. *Private Collection.*

A girl with a deer, very sparsely coloured. *c.* 1860-70. 298mm high. *Private Collection.*

Peace. A well modelled, if slightly sentimental
figure of a reaper with a sickle and a corn stook.
Apart from his yellow hat and pink breeches, the
figure is hardly coloured but the tree stump spill
vase has an orange interior. Made by Sampson
Smith. *c.* 1856. 395mm high. *Private Collection.*
One of a pair with WAR depicted by a Highland
soldier with drum, rifle and a pile of shells.

Pair of spaniels with black patches and gold chains round their necks. These were made in Staffordshire by Sampson Smith and other potters, and also in Sunderland. The greyhound was probably made in Staffordshire. *c.* 1850-60. Spaniels 260mm high. *Private Collection.*

A group of white earthenware cottages. The ones on the left and centre are pastille burners. All are decorated in enamel colours, with extruded strands of clay to simulate greenery. Made in Staffordshire. *c.* 1830-40. The tallest is 108mm high. *Private Collection.*
All three were later copied by Kent of Burslem and illustrated in their catalogue of 1955. From left to right they are listed by Kent as 'Small flowered No 195, Round No 197 and Château No 198'.

Castle of pale buff coloured clay decorated with extruded clay shavings to simulate greenery. The windows are outlined with gold and a red, white and blue flag droops from a tower. Made in Staffordshire. *c.* 1830-40. 137mm high. *Private Collection.*

White clay cottage decorated with extruded strands of clay to simulate creepers and with large flowers and leaves on the base. The door is orange-red and the outlining is gilt. 98mm high.

Plate 37. A pair of washerwomen. This piece has a
slightly different surface quality to the other pieces
illustrated here. It is much less shiny. Probably made
in Staffordshire. *c.* 1850. 260mm high. *Private Collection*.

Arctic Expedition in search of Sir John Franklin; engraving after a print by George Baxter. The scene depicted here happened on the expedition that sailed in 1848 and was led by the nephew of Sir John Rose in the ships *Enterprise* and *Investigator.* This pot-lid has been attributed to both T.J. and J. Mayer and Ridgways, but without any actual evidence. *c.* 1850. 75mm diameter. *Courtesy Sotheby's.*

A relish pot of pale blue earthenware decorated with a polychrome transfer showing 'The Fall of Sebastopol 8th September 1855'. Unmarked but like other Crimean War subjects probably made by T.J. and J. Mayer at the Furlong Works and Dale Hall Pottery, Burslem. 79mm high. *Private Collection.*

Guiseppi Garibaldi. The Liberator is standing with the dome of St. Peter's, Rome behind him. This lid, produced by F. and R. Pratt may well have been made in celebration of Garibaldi's visit to England in 1864. 108mm diameter. *Private Collection.*

Hauling in the Trawl. Engraved by Jesse Austin after a wood engraved reproduction of an anonymous painting 'Herring Fishing, Isle of Man' which appeared in *The Illustrated London News* in 1847. This was one of the Pegwell Bay Shrimpers' subjects. It was produced by F. and R. Pratt for Crosse and Blackwell in 1860. 108mm diameter. *Private Collection.*

20 Multi-coloured transfer decorated pot-lids and other ware

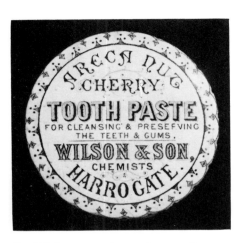

Pot lid from a toothpaste jar transfer printed in black only with hand drawn lettering and border. *c.* 1840-60. 76mm diameter. *Private Collection.*

A relish or mustard pot of pale blue with a two-colour transfer of men shooting. Registered mark 1856. 102mm high. *Private Collection.*

Before the days of plastic or cardboard containers and cartons, potted meats and relishes, sauces, pomades and toothpastes were packed in attractive pots made of white earthenware with decorative lids. Some of these were merely typographic with a variety of decorative letterforms, printed only in black. The most interesting pot-lids were multi-coloured, made first by F. and R. Pratt.

Felix Edwards Pratt (1813-94), the son of Felix Pratt of Fenton, whose factory had produced some of the distinctive underglaze coloured pottery mentioned in an earlier section of this book, was one of the first potters to make use of multi-coloured transfer printing. By 1847 the factory was decorating earthenware pot-lids as well for mustards, sauces, etc. Most of the designs were done by Jesse Austin, an artist who worked with the Pratts for many years.

Austin was also an engraver and he engraved the copper plates from which the transfer prints were taken. He usually used three or four colours and a dark brown or black. A plate was engraved for each primary colour, as well as for the key drawing and of course for every additional colour that was used. The colours were transferred separately, ending with the black or brown key drawing. Between each colour application the pot had to be dried (or the colours would have smudged). How the girls who put the flimsy transfer printed papers down and got them to register is something of a mystery, in spite of the registration marks, which were removed afterwards. These transfers were applied at the biscuit stage and then the pot was dipped in glaze and refired. If gold was used, a third firing was necessary. It was altogether a long and complicated process for something that was thought of as mere packaging. That the lids were appreciated for their aesthetic qualities is obvious by the number that have survived to this day, for they have for many years been collectors' pieces and their value like that of so much English pottery has increased over the years.

The earliest lids were for Bears' Grease, a pomade for the hair. The enterprising shrimpers of Pegwell Bay ordered pots by the thousands for packing their shrimps and fish paste. Their lids, naturally, were illustrated with fishing scenes and views of the local surroundings. The Great Exhibition of 1851 was commemorated on many lids and there were royal portraits, portraits of celebrities, country scenes, animals, birds, shells, flowers and engravings of famous paintings.

This colour transfer process was used on other things beside pot-lids and relish pots, including mugs, jugs, vases, trinket trays, tea and coffee and dessert services.

Pratt's rivals in this particular field were T.J. and J. Mayer and John Ridgway and Co. F. and R. Pratt continued in production until 1920 when they sold their business including all Jesse Austin's copper plates to Cauldon Potteries Ltd. For the next forty years Cauldon

227

Plate 38. *The ruined temple.* This anonymous engraving issued by F. and R. Pratt appeared only on plates, with differing coloured surrounds and borders. The border here is No 123 in the factory pattern book and is the same as that used on the mug illustrated on this page. 220mm diameter. *Private Collection.*

Plate 39. Large mug with a multi-coloured transfer print of a Continental village scene taken from a painting 'Val S. Nicola' by J.D. Harding. The other side is decorated with a print entitled *The Cattle Drover.* Made at the factory of F. and R. Pratt, High Street, Fenton. *c.* 1860-90. Printed mark on the base PRATT 103mm high. *Private Collection.*

123
FENTON.

Plate 40. *Shells and Seaweed.* This design appeared on pot-lids and other ware issued by F. and R. Pratt at Fenton, and by T.J. and J. Mayer and possibly other potters between 1860-90. 105mm diameter. *Private Collection.*

Large mug with a multi-coloured transfer printed scene of a windmill with horses and a cow on the other side 'The Cattle Drover' print inset on a strawberry ice-cream pink background. The prints and the top and bottom of the mug are encircled in gold, the handle is also gilded.
Printed mark on the base. F. & R. PRATT & CO
123
FENTON
c. 1860-90. 102mm high. *Private Collection.*

A blue earthenware or relish pot, decorated with a two-colour transfer of a wild boar hunt in black and yellow. Made in Staffordshire. *c.* 1870. 102mm high. *Private Collection.*

reissued a number of the Pratt pot-lids on a more porcellaneous and cream coloured body. In 1960 Cauldon was taken over by Coalport who continued with these reissues. In the 1970s Coalport had become part of the Wedgwood group. They also reissued, in limited editions, under the Coalport mark, about twenty of the F. and R. Pratt designs. These included the Bear Hunting design.

T.J. and J. Mayer were in production from 1843 to 1855. In 1855 the firm became Mayer Bros. and Elliot, then in 1861 Mayer dropped out and the firm continued under various owners until 1890 when Kirkhams took them over and remained in business until 1962, when the Portmeirion Potteries bought up the old pottery.

Between 1900 and 1960 Kirkhams reissued many of the Mayer designs, purely as decorations. They are distinguished by their flat tops and the fact that they are drilled with holes for hanging. On the verso there is usually a legend stating that the coloured prints are from Jesse Austin originals, or just that they were reproduced by Kirkhams Ltd., Stoke-on-Trent and the date.

For further reading

A. Ball. *The Price Guide to Pot-lids and other Underglaze Multi-colour Prints on Ware.* Antique Collectors' Club 1980.
A. Williams-Wood. *Staffordshire Pot-Lids and their Potters.* Faber 1972.
H.G. Clarke. *The Pictorial Pot-Lid Book.* Courier Press, London 1960.

A relish or mustard pot of pale blue earthenware with two colour transfer decoration (black and yellow) depicting a wild boar hunt. Registered at the Patent Office Design Registry on 18 August 1871. 98mm high. *Private Collection*.

A Fix. Engraved from Jesse Austin's original drawing adapted from J. Burnet's painting 'Playing Draughts'. Produced by F. and R. Pratt. The same design was issued by T.J. and J. Mayer omitting the barrel, broom and hat from the right hand side of the picture as well as other small modifications. Undated. 108mm diameter. *Private Collection*.

The Village Wedding. An engraving by Jesse Austin after a picture by D. Teniers the Younger (1610-94). Made by F. and R. Pratt at Fenton and registered on January 15, 1857. This subject was reissued many times over the years. In early editions of this design the registration mark is superimposed on the jug in the foreground. Lids without this mark date from after 1883. 108mm diameter. *Private Collection*.

Uncle Toby courting the Widow Wadman. A scene from *Tristram Shandy* by Laurence Sterne, an engraving after a painting by C.R. Leslie R.A. In this version Uncle Toby is wearing a purple coat. Made by F. and R. Pratt at Fenton. *c.* 1860-70. 105mm diameter. *Private Collection*.

21. Some factory made peasant wares

Cider or perry flagon banded in brown and blue with a feathered design in a greenish blue. Incised on the bottom in large letters, the initials J B and the date 1835. 159mm high. *Private Collection.*

Tankard with the verification mark and the word IMPERIAL sprigged on. (It actually holds three quarters of a pint.) The central band of coloured slip is café au lait, those at the top and bottom are blue, with black rings. Typical Mocha decoration applied as four 'trees'. Unmarked but made at Ynysmeudwy. 1850-55. 127mm high. *Private Collection.*

MOCHA WARE

Mocha ware was an intriguing but inexpensive and essentially utilitarian kind of ware. It was named after Mocha stone, a name applied to chalcedony with dendritic markings, said to have been originally from Mocha in Arabia. The dark marks simulating miniature trees and shrubs are caused by the infiltration of iron or manganese oxide solutions into the cracks in the stone. The decoration on Mocha ware closely resembles this type of chalcedony.

Decoration of this nature is said to have originated in the late eighteenth century at the factory of William Adams at Cobridge who was supposed to have used this Mocha decoration on cream coloured earthenware. But there seems to be no convincing proof of this.

This kind of pottery was so taken for granted that there are very few references to it in print and when Mr. Teulon-Porter began making his collection of this ware in the years just after the First World War, it was not easy to find even then.[1] Though throughout the nineteenth century and even up to about 1939, it was made in considerable quantities, mainly for use in public houses. In 1875 Mocha pint ale mugs could be purchased for 6d. and quart mugs for 10d. (less than a present day 5p piece). They must have been considered of little value or interest and were disregarded as rubbish as soon as they were cracked or chipped.

The body of the ware varied from the cream coloured earthenware of the early specimens to pearl ware, yellow ware, granite ware, chalkware and white ware. The earliest dated piece in a museum, so far recorded, is in Christchurch Museum, Ipswich and is inscribed 1799, though documentation exists proving 1793 as the earliest recorded date.

Though jugs and tankards are the most commonly found items, other things were made including lidded jars, butter pots, porringers, teapots, salt, pepper and mustard pots and dolls' or miniature pieces as well as spill vases and even chamber pots.

The basis of the design was a broad band of coloured slip, usually blue, greeny grey or coffee coloured, and on this band the trees or Mocha stone decorations were formed. The potter used a mixture, which he called 'tea' which was said to consist of tobacco juice, manganese and urine to make these decorations. While the band of colour was still wet a drop of the mixture was applied to it, this immediately fanned out and spread into tree-like fronds like the markings in the Mocha stone, the dark colour contrasting well with the coloured band on the white or light coloured earthenware. Rings of black were also added to complete the decoration.

---

1. The N. Teulon-Porter collection of mocha pottery is now in the City Museum and Art Gallery at Stoke-on-Trent.

Two early Mocha ware tankards, both made of cream coloured earthenware. The Mocha stone decoration and black rings are laid on an almost chestnut coloured background. The plain loop handles are uncoloured. *c.* 1795. Approx. 115mm and 132mm high. *City Museum and Art Gallery, Stoke-on-Trent.*

Tankard decorated with bands of blue, greeny grey and black with Mocha design on the widest band. There is a sprigged-on pad of clay with V R 1 IMPERIAL impressed on it. This tankard holds a quart of liquid and has the rare feature of three black lines above the base. The handle has carefully modelled leaf terminals. *c.* 1840-50. 153mm high. *Private Collection.* This matches similar examples from Ynysmeudwy in South Wales.

232

Each potter had his own recipe for the 'tea' that he used. Some are said to have used iron oxide mixed with orange or lemon juice or tobacco spittle, other recipes were said to have included tansy leaves. Nobody now remembers, though John Smith of Stourbridge, a practical potter who has done much experimenting with such things will no doubt have more to say about the subject when his book on Mocha ware comes out.

Some of the tankards are marked with small pads of clay with impressed lettering applied below the upper rim of the object. These clay 'badges' were not official and were the potter's way of indicating that the quantity was right. This was not an excise mark as such but merely a verification of true liquid capacity according to an official procedure of measurement. These marks do not occur earlier than Victorian times. False measures were also made with extra thick bottoms, for measuring out such things as shrimps, nuts or seeds. These purported to hold half a pint, but were intentionally never marked.

Mocha ware was illustrated in one of the pattern books belonging to the Leeds Pottery and it was made in Burslem by Edge and Malkin from about 1871-90, and by T.G. Green and Co. of Church Gresley in Derbyshire (founded in 1864 and still working today). Other makers included Broadhurst of Fenton, Pinder and Bourne of Burslem and Tams of Longton. In Newcastle upon Tyne it was made by Maling and Son.

Sherds of good quality yellow ware with Mocha decoration have been found fairly recently at Crew's Hole on the opposite bank of the Avon to Temple Parish, Bristol. This was the site of Anthony Amatt's pottery in the late 1790s. Mocha ware also appears to have been made at the South Wales Pottery at Llanelli and at the Ynysmeudwy pottery near Swansea from the middle of the nineteenth century.

It is interesting to note that fine examples of Mocha decoration on purely decorative examples of superb quality cream coloured earthenware were made in France *c.* 1800-10.

Small mug with brown, orange and blue slip decoration, achieved by dropping or splashing different coloured liquid clays on to the surface. This technique is sometimes given the name of 'Moco' and was in use from *c.* 1815-1860. 102mm high. *Crown copyright Victoria and Albert Museum.*

For further reading

N. Teulon-Porter. *The N. Teulon-Porter Collection of Mocha Pottery.* Museum and Art Gallery, Stoke-on-Trent, 1953. Reprinted 1971.

I am much indebted to the generosity of John Smith of Stourbridge for all the information concerning the dates, makers and places of origin of this ware, which, after years of detailed study he has compiled for his forthcoming book on industrial slip decorated ware. This is the first occasion on which this information has been released. He has also helped me with detailed descriptions of techniques.

Tankard decorated with bands of coffee and
blue slip and Mocha decoration on the coffee
coloured band. The sprigged-on verification
mark has ONE PINT impressed on it. The
handle has leaf terminals. Made at Bovey
Tracey. *c.* 1855. 127mm high.
Private Collection.

Mustard pot of putty coloured clay with
coffee, blue and black bands and Mocha
decoration. Probably made by Pountney and
Co., Victoria Pottery, Bristol. *c.* 1860.
51mm high. *Private Collection.*

Tankard with blue-green slip background and
Mocha decoration applied liberally to form a
wooded landscape. Made in Stoke-on-Trent.
1865-75. 127mm high. *Private Collection.*

Large milk or beer jug banded in greenish grey, blue and black with a decoration of white rings and ochre, black and white trailing design. Mid-nineteenth century. 229mm high. *Private Collection.*

Pepper pot banded in khaki, blue and black with dendritic markings. Mid-nineteenth century. 108mm high. *Private Collection.*

Jug with blue and greeny blue slip bands, black rings and Mocha decoration on the widest band. A red flower has been pencilled under the base. Made by T.G. Green of Church Gresley. *c.* 1910-23 and later. 121mm high. *Private Collection.*
The original shape of this jug dates from 1890.

Measham ware was closely connected with the Ashby-de-la-Zouche canal, which had been built to serve the collieries and limeworks at Measham, Donisthorpe and Moira. It ran from the Coventry Canal at Marston Bridge Bedworth, to Oakthorpe Fire Engine on Ashby Wolds, about a mile north west of the Moira Baths in the Parish of Ashby-de-la-Zouche.

This pottery, associated with the picturesque canal 'narrow' boats, only dates from the last quarter of the nineteenth century. Much of this ware was made at Church Gresley in Derbyshire. Pieces occur marked 'Mason Cash Co Church Gresley', though such marked pieces are extremely uncommon. The Victoria Pottery at Woodville quite near Church Gresley also made this type of ware.[1]

There used to be a shop on the Ashby-de-la-Zouche canal at Measham, on what the narrow boat men call the Moira Cut; this was also near Church Gresley and the canal folk could order from this shop special pieces inscribed with the names of friends or relations. These were put on by impressing printers' type into the damp clay. Often homely mottoes are to be found such as 'Love at Home' or 'Remember Me'. Some teapots are impressed with 'Diamond Jubilee 1887'.

The ware is dark brown and covered with a shiny 'Rockingham' glaze, except where the impressed flowers and birds in white clay are sprigged on, and these are painted with blue, green and pink.

The most spectacular objects made in this type of ware were immense teapots, some as high as 408mm, and holding half a gallon of tea. These pots were surmounted by another little teapot, in the form of a knob to the lid. Such vast pieces of ware must have dominated the tiny crowded cabins. They were, however, a reflection of the love of decoration that the narrow boat people showed in their daily lives. The cabin sides and doors of the boats, the buckets and the basins were covered with paintings of pastoral scenes, of roses and castles. This primitive painting had much of the fairground about it. The Measham ware was all part of this tradition. It was also in the tradition of the sprig decorated red wares of John Astbury (see page 82).

Measham ware kettles and chamber pots, jugs and tobacco jars are also to be found. Production of this naïve but interesting type of pottery ceased in the 1920s.

---

1. This statement was made by the late Mr. Pascoe Tunnicliffe, whose father once owned the Woodville Pottery. There is also a letter in the Stoke-on-Trent Museum, from a lady whose mother used to work on these kind of teapots at Newcastle-under-Lyme. She said that the painting of the flowers and birds was done by the men in the pottery and not the women. The pottery has not been identified.

Tobacco jar, teapot and small jug in the form of an owl. The owl jug is interesting in that the inscription 'HAFODLWYFOG' is the name of a farm near Nant Gwynant in Snowdonia, well-known to climbers. The ware was obviously not entirely confined to the people on the canal barges. Height of teapot 197mm; tobacco jar 178mm; jug 117mm. *Private Collection*.

Measham ware kettle-shaped teapot. It is interesting to compare that with the Astbury kettle on page 82. *c.* 1890. 210mm high. *Private Collection*.

Plate 41. Measham ware teapot with relief decorations
sprigged on. The teapot is covered with a shiny brown
Rockingham glaze and the flowers and birds are painted in
blue, pink and green. 'A PRESENT FROM A FRIEND' is
impressed and filled in with blue. Unmarked, but probably
made in Church Gresley. *c.* 1890. 407mm high.
Private Collection.

Three jugs, two of which are inscribed 'LOVE AT HOME'
impressed blue lettering. Brown shiny glaze and flowers
picked out in blue, green and pink. All unmarked, but
probably made in Church Gresley. *c.* 1890. Height of
tallest jug 204mm. *Private Collection.*

Chamber pot of Measham ware, the interior washed
with white slip and decorated with an array of frogs and
lizards. Round the rim is the couplet
   'Pick me up and use me well
    And what I see I never will tell'
Obviously from the same pottery as the teapots, the
circular flower is identical. 140mm high.
Private Collection.

A six-piece smoker's compendium of grey stoneware with white applied decorations and 'CHARLIE REVILL 1897' impressed in black on scrolls. Unmarked. 432mm high.
Private Collection.

When separated, the compendium provides the smoker with a candlestick, a mug, an ashtray, a tobacco jar, a spittoon and a match holder. But who was Charlie Revill? These smoker's sets are sometimes known as the 'Bargee's Companion'.

22. Decorative Victorian tiles

Encaustic floor tile made by Minton.
c. 1850-60. 152mm square.
Courtesy Minton Museum.

Left: Glazed encaustic floor tile, white,
ochre and sepia, made by Minton.
c. 1860-80. 152mm square.
Centre: Glazed encaustic floor tile,
white, ochre and sepia, made by
Minton. *c.* 1860-80. 152mm square.
Right: Unglazed encaustic floor tile,
ochre and terracotta, made by Maw and
Co. *c.* 1860-80. 152mm square.
Courtesy Ian Craig.

By the end of the nineteenth century, there were decorative tiles in practically every house built within the previous twenty-five years and in many public buildings as well. Tiles were used on the walls of entrance halls, kitchens, bathrooms and lavatories and extensively on hearths and round fireplaces. In addition, the furniture of the period was often embellished with tiles, the backs of hall and wash stands, doors of sideboards, tops of occasional tables and teapot stands, jardinières and even the backs of chairs. Porches and conservatories were floored with encaustic tiles in sombre reds, buffs, greys and blues laid in elaborate geometric patterns. Interiors, and sometimes the exteriors as well, of butcher's shops, fishmongers, dairies and even restaurants were lined with tiles.

The inspiration for this ubiquitous use of ceramic decoration came from the writings of Augustus Welby Pugin and Sir Henry Cole, whose common theme was the improvement in taste of manufactured articles for the mass market. The influences on the design of these tiles came from various sources, from the Gothic Revival, from the Arts and Crafts Society and the work of William Morris, from the Art Nouveau Movement and from the Near and Far Eastern influences of the Aesthetic Movement.

Encaustic tiles had been made by monks for the paving of the floors of churches and other monastic buildings from about 1200 until the middle of the sixteenth century (see page 23). Encaustic literally means 'burnt in'. The tiles were made of red clay with an impressed or incised pattern filled in with white clay. The design fused together in the firing and the tile was subsequently glazed with a greenish or yellowish lead glaze as a protection from dirt.

It was not until the beginning of the Gothic Revival in the 1820s that there was an awakened interest in encaustic tiles. Pugin, the architect of so many of the Gothic Revival churches, was the first to think of

Dust-pressed tile with Japonaiserie design printed in sepia made by Maw and Co. *c.* 1880.

Dust-pressed tile made by Wedgwoods. 'May' from a series of the months. 1878.

Dust-pressed tile made by Wedgwoods. 'Peaseblossom' from a series of *A Midsummer Night's Dream* characters designed by Thomas Allen. 1878.

One of a set of four dust-pressed tiles representing the Elements. Decorated with an underglaze transfer print and colour painting. Unmarked. *c.* 1880. All tiles 152mm square. *Courtesy Ian Craig.*

specifying this kind of tile in his buildings. The art of making them had been completely lost. Herbert Minton (the son of Thomas Minton), one of Josiah Spode's great rivals in Staffordshire was a friend of Pugin and the latter encouraged him and inspired him to experiment with tile manufacture. Herbert Minton began to do this in 1828.

At the same time, but quite independently, Samuel Wright of Shelton was granted a patent for the manufacture of encaustic tiles. There were considerable technical difficulties to be overcome and both men suffered many disappointments. However, within a few years Minton had perfected the technique and his firm laid down a floor at the Temple Church in London in 1841 and another at Osborne House in the Isle of Wight for Queen Victoria in 1844. Wright's patent ran

Dust-pressed tile with sepia transfer print. *c.* 1885.

Dust-pressed tile with hand-coloured sepia transfer painted in brown, navy blue and yellow. A. Simpson, Hanley. *c.* 1880.

Dust-pressed tile with a green transfer printed decoration. T. and R. Boote Ltd. *c.* 1885.

Dust-pressed screen printed tile with a mosaic design in blue, grey and rust. Craven Dunnill and Co. *c.* 1890. All tiles 152mm square. *Courtesy Ian Craig.*

out in 1844 and a half share was bought by Herbert Minton, the other half being taken up by the Worcester firm of Chamberlain, who ceased production a few years later.

Decorative wall tiles did not come into general use until the late 1860s. Their widespread use was made possible by a new and most important development. Formerly tiles had been made by pressing clay into metal frames, larger than the finished tile to allow for shrinkage. The tiles then had to be dried for two to three weeks before they could be fired. In June 1840, Richard Prosser of Birmingham patented a method of making buttons, whereby almost dry powdered clay was put between two metal dies and subjected to pressure. The result was a clay button that was instantly ready for firing. Herbert Minton at once saw

243

Art nouveau slip-trailed tile. Possibly designed by Louis Solon and made by Minton. *c.* 1890. 457mm x 305mm.
Courtesy of the Minton Museum.

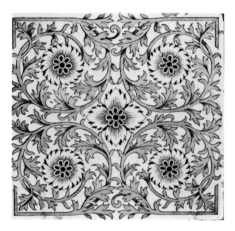

Dust-pressed tile with a design in two shades of blue on a cream background. Impressed in relief on the back JOSIAH WEDGWOOD & SONS ETRURIA. Also the name of the pattern BELLFLOWER has been stamped in blue capitals. *c.* 1870. 152mm square. *Private Collection.*

Dust-pressed tile decorated with a finely engraved floral pattern in shades of green on a cream coloured background. Impressed on the back MINTON CHINA WORKS STOKE-ON-TRENT and a circle with MINTON across the centre with Stoke-on-Trent and WALBROOK LONDON. *c.* 1870. 152mm square. *Private Collection.*

A dust-pressed, hand-painted imitation Delft tile with overglaze decoration in pink. Made by Robert Minton Taylor. *c.* 1875. 152mm square. *Courtesy Ian Craig.*

Opposite page: Typical of the Aesthetic Movement. A fireplace panel of five dust-pressed tiles decorated with a sepia transfer and hand-coloured with green, orange, yellow and red enamel colours. Decorative Art Tile Co. 1887. 762mm high. *Courtesy Ian Craig.*

the possibility of adapting this technique for the making of tiles. He bought a share of the patent and within a few weeks had installed a press and the manufacture of dust-pressed tiles had begun. These tiles could be made much thinner than the old type of flooring tile and the drying time was very much curtailed. The backs of the tiles were impressed with some kind of keying design to enable them more easily to be stuck to a wall.

Mintons started transfer printing on wall tiles in the 1850s but it was not until the late 1860s, after Herbert Minton's death, that they began to produce every kind of decorated tile. The history of the firm at this time is very complicated. The name of Minton was used by three different firms; Herbert Minton had taken his nephew Michael Hollins into partnership in 1845 and their firm was known as Minton Hollins, trading in partnership with Minton and Co. In 1868 the firm split up, Michael Hollins taking the tile business and Colin Minton Campbell the China Works. Soon after this Colin Minton Campbell started mass production of decorative wall tiles at the China Works. There were numerous legal disputes as to who had the right to use the name Minton on tiles. Eventually Hollins was successful in law, but the litigation had lost his firm much business. Colin Minton Campbell joined forces with Robert Minton Taylor and established the Campbell Brick and Tile Company.

All these family squabbles were greatly to the benefit of Maw and Company and the other tile making firms, such as Craven Dunnill of Jackfield, T. and R. Boote of Burslem (who tiled the Blackwall Tunnel) and the Architectural Pottery at Poole in Dorset. Copelands, who had always been Mintons great rivals, and also Wedgwoods both made good quality decorated tiles and must have benefited by Minton's difficulties.

The designs on the tiles were very varied. Many tiles were designed to make up into repeat patterns to give a wall-papered appearance. The designs were geometric, floral or pictorial. The colours used were infinite in their variety. Enamel colours were used over the glaze as well as underglaze colouring. Sometimes the tiles were embossed, the glaze deepening in the lower parts of the design and so giving it a toned effect. The artistic trends of the times, the Aesthetic Movement, the Art Nouveau Movement and so on were mirrored in the tiles. Lilies and sunflowers blossomed all over the place and Oriental motifs were popular.

Mintons were the first of the firms to employ artists of note. In 1870 they took on the French designer, Marc Louis Solon whose pâte sur pâte tiles were a technical *tour de force*. Leon Arnoux, another Frenchman, was for many years Minton's Art Director. He perfected certain glazing techniques in imitation of Hispano-Moresque tiles.

245

J. Moyr Smith was retained by Mintons and he produced a number of transfer printed tiles for them during the '70s and '80s. In 1871 Mintons opened their Kensington Gore Art Pottery Studio in Queen's Gate. It only lasted for four years, but it was there that Hannah Barlow (who also worked for Doultons), William Wise and Moyr Smith did so much of their work.

Doultons were responsible for some remarkable ceramic murals. They had a studio in Lambeth, which they ran in association with the Lambeth School of Art. Their most successful artist was W.J. Neatby, who became head of their Architectural Department in 1890. Neatby was a highly competent craftsman as well as a talented, self-taught artist. He had learned his trade at Burmantofts in Leeds. He was responsible for the Doulton ceramic murals at Frascati's Restaurant, the Meat Hall at Harrods and the Winter Garden at Blackpool.

Pilkington's Tile and Pottery Company at Clifton Junction, Manchester embarked on tile manufacture in 1893. At various times they employed Walter Crane, Frederick Shields, Lewis F. Day, C.F.A. Voysey and Alphonse Mucha, the great Czech poster artist, who designed a set of panels made up from six inch square tiles, the subjects being the Carnation, the Lily, the Iris and the Rose. Mucha, one of the most interesting of the Art Nouveau artists, set the seal of artistic approval for the style of most of the late Victorian tiles. The swirling lines of Art Nouveau were well served by the tube-lined or moulded techniques, combined with thick translucent maiolica glazes. Tube-lining was a technique comparable to that used by a pastry cook forcing icing patterns on to a cake.

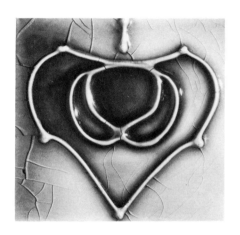

Dust-pressed tile decorated with the tube-lining technique and glazed with a rich yellow brown maiolica glaze. *c.* 1890. 76mm square. *Courtesy of the Gladstone Pottery Museum, Stoke-on-Trent.*

Plate 42. Opposite: A collection of typical late Victorian dust-pressed decorative tiles, showing different methods of surface treatment and design.

All tiles 152mm square. *Courtesy Ian Craig.*

Top row left to right:
Moulded 'Isnik' design. Made by Maw and Co. *c.* 1880.
Hand coloured sepia transfer printed decoration of a decadent poppy. *c.* 1885. Maker unknown.
Art nouveau design, moulded in low relief. Maker unknown. *c.* 1895.

2nd row left to right:
Hand coloured sepia transfer printed decoration. Made by Flaxman Tile Works. *c.* 1890.
Flower design made by coloured raised slip. Made by Wedgwoods. 1885.
Hand coloured sepia transfer printed design made by Minton Hollins. *c.* 1880.

3rd row left to right:
Hand coloured transfer printed 'aesthetic' design. Maker unknown. *c.* 1880.
Hand coloured transfer design printed in sepia by Sherwin and Cotton. 1880.
Hand coloured transfer design printed in sepia also by Sherwin and Cotton. 1888.

Bottom row left to right:
Coloured transfer printed design, possibly by Lee of Tunstall. *c.* 1896.
Hand coloured sepia transfer printed design by The Decorative Art Tile Co. 1887.
Moulded design in low relief made by Minton. *c.* 1880.

Dust-pressed tile decorated in the 'cuenca' technique. This is the Poppy, one of a set of six tiles called 'Flora's train' designed by Walter Crane for Pilkington. The design is impressed to leave thin walls of clay separating off the various green and red glazes. *c.* 1893. 152mm square. *Crown copyright Victoria and Albert Museum.*

Dust-pressed tile with an art nouveau floral decoration in high relief, coloured blue, orange and an acid green on a pale green background. Impressed mark on the back MINTON HOLLINS & CO STOKE-ON-TRENT No 2 Patt No 1557 W. *c.* 1895. 152mm square. *Private Collection.*

Dust-pressed tile with an asymmetric floral design in low relief coloured with greens and yellow on a green background. Impressed mark on the back A.M. LTD ENGLAND 4 and A 1: a mark used by Alfred Meakin and Co. *c.* 1895. 152mm square. *Private Collection.*

Dust-pressed tile with a design in high relief and coloured with a pale and a dark toffee colour with dark green on a paler green background. Stamped on the back the impressed mark of a couchant greyhound, one of the marks used by T. and R. Boote Ltd. between 1890 and 1903. 152mm square. *Private Collection.*

Two other distinguished illustrators to become involved in tile decoration were Kate Greenaway and R. Anning Bell. In 1881 Kate Greenway drew the designs for a set of The Four Seasons for T. and R. Boote and drew a further set of designs for Mintons which were engraved by William Wise, who was himself responsible for the designs of many tiles. Anning Bell was responsible for numerous tile designs for the firm of Della Robbia at Birkenhead. He had a close association with this pottery at the time when he was the Principal of the Liverpool College of Art. Among the many series of designs for tiles produced by Copelands, was one depicting musicians. Wedgwoods commissioned a series of illustrators for Shakespeare's plays. Minton's elaborate maiolica designs after the style of the fifteenth century Italian ceramic artist Luca della Robbia can still be seen and admired in some of the corridors and on the stairways of the Victoria and Albert Museum.

The tiles offered today are mostly poor palid things compared with the richness of effect produced in the last century, though Spain, Portugal, Italy and Mexico still make traditional, colourful and satisfying designs.

It is, however, still possible to find old Victorian tiles, and not just in antique shops and at auction sales. In junk shops one may come across battered old washstands with the tiles still in place. In builders' yards one may still find the remains of tiled fireplaces, and wherever Victorian buildings are being demolished there is a chance of getting hold of tiles from old hearths or walls or even from shop or factory fronts. But arrive before the bulldozers of the demolition gangs.

There are fine displays of Victorian tiles at the Gladstone Pottery Museum, Stoke-on-Trent and at Maw's Tile Museum, Coalport, Telford, Shropshire.

For further reading

Julian Barnard. *Victorian Ceramic Tiles*. Studio Vista 1972.
Terence A. Lockett. *Collecting Victorian Tiles*. Antique Collectors' Club 1979.
J. and B. Austwick. *The Decorative Tile*. Pitman House 1980.

Dust-pressed tile with a design in low relief, coloured blue and green on a cream background. Impressed on the back a rampant lion device in a shield and ENGLAND with an 's' and 'c' and 51, a mark used by T.A. Simpson and Co. *c.* 1900. 152mm square.
Private Collection.

Tea set designed by Sir Henry Cole (Felix Summerly) and made by Mintons in 1846. This was the tea set that won the Society of Arts prize and gave Cole the idea of starting Summerly's Art Manufactures.
Crown copyright Victoria and Albert Museum.

'The Hop Jug', designed and modelled by H.J. Townsend and made in cane coloured earthenware with coloured glazes. Commissioned by Sir Henry Cole for Summerly's Art Manufactures and made by Mintons. *c.* 1855. 267mm high.
Crown copyright Victoria and Albert Museum.

Opposite:
Brown salt-glazed stoneware vase by Mark V. Marshall. *c.* 1875. 254mm high. *Doulton and Co. Ltd.*

23. Artist potters and art pottery

A Minton maiolica seahorse and Cupid group modelled by A. Carrier de Belleuse and decorated in coloured glazes. It bears the Minton date mark for 1859. 407mm high. *Crown copyright Victoria and Albert Museum.*

One of the first people in the mid-nineteenth century to attempt to improve the standard of public taste was Sir Henry Cole. He had won a prize given by the Society of Arts in 1846 for the design of a tea set which he had entered for a competition under the pseudonym of Felix Summerly. In the following year he started Summerly's Art Manufactures and commissioned various artists and sculptors to produce designs for industry. The venture only lasted about three years, perhaps because Cole became absorbed in the organisation of the 1851 Exhibition. He later became Director of the South Kensington Museum (now the Victoria and Albert Museum).

Two of the designs sponsored by Cole were Henry Townsend's two jugs, the Hop design and the Two Drivers jug. Both these were made by Mintons. Mintons produced their first maiolica pieces in time for the Great Exhibition of 1851. The bright green, brown, orange and yellow glazes became immensely popular and figures were produced (some almost life size) as well as numerous aspidistra pots and elaborate table centre pieces. Mintons had working for them some French sculptors including Leon Arnoux and Albert Carrier de Belleuse, who were responsible for many of the designs.

In 1862 Alfred Stevens designed a series of painted maiolica plates and vases in the Italian Renaissance style which Mintons showed at the International Exhibition of that year. These intricate designs must have been very time taking to execute and were therefore expensive; they were not made in large quantities.

About 1867, Henry Doulton, inspired by John Sparkes, the Principal of the Lambeth School of Art, and with the help of a group of his students, established a studio at his Lambeth Pottery for the production of Art Wares. With the arrival of George Tinworth, a semi-literate son of a South-London wheelwright, the success of the studio became assured. While still a boy Tinworth showed a great talent as a carver, but his severe and limited father broke up every carving the boy made, thinking such frivolities were no help towards the wheelwright's trade.

Tinworth was described by Sir Henry Cole, when he visited the Lambeth studio in 1878, as 'an untutored genius', though in fact he had studied sculpture at the Royal Academy Schools. Tinworth was as much at home designing and modelling terracotta bas reliefs of religious subjects, which he did with the utmost sincerity, as he was producing groups of drunkards, gossiping old ladies or comic mice and frogs. Among the artists who worked for the Lambeth Pottery studio were Hannah, Florence and Arthur Barlow and Mark V. Marshall.

The success of Doulton's studio inspired many potters, either on their own, or as part of a larger concern to venture into this profitable and exciting field of Art Pottery.

Painted earthenware vases and plates designed for Mintons by Alfred Stevens. Inscribed 'February 1864' on the two plates and the tallest vase. They are all copies of the prototypes that were made from Stevens' designs and shown at the International Exhibition of 1862. They were never actually mass produced. Height of tallest vase 432mm. Diameter of plates 279mm.
Crown copyright Victoria and Albert Museum.

Vase, richly coloured in dark green, dark blue and ochre, impressed mark on the base Lambeth Doulton Faience in a circle, and lettered with the initials of the decorator MBS (Mildred Smallfield) and the date 1882. 195mm high.
Courtesy Kate Carter.

Buff coloured stoneware jug with pale blue applied flowers and dark blue glazed bands. The top of the neck has slots to accommodate a metal lid. Impressed mark on the base DOULTON LAMBETH ENGLAND a lower case '1' and an 'e' and 8831. These were the marks of Ada London and Bertha Evans both listed as Senior Assistants in 1882. *c.* 1882-87. 191mm high. *Courtesy Kate Carter.*

Stoneware tankard decorated by George Tinworth for Doultons in 1874. The incised monogram G T appears near the base. Impressed mark Doulton Lambeth 1874. 263mm high. Two vases and an owl in stoneware made by the Martin brothers at Southall, Middlesex. The owl was modelled by Wallace Martin. He made many more grotesque birds than this. *c.* 1899.
Crown copyright Victoria and Albert Museum.

Quite a different kind of ware from the London stonewares was also being made in the 1880s. This was earthenware decorated with rich, dark and sometimes brilliant glazes. Most of the designs were following the art nouveau fashion of the time and some were very successful. Small factories specialising in this kind of art pottery sprang up all over the country; among the most successful of these were the Linthorpe Pottery at Middlesbrough, Wilcock's Burmantofts pottery near Leeds, the Bretby Art Pottery at Woodville, Ault's pottery at nearby Swadlincote in Derbyshire and the Della Robbia at Birkenhead. There were of course numerous others, but hardly any in Staffordshire.

THE MARTIN BROTHERS

Stoneware dish with a fish and scrolled weeds on a blue ground. Inscribed: Martin Bros. London & Southall.
c. 1900. 149mm diameter.
Crown copyright Victoria and Albert Museum.

Wallace Martin, after some training at Lambeth School of Art and working as a sculptor's assistant, went to work at the Fulham Pottery (where John Dwight had worked). In 1873, he set up a workshop in King's Road, Fulham with his two younger brothers, who had been working at Doultons. The firing was done at the Fulham Pottery. Finally in 1877 they moved to Southall. Wallace was the head of the firm and was responsible for the modelling. Walter did most of the throwing, glazing and firing and Edwin did most of the decorating. The other brother Charles ran a shop that they had acquired near High Holborn. Wallace was the originator of the grotesque birds with big beaks and sly eyes as well as the jugs in the shape of human heads with leering expressions. Much of the Martins' early work was blue and grey, later a dark brown was used and later still greens and blues and browns. The colouring was always very low in tone. Relief and incised

253

Earthenware dish designed by Lewis F. Day who was a founder member of the Arts and Crafts Exhibition Society. 1877. 260mm diameter.
Crown copyright Victoria and Albert Museum.

White stoneware vase decorated with a resist design of birds and flowers on a dark blue ground. Marked: Martin Brothers London and Southall 1-1878. 381mm high.
Courtesy of the Trustees of the British Museum.

Four pieces of stoneware by the Martin brothers, each from a different period. The jug on the left was made by Wallace Martin in 1874 at the Fulham Pottery. 216mm high. The vase next to it was made at Southall in 1886. The jug with the human face was made by Wallace Martin in 1900 at Southall. 222mm high. The vase on the right which is a pleasant green is typical of their 'vegetable' period and was made by Edwin Martin in 1903. 254mm high. *Crown copyright Victoria and Albert Museum.*

Part of a dessert service designed by William de Morgan in the Isnik style with thistles in alternate blue and turquoise panels radiating from a central medallion, painted by Charles Passenger whose black monogram appears on the bases, with WILLIAM DE MORGAN & CO. After 1888. (The & Co. was added in that year to the pottery's mark.) Diameter of bowl 165mm. *Courtesy Christie's.*

Tile designed by William de Morgan and decorated with blue and green colouring. Marked with the impressed mark of the Sands End Pottery. *c.* 1888-98. 152mm square. *Private Collection.*

decoration was used, much of it with floral forms. Some of the later pots and vases were inspired by vegetable forms like gourds and marrows with vertical ribbed designs and textured surfaces. They made many miniature versions of their wares which are particularly attractive and quite as well finished as the larger pots, for the Martins were all expert craftsmen. They worked together perfectly as a team. Charles died in 1910 and Walter in 1912. They were sadly missed by the others. After the death of Edwin in 1914, only one more kiln was fired. Walter lived on until 1923. Most of their work is marked on the bottom in a cursive hand with the date and the name of the firm. Their pots are now much sought after. There is a fine collection of Martin ware in the Southall Public Library.

WILLIAM DE MORGAN

William de Morgan was perhaps the most outstanding of all the artist potters of the late nineteenth century. He studied at the Academy Schools. He met William Morris and possibly under Morris's influence took up pottery rather than painting. He began in quite a

Plate decorated in ruby lustre by William de Morgan, probably at Merton Abbey between 1882-88. 365mm diameter. *Crown copyright Victoria and Albert Museum.*

Vase with design by William de Morgan, painted in blues and greens. *c.* 1888. 229mm high. *Private Collection.*

Vase made by Bernard Moore of a fine hard earthenware with a *rouge flambé* glaze, very glowing and intense, specked with golden lights. Marked B. Moore on the base. *c.* 1904. 235mm high. *Private Collection.*

small way in 1864 making tiles, vases and dishes inspired by Persian pottery and decorated with animals, birds, flowers, and fishes in greens, pinks and blues. He also made some fine dishes in a ruby red lustre on a cream coloured earthenware. Although de Morgan produced a certain amount of beautiful work, he never had very much financial success, though his work became well-known in his life time. In 1888 he went into partnership with the architect Halsey Ricardo and they founded the Sands End Pottery at Fulham, where many of the tiles de Morgan designed were painted. His health was not good, and by 1892 he was obliged to spend the winters abroad, which made organising the work difficult. By 1907 his health had broken down and he was forced to give up. Among the painters who worked for him were Fred and Charles Passenger, Joe Juster and Jim Hersey. Their initials are frequently to be found on the base of de Morgan pots.

BERNARD MOORE

Another potter who was fascinated by colour was Bernard Moore. He and his brother Samuel had taken over their father's factory at Longton in Staffordshire in 1870 and ran it until 1905. After this, he set up his own workshop. He had always been interested in glazes, particularly those used by potters in the Far East and he became famous for his experiments with these. He produced some technically remarkable pieces with *flambé* and *sang de boeuf* glazes. Until the 1914 war he employed artists to make decorative pieces for exhibitions. His work is signed B M or with his whole name in capital letters.

Plate 43. Panel of tiles in typical Persian colouring. Designed by William de Morgan. Probably made at the Sands End Pottery between 1888-98. Each tile is 152mm square. *Private Collection.*

Two vases by Owen Carter. The one on the left is cast and finished in a red copper glaze with a slight lustre effect. The one on the right is thrown and produced by the same method using a reducing atmosphere in the kiln. Both show the influence of the art nouveau movement. *c.* 1906. 305mm high.
Carter, Stabler and Adams.

A teacup and saucer and teapot, designed by Roger Fry and made at the Omega Workshops. *c.* 1913. Teapot 159mm high. *Private Collection.*

POOLE POTTERIES

In the year 1855 the Patent Architectural Pottery was established at Hamworthy on the west side of Poole in Dorset by a group of men including John Ridgway of Hanley. In 1861 when Ridgway retired, James Walker, the chief technician left the pottery to set up his own tile making business a mile away on the East Quay. When in 1873 Walker's business failed, it was bought by Jesse Carter, a prosperous builders' merchant from Weybridge. Two of his sons, Owen and Charles, worked for the firm. In 1895 Jesse Carter bought up the Architectural Pottery as well. This was the same firm that had been supplying William de Morgan with blank tiles for decorating since the early 1870s. Later he also bought bowls and dishes from them.

In 1900 Owen Carter, the artist of the family, started experimenting with lustre glazes and his pots became a solid part of the firm's output. Meanwhile the Hamworthy works went on making tiles in great variety, mosaic, encaustic, embossed, printed and hand painted.

It was just before the Great War that the firm developed a tin glaze. This was taken up by Roger Fry at the Omega Workshops and was to have a profound effect and influence on the future productions of the Carter Pottery. (See pages 340-1).

OMEGA WORKSHOPS

In 1913 the painter and art critic Roger Fry started the Omega Workshops. After some preliminary instruction from a potter at Mitcham in Surrey, he met Roger Carter, Owen's nephew, and went down to Poole to further his knowledge.

In his advertising leaflet, published in 1915, Fry wrote:

> 'The Omega Workshops Limited is a group of artists who are working with the object of allowing free play to the delight in creation in the making of objects in common life...They try to keep the spontaneous freshness of primitive or peasant work, while satisfying the needs and expressing the feelings of the modern cultivated man ...Omega pottery is made on the wheel by artists and is not merely executed to their designs...It is made for the most part with a white tin glaze analogous to that of old Delf.'

The firm had considerable success during the Great War, in spite of the crudity of their wares. However, the burden of running Omega and the Quaker Relief Fund in France proved too much for him and in June 1919 the Omega Workshops closed down.

Plate 44. Royal Lancastrian pottery vase with a blue glaze and gold lustre decoration of four sailing ships and the inscription round the top JUVA FORTES FORTUNA. Made by Pilkington's and decorated by W.S. Mycock, whose monogram is to be seen on the base with the number 288 impressed. *c.* 1920. 319mm high. *Private Collection.*

Plate 45. Yellow vase with gold lustre decoration by Richard Joyce at Pilkington's Royal Lancastrian Pottery. Signed with his initials on the base and a lustre silhouette of a deer, signifying the date of manufacture as 1909. Also the numbers 2112 and IX. 222mm high. *Private Collection.*

Plate 46. Six handled vase with mottled red, blue and green glazes over incised decoration built up with coloured slip. Made by Sir Edmund Elton at the Sunflower Pottery. *c.* 1890-1900. Approx. 150mm high. *Courtesy Sir Charles Elton, Bart.*

This curious pot was made by Sir
Edmund Elton at the Sunflower Pottery
at Clevedon Court near Bristol. It was
copied from an ancient Cypriot oil lamp
which was given to him shortly after its
excavation in 1914. It shows an
extraordinary technical achievement.
This was one of Elton's most successful
gold and platinum lustre effects. *c.* 1916.
222mm high.
Courtesy Sir Charles Elton, Bart.

Right:
Two handled vase with green and blue
marbled glaze and a red and green
flower design built up with layers of
coloured slip. Made by Sir Edmund
Elton at the Sunflower Pottery. *c.* 1900.
394mm high.
Courtesy Sir Charles Elton, Bart.

SIR EDMUND ELTON

Sir Edmund Elton started the Sunflower Pottery at his home Clevedon
Court near Bristol in 1881, after seeing tiles being made at the local
brickworks. He taught himself to throw, to build kilns, to decorate and
to glaze. He used the clay from his estate and with the help of a small
hunch-back called George Masters worked away tirelessly every
morning for about forty years. At first there were many failures and
disappointments which only spurred him on to further experiments.
He made mainly decorative ware. His pots were decorated with incised
patterns, usually based on floral forms and somewhat in the art
nouveau manner. The designs were built up with coloured slips which
he modelled and carved and then fired to fix the colours, re-firing with
a lead glaze to 1050° – 1100°. From 1902 he experimented with gold
and platinum lustre and crackled glazes. His work is quite distinctive
and all the pieces he actually made himself are signed 'Elton' on the
bottom.

After Sir Edmund's death in 1920 his son, Sir Ambrose Elton,
attempted to carry on the pottery with the help of the charming and
intelligent W. Fishley Holland (the grandson of Edwin Beer Fishley of
Fremington). Sir Ambrose signed his pieces with Elton + , but they
are distinguishable as being poor derivatives of his father's work.

With the death of George Masters in 1921, the enterprise came to
an end and Fishley Holland set up his own pottery about a mile away.

Vase with sgraffito decoration and an ochre coloured glaze, made at the Linthorpe Pottery. Marked on the base Linthorpe Chr. Dresser and a monogram of HT (Henry Tooth) and the number 85. *c.* 1879-82. 190mm high.
Courtesy Dorman Museum, Middlesbrough.
Copyright Cleveland County Council.

Jug with a fine ochre, green and brown mixture of glazes made at the Linthorpe Pottery. Marked on the base Linthorpe, Chr. Dresser and a monogram of HT (Henry Tooth) and the number 783. *c.* 1879-82. 145mm high.
Courtesy Dorman Museum, Middlesbrough.
Copyright Cleveland County Council.

Earthenware jug designed by
Dr. Christopher Dresser, showing
Amerindian influence, for the Linthorpe
Pottery. *c.* 1880. 165mm high.

LINTHORPE ART POTTERY

In 1879 Dr. Christopher Dresser (1834-1904) a well-known Orientalist and consultant designer to various firms including Tiffanys of New York and a Fellow of the Linnean Society, was visiting Mr. John Harrison at Linthorpe near Middlesbrough. He was moved by the sight of the unemployed ironworkers and noting the clay soil on the estate where there had been a brick works suggested to Harrison that they started a pottery there. This would provide work for some of the former ironworkers.

Harrison agreed and on Dresser's advice engaged Henry Tooth to be the pottery manager. Tooth had worked as a scene painter during the sixties in London and later as an interior decorator at Ryde in the Isle of Wight. He was a man of considerable talent and energy. At fourteen years of age he had been employed in a brickworks. His father then apprenticed him to a butcher. Having no liking for that trade, and inspired by Dr. Dresser's writings, he turned to art as a career.

In 1879 on his way to Middlesbrough Henry Tooth visited Stoke-on-Trent and learned much about the pottery trade. Within a few months he had converted the old brick yards at Linthorpe into a pottery and though he had never made a pot in his life, using the common brick clay, he was soon modelling, decorating and firing the ware himself. Harrison appointed Dresser as Art Director of the pottery for life. However, Dresser was occupied with other things. Within a couple of years his influence declined, he rarely visited the pottery, contenting himself with sending Tooth his designs which the potters and decorators would copy. These were under the direction of Richard Patey who Tooth had brought from the Isle of Wight to oversee the modelling. Patey later became manager after Tooth left in 1882 to start his own firm.

By 1885 the Linthorpe Pottery was employing between eighty and one hundred hands. It had become the largest pottery on Teeside. By this time they were importing white clay from Cornwall to supplement the brick clay. Linthorpe's wares, influenced by Middle Eastern and Oriental designs, with their richly coloured glazes, were something new to the English market and soon became very popular. They used low toned reds, mottled olive greens, browns and yellows and also made incised and perforated wares.

The Linthorpe Art Pottery was the first pottery in England to use gas-fired kilns. This go-ahead firm should have prospered but Dresser's glazes proved very costly and breakages during firing were common. In 1889 John Harrison went bankrupt, for reasons unconnected with the pottery. He could no longer supply any support and it closed in that year. In spite of its short life its influence was great.

The mark used by the firm was the word LINTHORPE impressed.

Jardinière covered with Indian red, yellow and green streaked glazes. Marked with the rising sun mark of the Bretby Pottery impressed on the base and 1222K ENGLAND Rd 338766. *c.* 1891-1900. 235mm high. *Courtesy Kate Carter.*

Top left: Pot covered with a fine green glaze, made by Tooth and Co. The Bretby Art Pottery, Woodville, near Burton-on-Trent, Derbyshire. Marked with the rising sun mark and 1782 on the base. *c.* 1884. 113mm high.
Courtesy Castle Antiques, (Warwick's Art Deco Shop), Warwick.

Jewelled ware vase. This ware was made of red clay and finished with a lustrous brown glaze to simulate iron or bronze. The applied 'jewels' are large cabochons made of ceramic, enamelled and glazed to represent turquoise (round the top) and opals at the bottom. Though the 'jewels' were made at Howson Taylor's Ruskin Pottery, the vase is marked with the rising sun mark of the Bretby Pottery, the number 16760 and the word ENGLAND. *c.* 1909. 260mm high. *Courtesy Castle Antiques, (Warwick's Art Deco Shop), Warwick.*

Advertising leaflet showing the change of address issued by Henry Tooth on the occasion of moving his London showrooms to 9 St. Andrew's Street, Holborn.
This photomontage was designed by Henry Tooth and shows him wearing his characteristic wide brimmed hat. *Courtesy Bretby Art Pottery, Tooth and Co. Ltd.*

In 1882, after leaving the Linthorpe Pottery, Henry Tooth went into partnership with William Ault, who had worked for T.G. Green at Church Gresley. In the following year they designed and built the Bretby Art Pottery. Tooth and Ault were very different kinds of men. Ault, though trained as a potter was a businessman, Tooth was an artist. After four years Ault left Bretby to set up his own pottery at nearby Swadlincote.

From then on, Tooth traded as Tooth and Co., producing ornamental pottery in a variety of glazes and colours. The pottery expanded from the ten workers they had in 1883 to upwards of seventy employees. Most of their wares were press moulded or slip cast. Some of these can still be seen in the showroom that Henry Tooth had designed and built in 1883. The room is a marvellous evocation of the age with its display of art pottery, its poker work doors and mural scenes by Henry Tooth of the potters at work. A bust of Henry Tooth in a wide brimmed hat still dominates the scene. He must have had a dynamic personality. Coming into the pottery trade with no knowledge of it, his only qualification was that he was an imaginative and versatile artist. He had the advantage of being unfettered by tradition.

There was an immediate demand for Bretby ware both at home and abroad. Henry Tooth concentrated solely on ornamental wares with no distracting side lines. The Bretby Art Pottery won numerous medals at International Exhibitions for their elegant tall vases and other ware in blues, reds, greens and yellows and splashed and mottled glazes.

Henry Tooth was assisted by his second daughter Florence who was a skilled modeller and decorator and by his son who at the end of the great war took over the management of the business. In 1933 The Bretby Art Pottery was bought by Mr. Fred Parker, whose family still run it. The mark, both impressed and printed is a rising sun above the word BRETBY. It has been in use from 1891.

Vase with a powder blue
glaze, made by William Ault
at Swadlincote in Derbyshire.
Impressed mark on base.
c. 1900. 155mm high.

Small scallop shell form vase
with a yellowish green glaze
made by William Ault at
Swadlincote in Derbyshire.
Impressed mark on base
with Rd 195321. *c.* 1890.
67mm high. *Private Collection.*

Jardinière of cream coloured
earthenware with brown and
green glazes. Made at
Wilcock's Pottery at
Burmantofts near Leeds.
c. 1890. Height of pot
275mm. Height of matching
pedestal opposite 660mmm.
*Courtesy Abbey House Museum,
Kirkstall, Leeds.*

AULT'S POTTERY

William Ault was born in Burslem in 1841. In 1863 he was given a responsible job at the Church Gresley Pottery, which shortly after his appointment was bought by T.G. Green. Ault stayed there until 1867 when he left to attend a business and accountancy course at Liverpool. At T.G. Green's request he returned to the newly built Church Gresley works and remained there until 1881. He joined Henry Tooth in 1882 in the founding of the Bretby Art Pottery.

William Ault opened his own pottery at Swadlincote in 1887. There he manufactured ornamental wares, vases, plant pots and pedestals, which were known as 'Ault Faience'. Mostly press moulded, they were of simple shapes and rich colours. Dr. Christopher Dresser supplied him with many of his designs. In 1893 his faience received the highest award at the Chicago World Fair. Ault was not content with being a successful pottery manager, but experimented with a variety of glazes. The firm prospered. Their mark was AULT on a ribbon under a reeded vase. Some of the Ault wares carry an impressed facsimile of Christopher Dresser's signature. In 1923, the firm took into partnership Pascoe Tunnicliffe and became Ault and Tunnicliffe. A brochure dated 1924 shows that they were still making elaborate jardinières and jug and basin sets in the art nouveau manner.

BURMANTOFTS POTTERY

The pottery at Burmantofts near Leeds had been making salt-glazed pipes and firebacks etc. since the 1850s on a hundred acre site where both coal and clay were in abundant supply. In 1882 Messrs. Wilcock and Co. decided to start the production of art pottery here. The manager from 1879 to 1890 was James Holroyd Snr., succeeded by his son James Holroyd Jnr. from 1890 to 1896, when Robert Bond took over. William J. Neatby was an artist employed there from 1883 to 1890. Some of the employees from the recently defunct Linthorpe Pottery came to work here in 1889.

Some of the large jardinières that the pottery produced were remarkable pieces of ceramic engineering with their fine mouldings and tall pedestals. The glazes were a real feature of the Burmantofts pottery; the colours used were a brilliant turquoise blue, an orange, a fine pale yellow and a *sang de boeuf* red. Sometimes several colours were blended together. Unfortunately economic pressure overcame them and the making of pottery ceased in August 1904. They continued making a certain amount of architectural faience until the 1950s. One of the last jobs was the lining of the Empire Pool, Cardiff for the Commonwealth Games in 1958. The mark was BURMANTOFTS or the monogram BF. FAIENCE

Large lustre jar with a design made up of a frieze of leopards in black, grey and tawny brown. Designed and executed by Richard Joyce. *c.* 1912. 229mm high.
Private Collection.
Richard Joyce worked at Pilkingtons from 1903-31. He had studied at the Swadlincote School of Art and had worked at Henry Tooth's Bretby Art Pottery before this. His real speciality was animal forms, which he drew with verve and sensitivity.

Below left: Royal Lancastrian pottery vase, grey-green with gold lustre decoration after Walter Crane's 'Sea Maiden' design, by William S. Mycock for Pilkington's. Dated 1916. 267mm high.
Private Collection.

Below right: Grey-green lustre decorated bottle with an all-over design of conventional flowers by Charles Cundall RA. *c.* 1909. 229mm high.
Private Collection.

Blue vase streaked with an almost golden green matt glaze. Made by W. Howson Taylor at the Ruskin Pottery. Impressed mark on the base RUSKIN ENGLAND and the date 1932. 273mm high.
Courtesy Kate Carter.

Tall, slim vase with a band of floral decoration inspired by *l'art nouveau*. This was designed and painted by Gordon M. Forsyth in particularly beautiful shades of blue. *c.* 1907. 419mm high.
Private Collection.

RUSKIN POTTERY, SMETHWICK NEAR BIRMINGHAM

W. Howson Taylor started his pottery in 1898, first using local clay and then later imported china clay with calcined flints. His work consisted of three main types; soufflé wares decorated in single and shaded colours, lustred wares and high-fired wares with mottled glazes and brilliant colours. The Ruskin Pottery closed in 1935 on Howson Taylor's death. Just before he died, emulating Cobden-Sanderson in another field of design, he destroyed all his recipes and materials.

Ruskin wares from 1898-1904 are marked TAYLOR or with a monogram WHT and after 1904 the word RUSKIN appears, sometime after 1920 with W. HOWSON TAYLOR above and ENGLAND below.

PILKINGTON'S LANCASTRIAN POTTERY

Towards the end of the century in 1893 the Pilkington Pottery was opened at Clifton Junction near Manchester. To begin with they made glazed bricks and tiles, but soon the pottery began to experiment with decorative ware under the leadership of William and Joseph Burton. Both the Burtons were chemists, William having worked at Josiah Wedgwood and Sons for five years. During the first two decades of the twentieth century many famous artists designed for them including Gordon Forsyth, Lewis Day, Walter Crane, Richard Joyce and W.S. Mycock. Experiments were made with many different kinds of shapes and glazes, including lustred wares. At one time double thrown pottery was produced, the outer skin pierced to reveal the inner, the whole being glazed with plain, mottled or onyx glazes, though this was discontinued soon after the First World War. Ware was also decorated with *sgraffito* designs. But the main feature of the pottery was the variety and beauty of the glazes that were used and the precise and jewel-like quality of the lustred designs.

In 1913 with the award of a Royal Warrant from George V, Pilkington's ware became known as Royal Lancastrian. In 1937 the pottery section of the factory was closed down and in the following February the company's name was changed to Pilkington's Tiles Ltd. The tiles business expanded and in 1964 the company merged with Carters of Poole, Dorset. The company still flourishes today.

THE DELLA ROBBIA POTTERY, BIRKENHEAD

Another short lived pottery that started off with noble aims and high ideals was the Della Robbia Pottery at Birkenhead. The pottery was founded in 1894 by the talented but somewhat eccentric artist Harold Rathbone and the sculptor Conrad Dressler, to employ local artists to make beautiful artifacts out of local clay (which however proved to be unsatisfactory), in a happy working environment. Conrad Dressler was mainly concerned with the architectural side of the business which

Plate 47. Della Robbia pottery.
Left to right: Small vase with Celtic decoration inscribed in monogram CJ and dated 1902. 200mm high.
'Manzoni Vase' the portrait is after Andrea del Sarto's painting of Lucrezia di Baccio del Fede and was probably inscribed by Carlo Manzoni. The remaining decoration is the work of Cassandia Annie Walker. Inscribed CAW and dated 1903. 377mm high.
Spoon warmer in the shape of a fish. Inscribed CAW (Cassandia Annie Walker) and dated 1900. Painted mark EMW (Miss E.M. Wood). 310mm long.

Clock case signed Ruth Bare and dated April 1904. The inscription 'Il Progresso Sia Il Nostro Scopo' (Let Progress Be Our Aim) was a devotion of the Positivist Movement. 460mm high.
Small two-handled classically shaped vase decorated by Cassandia Annie Walker. Inscribed CAW and dated 1897. 243mm high.

Williamson Art Gallery and Museum, Birkenhead, Wirral Borough Council Dept. Leisure Services and Tourism.

Two vases made at the Della Robbia Pottery, Birkenhead. The one on the left is decorated by Cassandia Annie Walker and Charles Collis; on the base is the incised galleon mark and painted artists' initials. The colours are green predominating with pink and yellow. *c.* 1900. 334mm high. *Courtesy Sotheby's.* The one on the right was decorated by Jack Ford and H. Jones, whose initials appear on the base with the incised galleon mark. Same colour scheme as the other one. *c.* 1900. 313mm high.

'Florian' ware vase, coloured in two tones of blue. Made by William Moorcroft. 1898. 230mm high. *Courtesy Beatrice Moorcroft.*

comprised wall panels, fountains, etc. but which never reached its potential; he only stayed about three years.

About 1898 Carlo Manzoni went to work at the Della Robbia Pottery and stayed there until it closed in 1906. The pottery employed artists including Anning Bell and girls from the local art schools and nearby district. As well as being a talented lot some of the girls were very attractive, judging by old photographs. Technical staff were imported from Staffordshire and John Bowers, the first thrower came from Doultons. The number of members of staff fluctuated, some only remaining a short time, but there seem to have been a nucleus formed by a faithful few including Charles Collis, Cassandia Annie Walker, Ruth Bare and Violet Woodhouse.

The vases, plaques and other pieces made at the pottery show a strong art nouveau influence in their use of natural forms. The colouring tended to be restricted to blues, greens and yellows and individual artists were encouraged to sign their own designs.

The Della Robbia marks consisted of a number of sailing ship motifs, with a D on one side and an R on the other and the monogram of the potter. The decorator's initials were also pencilled on.

WILLIAM MOORCROFT

One of the artist potters who actually came from the pottery district of Staffordshire was William Moorcroft, born at Burslem in 1872. His first job was as a designer at James Macintyre's Washington Works at Burslem. Here he was given a free hand to experiment with clays, slips, colours and glazes and encouraged to develop his own style. In his early pieces the drawings were outlined in trailed slip on the pots (much in the same way that tube-lined tiles were decorated).

He set up his own workshop in 1913 and continued to design all the pots and their decoration, colouring and glazes, working alongside the craftsmen he employed. Moorcroft said that he was influenced by Chinese art. The colours he used on his early 'Florian' ware were limited to blues, greens and yellows, for they were the only underglaze colours known to him at the time to withstand the high temperature firing. Over the years he built up a much more extensive colour range and the rich dark colours he used in the early twenties were more massed and bolder in treatment than the linear designs he had developed earlier.

William Moorcroft signed practically all his decorative pottery, except for experimental pieces and those with which he was unsatisfied; also most of the plain lustre and slipware produced between 1915 and 1924. The early signature or initials was followed by 'des' for designer, until 1906 when this was dropped.

271

Left: 'Florian' ware vase with raised decoration and coloured with blue, green and ochre. Signed W. Moorcroft des. No trade mark but the Rd No 347807 1899. 280mm high.

Right: 'Florian' ware vase with raised decoration coloured in tones of blue. Designed by William Moorcroft and made by him at his department at James Macintyre and Co., Burslem. Initialled on the base W.M. des and Macintyre's Florian Ware backstamp. 1898. 280mm high.

Left: 'Hazledene' vase coloured with blue, green and ochre glazes. Signed W. Moorcroft. This was one of the pieces made specially for Liberty and Co. 1904. 310mm high.

Right: 'Eighteenth century' design vase made by W. Moorcroft. The colouring is red, green and blue with the addition of gilding. Signed on the base W. Moorcroft and bearing the Macintyre mark. 1906. 310mm high.
All photographs courtesy Beatrice Moorcroft.

Vase with a rich dark blue glaze and a decoration of pansies coloured with pink, a mauvy blue and green. Made by William Moorcroft. Impressed mark on base MOORCROFT MADE IN ENGLAND and his initials pencilled in blue. *c.* 1921-30. 160mm high. *Courtesy Kate Carter.*

The early 'Florian' ware 1898-1905 was marked with a printed backstamp in the form of a cartouche with James Macintyre and Co. Burslem England. The later Macintyre trade mark consisted of J.M. & Co in a circle and this replaced the Florian backstamp in 1906, though the marking of the ware was somewhat erratic and some pieces escaped being marked altogether. Impressed MOORCROFT marks in various styles date from 1915-45.

Macintyre also on occasions printed the retailer's name, by request on the base of pieces, the most frequent being 'Made for Liberty & Co'. Libertys still stock contemporary Moorcroft ware.

In 1937 William Moorcroft was joined by his son Walter, who continues to direct the pottery today with the help of his brother John. William Moorcroft died in 1945. For the last twenty years of his life he concentrated on the *flambé* glazes which interested him most. Moorcroft's work was largely exported and is probably better known abroad than in his own country.

For further reading
Hugh Wakefield. *Victorian Pottery*. Herbert Jenkins 1962.
William Gaunt and D.E. Clayton-Stamm Maxwell. *William de Morgan*. Studio Vista 1971.
J. Catleugh. *William de Morgan Tiles*. Trefoil 1983.
Malcolm Haslam. *English Art Pottery*. Antique Collectors' Club 1975.
E. Lloyd Thomas. *Victorian Art Pottery*. Guildart, n.d. c.1975.
James H. Rushton. *Ruskin Pottery*. Metropolitan Borough of Sandwell 1975.
Desmond Eyles. *The Doulton Lambeth Wares*. Hutchinson 1975.
A.W. Coysh. *British Art Pottery 1870-1940*. David and Charles 1976.
Malcolm Haslam. *The Martin Brothers Potters*. Richard Dennis 1978.
A.J. Cross. *Pilkington's Royal Lancastrian Pottery and Tiles*. Richard Dennis 1980.
Richard Dennis. *Pilkington's Royal Lancastrian Ware* (Exhibition Catalogue) pub. Richard Dennis 1971.
R. and Jessie Dennis. *Christopher Dresser*. Dennis 1972.
R. Dennis. *William and Walter Moorcroft 1897-1973*. n.d.
Julia Elton. 'Eltonware at Clevedon Court'. *National Trust Journal* Autumn 1980.
Aileen Dawson. *Bernard Moore, Potter*. 1982.
Della Robbia Pottery, Birkenhead 1894-1906 (An interim report) pub. Metropolitan Borough of Wirral. c.1981/2.
I. Bennett. *Ruskin Pottery and the European Ceramic Revival*. Haslam and Whiteway 1981.
A. Garlick et al. *Burmantoft's Pottery*. Bradford Art Galleries and Museums 1983.

Posset pot decorated with a frieze of couples, hand in hand. The lid is surmounted by a happy fiddler and is inscribed 16 I H 87. This pot was probably made to celebrate the betrothal of John Hammet and Judith Rice who were married at Fremington on 4 September 1689. Both bride and groom were members of local potting families. Made in North Devon 1687. 413mm high.

The red clay body has been dipped in white slip, the inscription and details have been incised through and the whole covered with a lead glaze. A technique used by the Devon potters until the present day.
Royal Albert Memorial Museum, Exeter.

24. Some country potteries

As well as the artist potters there is a small group of craftsmen whose work should not be completely ignored. These are the real country potters. Small potteries in obscure villages run by one man with the help perhaps of a member or two of his family, their survival depending on producing ware for local use. These men were artists in their way and made their pots because they liked to do so. Some of these such as Brannams of Barnstaple developed into larger concerns.

Barnstaple and Bideford were the main West Country pottery centres from the 15th to the mid-19th centuries. Local red and white clays were used for the manufacture of domestic and ornamental pots. Cornish or cloam ovens for baking bread were made by the local potteries and not only used all over the West Country but exported to Wales, Ireland and America.

THE FISHLEYS OF FREMINGTON

George Fishley had opened a pottery at Muddlebridge about three miles from Barnstaple by about 1800. This he soon abandoned for another pottery near Fremington where there was a particularly fine red clay. His productions were mainly of domestic ware for use by the local farmers and fishermen. By 1840 his sons Edmund and Robert were working in the pottery, leaving their father time to produce many individual pieces, highly decorated but somewhat naïve in character. These were formed of different coloured clays and lead glazed. Edmund Fishley also decorated many pieces including Harvest jugs and posset pots. The pottery flourished under his direction but he died tragically in 1860 and his only son Edwin Beer Fishley took over the management. In the 1880s he began to make art pottery which he decorated with rich green and blue glazes. The pottery also continued to make coarse domestic wares.

Mantelpiece ornaments made by George Fishley. Both lead glazed. The one on the left has four animals reclining on the base. The decorations are made of dark brown and white clays. Impressed 'G * FISHLEY/ FREMINGTON/ DEVON' and incised '1770/1855' on the back. 170mm high.
The one on the right also supports four reclining animals. The decorations are also dark brown and white clays. Impressed 'G * FISHLEY FREMINGTON' and 1849 incised on the base. 220mm high.
Royal Albert Memorial Museum, Exeter

Jug with a globular body made by Edmund Fishley covered in a white slip and lead glaze with numerous incised inscriptions. On the front 'Wm Mildon Hallswell Chittlehampton 1839' and on the other side 'Rebecca Searle/June 6th/1839'. Impressed 'Edmund Fishley/Maker/Fremington June 6th 1839'. 325mm high. *Royal Albert Memorial Museum, Exeter.*

Three handled mug, puzzle jug, bowl and cover and plate, all by Edwin Beer Fishley. The mug and the puzzle jug are both inscribed with incised lettering. The plate which has a wavy motif must have been an inspiration to Michael Cardew when he visited the pottery as a boy. All the pieces are green glazed and impressed 'E.B. Fishley/Fremington/N Devon'. *c.* 1900. The mug is 165mm high. *Royal Albert Memorial Museum, Exeter.*

It was at the Fremington Pottery that Michael Cardew, when a boy, developed his interest in the craft. Fishley's influence can be seen in some of Cardew's later pots. At Edwin Beer Fishley's death in 1912 the pottery was sold up, firstly to a Staffordshire man and subsequently to Brannams of Barnstaple who only used it for making ovens. These continued in production until the early 1930s when most of the buildings were demolished.

THE BRANNAM POTTERY BARNSTAPLE

There had been a family of Brannams potting in Devon since the end of the 18th century. By 1840 Thomas Brannam had bought a pottery in Litchdon Street, Barnstaple. He manufactured pitchers, pots and pans and other peasant pottery for local consumption. He exhibited some Harvest jugs at the Great Exhibition of 1851. In 1879 Thomas Brannam's son, Charles Hubert, took over the pottery and started to make art pottery. He had a fine sense of form and colour. He used dark blues and greens and lighter shades applied with coloured slips with *sgraffito* patterns which revealed the red body of the ware. He named his pottery Barum Ware after the Roman name for Barnstaple. At the

Vase with a brown and blue mottled glaze and three swirling handles round the top. Underneath are the incised words 'Barum Barnstaple'. Made by C.H. Brannam. *c.* 1904. 178mm high. *Private Collection.*

Small red ware Toby jug covered with dark blue and green glazes. Made by C.H. Brannam at Barnstaple and incised in the base 'C.H. Brannam Barum 1899'. 150mm high. *Courtesy Kate Carter.*

same time he continued with the production of peasant pottery with a growing work force.

In 1885 William Baron joined the firm as a decorator. The actual production of art pottery was a slow business. The vases etc. had to be in the decorating room for up to fourteen days, with one colour being laid and then allowed to dry before the next was applied. The ware had to be kept damp for the whole time it was being decorated. Most of the pots were thrown, though moulds were used for three-dimensional details.

In 1898 Baron quarrelled with his employers and departed to set up a pottery on his own. Brannam's art pottery was sold by Liberty's in London. Most of it was marked 'C.H. Brannam Barum Ware' and was often dated. Some of the pieces also carried the initials of the artist who had decorated them.

A blue glaze applied over a white slip was introduced to make a very rich dark blue colour. Other colours were a 'Liberty Green' and 'Old Gold' achieved by adding metallic oxides to a raw maiolica glaze, which gave a brilliant surface but had a high lead content and a tendency to craze.

C.H. Brannam retired in 1914 and the pottery was taken over by

Tall three handled vase covered with a mottled pink glaze. Made by Brannam and marked 'Barnstaple Barum' on the base. 309mm high. *Courtesy Castle Antiques, (Warwick's Art Deco Shop), Warwick.*

Earthenware vase with bands of white slip and sgraffito decoration made at the Watcombe Pottery. *c.* 1885. 102mm high.

278

his two sons, Charles and Jack. Charles managed the business side, Jack the works and they were permanently at loggerheads. In the 1920s flower pots had become their main product, but they continued to make art pottery. Jack Brannam introduced some fine mottled glazes and substituted simple contemporary shapes for the ornate Victorian pieces. Many of these were commissioned by Heal's of Tottenham Court Road, London. Various other new glazes replaced the old shiny greens, blues and yellows. One colour remained, a rich dark blue which became the hallmark of the firm. Another distinctive colour was a fine orange made from uranium oxide, in a glaze with a high lead content. The use of these lead based glazes ended in the late 1940s because of strict government regulations.[1]

In 1979 Peter Brannam, a grandson of C.H. Brannam, retired. Peter Brannam, engineer, business man and potter had been in charge of the works for some years and had cleverly replanned the layout of the factory turning more and more to the manufacture of flower pots. On his retirement the firm was taken over by Candy and Co. of Newton Abbot, part of the group operated by the Fox family of Wellington, Somerset. Today Brannams are the last firm in England to make earthenware flower pots. However, they still make fine great jars glazed with blues, green and browns with three characteristic twisted handles. It is a real old fashioned pottery and they are still using one of their old bottle ovens which takes three men two days to fill and sixteen hours to fire.

BARON POTTERY BARNSTAPLE

This pottery was opened by William L. Baron in 1893, after he had left Brannams. In 1899 he became established in new premises at Rolle Quay, his pots were very similar to Brannams and he was in hot competition with his old firm. He used to bribe the local coach drivers to bring tourists to his pottery. Brannams in turn out-bribed him!

In 1910 Frederick Baron joined his father and the firm continued to make ornamental ware. William Baron died in 1938 and in the following year Brannams took over Baron's Pottery. Some of Baron's ware is displayed in the Royal Albert Memorial Museum, Exeter, including some red ware covered with a white slip and *sgraffito* decoration with designs of fishes.

THE WATCOMBE POTTERY

This pottery was established in 1867 as a result of the altruistic aims of G.J. Allen, former master of Dulwich College. Allen found a site for

1 See Peter Brannam *A Family Business: the story of a pottery.* Barnstaple 1982.

Elegant earthenware vase of fine red clay made at the Watcombe Pottery. *c.* 1880. 153mm high.

Two typical Aller Vale pieces, on the left a small 'motto' ware jug with sgraffito decoration and an amber glaze. On the right a vase with a slip-trailed dolphin design. The taller piece approx. 160mm high. *c.* 1900. *Royal Albert Memorial Museum, Exeter.*

Red earthenware sugar basin covered in a cream coloured slip and banded in blue with sgraffito lettering. On the other side is the phrase 'Sweeten to your liking'. On the base, stamped in black is

WATCOMBE
TORQUAY
ENGLAND

and 176. Made after the amalgamation with the Aller Vale Pottery. *c.* 1920-30. These West Country tourist pieces must have been made in their tens of thousands.

a house in the vale of Watcombe, just north of Torquay, where there proved to be an outcrop of red clay. Mr. Allen saw the obvious possibilities for pottery making and founded a company with seven of his friends. They took on the best modellers, throwers and decorators that they could find. Charles Brock, an experienced potter, was appointed as the first manager and soon had a successful enterprise under his hands. He found that the local red clay mixed with lighter clays produced a fine, smooth terracotta ware. Some of the Watcombe wares were decorated with bands of white slip.

Christopher Dresser is said to have provided the Watcombe Pottery with designs. In 1901 the pottery joined up with the Aller Vale Pottery to become the Royal Aller Vale and Watcombe Pottery Company.

THE ALLER VALE POTTERY

This was probably the most prolific of the South Devon potteries. It was established in 1881 at Kingkerswell near Newton Abbot and turned out masses of red ware slip-dipped and with *sgraffito* decoration and mottos for the tourist trade. 'Drink like a fish – but only water' was a typical one. In 1901 it merged with the Watcombe Pottery to become the Royal Aller Vale and Watcombe Pottery Company. It closed in 1962.

Jug made of white earthenware with green, brown and yellow slip decoration. Inscribed on the base 'Lauder, Barum'. Late 19th century. 215mm high.
Royal Albert Memorial Museum, Exeter.

LAUDER POTTERY, BARNSTAPLE

Alexander Lauder, an architect, opened this pottery in partnership with a man called Smith in 1876. To begin with they specialised in large terracotta panels and other architectural ornaments. During the 1880s Smith left the firm and Lauder turned to the production of ornamental pots. He called these 'Devon Art Pottery'. The ware was very similar to Brannams. Two very elegant little jugs with rich green, brown and yellow glazes are on show in the Royal Albert Memorial Museum, Exeter.

In the 1880s Lauders were employing about forty hands, many of them women specialising in naturalistic designs. In 1914 the pottery closed. Their marks consisted of 'Lauder' and references to the design number scratched on the base.

THE DEVON ART POTTERY

This was started in the Exeter area in 1896 by William Hart and Alfred Moist. They produced wares very similar to those made at Aller Vale.

THE LONGPARK POTTERY

This was established in about 1883 and was housed in one of Brunel's derelict pumping stations. This pottery also made *sgraffito* motto ware similar to that made at Aller Vale. Production ceased in 1957.

RYE POTTERY

There had been a pottery at Rye in Sussex since the fifteenth century. Sometime about the beginning of the nineteenth century a pottery was established at the Cadborough Brickworks. In 1830 the manager there was William Mitchell, who finally bought the pottery in 1840. Mitchell had two sons, Frederick and Henry. In 1869 Frederick started the Belle Vue Pottery at Rye. In addition to making Palissy-like ware decorated with lizards etc. the pottery made many other pieces decorated with three-dimensional botanical forms in a naturalistic colouring against the dark brown glazed background. The hop was a favourite motif. After Frederick's death in 1875 his wife carried on working the pottery until she was joined by her nephew Frederick Thomas (Henry's son) in 1882, who continued to run it until his death in 1920.

The hop ware made by F.T. Mitchell was perhaps modelled in greater detail, but lacks the softness of colouring of the older Frederick's pieces.

EDWARD BINGHAM'S POTTERY, CASTLE HEDINGHAM

Another of these country potteries existed in Essex, in a ramshackle collection of buildings at Castle Hedingham, the walls of which were covered with scriptural texts. There was a small showcase at the end

A brown earthenware jug with a tortoiseshell manganese glaze, and hops modelled and coloured naturalistically in green. Made at the Rye Pottery and incised on the base 'Sussex Ware 1901 F.E. Mitchell'. 299mm high.
Private Collection.

A group of Mitchell ware made at the Rye Pottery by Frederick Mitchell. The hops and leaves are naturalistically coloured and the body of the ware is glazed with a manganese brown tortoiseshell glaze. *c.* 1870. Jug is 229mm high.

A collection of Castle Hedingham ware, made between 1870-1900 by Edward Bingham at Castle Hedingham. Some of the relief designs are in white clay. The glazes are blue, grey-green, brown or yellow. The Essex jug at the back shows Boadicea in a chariot on the central medallion and all round are the arms of Essex families and the symbols of the produce of the county. 330mm high. *Private Collection.*

Teapot of red earthenware with applied decoration in brown and white clays. Some of the white clay motifs have been painted with a green glaze. Signed with the Castle Hedingham castle and the EB monogram of Edward Bingham. Late 19th century. 216mm high.
Crown copyright Victoria and Albert Museum.

of the garden which bore the inscription 'Original, Quaint and Classical'. This pottery was owned by a somewhat eccentric Plymouth Brother, whose father, also a potter, had settled in Castle Hedingham in the 1830s. Edward Bingham was working from about 1864 to 1905. He made from the local clay, which he and his family dug and refined, the most elaborate pieces with moulded applied decoration, sometimes in white clay with coloured glazes: blue, grey, green and brown. He was interested in history and loved to copy coats of arms and motifs from classical sources. Some of his pieces have an almost surrealist quality. There is an extraordinary teapot by him in the Victoria and Albert Museum that is nightmarish in its absurdity. Bingham was no business man and found it difficult to market his wares; by the beginning of the twentieth century the pottery was in difficulties and his children emigrated to America. In 1905 he joined them. His ware was marked with a small relief of Hedingham Castle, and usually his initials or signature.

For further reading
William Fishley Holland. *Fifty Years a Potter.* Pottery Quarterly 1958.
P.C.D. Brears. *The Collector's Book of English Country Pottery.* David and Charles, 1974.
J.M. Baines. *Sussex Pottery.* Fisher Publications, 1980.
Peter Brannam. *A Family Business: the story of a pottery.* Barnstaple 1982.
E. and D. Lloyd-Thomas. *The Old Torquay Potteries.* n.d.

25. The modern artist potter

Vase with a wax resist decoration and a red glaze. Incised mark W.S. Murray London 1923. 153mm high. *City Museum and Art Gallery, Stoke-on-Trent.*

In the years following the First World War, a number of artist-craftsmen turned their attention to the making of pottery. The inspiration for this came largely from Bernard Leach and William Staite Murray, whose ideas on the subject were utterly different.

Staite Murray began to make pottery in 1912; though he attended the Camberwell School of Art for a time, he can be said to have taught himself through his own persistent experiments. In the 1920s he was also influenced by the work of the Japanese potters, and much of his work has an art nouveau flavour but is quite unlike that of Leach. Staite Murray managed to persuade some London art dealers to show his work in company with that of the more promising young painters of the time. In this way he contributed much to the idea that studio potters should be considered as serious artists and not merely as practitioners of a quaint craft. Staite Murray had no interest in the making of useful wares.

In 1925, he became the head of the ceramic department at the Royal College of Art, where he had a marked influence on many students. In 1940, Staite Murray left England and went to live in Southern Rhodesia. The students who came in contact with Leach and Staite Murray, in addition to producing much interesting work themselves, have passed on their knowledge and interest to further generations of artist potters.

Bernard Leach had studied the making of stoneware in the Far East and when he returned to this country in 1920, he set up a pottery near St. Ives, with the assistance of a young Japanese potter called Shoji Hamada. For some time Leach made stoneware in the Japanese manner and then turned his attention to slip-decorated earthenware in the English tradition. Leach trained many pupils at his pottery where he ran a summer school for a small group of students and teachers. His wish was to make well-designed and reasonably priced pottery that would be in everybody's reach. In the early 1930s he started the Shinner's Bridge Pottery near Dartington, before revisiting the Far East. He later returned to St. Ives to the pottery which he ran with a team that included his sons David and Michael. The pottery is now run by his American widow, Janet Leach.

Henry Fauchon Hammond was a pupil of Staite Murray's at the Royal College of Art, and though Hammond stuck to the stoneware tradition, he mainly confined himself to the making of bowls and vases. The most notable thing about his work is the extreme dexterity of his brushwork decorations. As for many years he was the head of the Ceramics Department at the West Surrey College of Art and Design, he has not had time in recent years to devote himself solely to his craft, though many students have benefited from his teaching.

In 1956 David Leach started his own workshop in Bovey Tracey, where he continues to make well-designed stoneware and porcelain, both domestic ware and fine individual pieces. David's three sons have all become potters. In addition to the Leach family the tradition is still carried on by such potters as Michael Casson and Richard Batterham who both make useful stoneware pieces in their own individual manners. There are also many lesser talents working in the same field whose imitations have little appeal.

A whole generation of potters who took the vocational course at the Harrow School of Art originally set up by Michael Casson and Victor Margrie were inspired to return to the old technique of salt glazing. These include Walter Keeler, Jane Hamlyn and Sarah Walton who have all developed their own individual means of expression.

Strong influences tend to invoke strong reactions. In the late 1950s the students at the Royal College of Art (and many other art schools as well) began to reject the wheel in favour of less mechanical methods of handling clay and also to turn away from the heavy dark colours that had come to be associated with stoneware.

The inspiration for this new outlook must have come partly from the work of Lucie Rie, a potter from Vienna, whose delicate stoneware with its finely incised decoration has influenced the work of many followers. An even more powerful influence has been the work of Hans Coper who came to England in 1939 and was taught by Rie, with whom he worked. Coper's beautiful and sensitive coiled pots have proved a lasting inspiration for a great number of potters as well as the students who were lucky enough to come in contact with him when he was a tutor at the Royal College of Art in the 1960s. Elizabeth Fritsch, the most talented of all his students, acknowledges her debt to Coper.

'He was a kind of guru figure,' she said, 'he managed to drag talent out of us that we did not know we had,' surely the highest compliment that can be paid to any teacher.

Although this book is about pottery, so many potters are now making porcelain that it seemed a pity to exclude their work completely. The line between fine stoneware and porcelain is, after all, a very slender one.

Whether or not it is a reaction from the technological age in which we live, the desire to learn pottery making is very strong today. The craft is being taught well, in many schools as well as in art colleges and polytechnics, with the result that there are many more artist potters at work in Britain now than there ever have been.

During the last twenty years, ceramic sculpture has taken many forms. Though useful ware will always be needed and appreciated, more and more people are deriving pleasure from hand-made individual pieces.

Stoneware pot made by Hans Coper
c. 1972. 240mm high.
Reproduced by kind permission of the Museum für Kunst und Gewerbe, Hamburg.

I have tried to show as wide a range as possible of the work of recent years, not only from that of the well-known and established potters but also from the promising younger generation. The productions of small potteries where the work is designed by the principal and carried out by himself with his wife or an assistant has also been included, as well as the work of some of those who teach pottery. Inevitably the pictures shown here are but a cross section of the work of only relatively few of our artist potters, but I think there is enough evidence to show the vitality and ingenuity of the work of contemporary potters and to suggest that here are pots just as worthy of collection as anything that came from the hands of Toft, Whieldon or Wood.

Stoneware vase with sgraffito decoration and temmoku glaze. Made by Bernard Leach. *c.* 1957. 343mm high.
Crown copyright Victoria and Albert Museum.

Tall stoneware jar with sgraffito decoration combed into the surface and a poured temmoku glaze, made by Bernard Leach, with two impressed seal marks near the base. *c.* 1965. 483mm high. *Courtesy David Leach.*

Top left: Stoneware vase made by W. Staite Murray. *c.* 1938. 292mm high. *Crown copyright Victoria and Albert Museum.*

Brown stoneware jar with a black glaze and sgraffito decoration. Made by Bernard Leach in Japan in 1954. *Private Collection.*

Plate 48. Tall vase with temmoku glaze made by David Leach at the Lowerdown Pottery, Bovey Tracey. 1984. 465mm high. *Private Collection.*

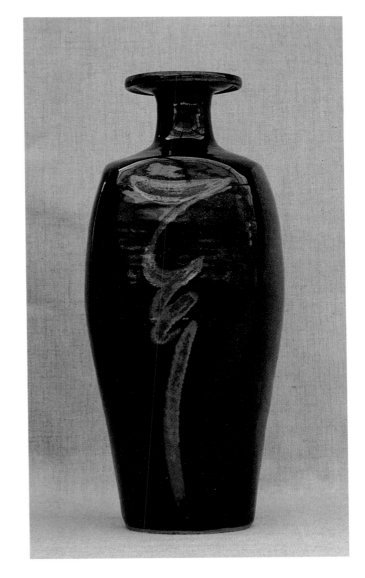

Plate 49. Wheel-thrown storage jar with a red stoneware body. The design has been incised into the damp clay. The dry glaze is composed of wood ash and clay. Fired in an oil burning kiln in a reducing atmosphere to 1260° to 1280°. Made by Michael Casson, whose impressed seal mark appears near the foot. 1980. 240mm high. *Private Collection.*

Red earthenware charger with slip decoration and a slightly mottled green glaze. The design has been incised through the layer of white slip covering the front of the dish. Made by Michael Cardew at the Winchcombe Pottery and impressed with his initial seal as well as the impressed initial stamp of the pottery. *c.* 1930. 420mm diameter. *Jasper Pearce Collection.*

Earthenware jar with slip decoration made by Michael Cardew. *c.* 1950. 365mm high.
Crown copyright Victoria and Albert Museum.

Michael Cardew learned to throw at the Braunton Pottery, not far from Fremington in Devon. He later joined the Leach Pottery, where he worked for three years before starting up on his own at Winchcombe in Gloucestershire. His pottery had a large kiln capable of holding up to three thousand pieces which Cardew's energy and drive enabled him to fill every two or three months. He made mainly slip decorated useful ware in the English tradition, some of his pieces were very large.

From 1942 to 1950 Cardew worked in Ghana and then in Nigeria. He returned to England and re-opened the Wenford Bridge Pottery where he worked with his son and one or two assistants until his death in 1983. His work is to be seen in many public collections.

Large stoneware bowl by Michael Cardew with yellow and brown finger decoration 'basket pattern'. 1970.
406mm diameter.

Three stemmed coffee bowls made by Michael Cardew. White glazed with oxide design, inspired by Minoan pottery. 1974. 140mm high.

Henry Fauchon Hammond studied at the Royal College of Art under Staite Murray. He was also helped and encouraged by Bernard Leach, who had a powerful influence on his work. For many years he was the head of the Ceramic Department at the West Surrey College of Art and Design at Farnham in Surrey. For some time he shared the Oast Pottery at Bentley with Paul Barron, where he produced mainly reduced stoneware with brush decoration very much in the Japanese manner. He has exhibited widely and his work is to be seen in many public as well as private collections.

Stoneware bowl with a matt glaze and brush stroke decoration in cobalt. Made by Henry Hammond. *c.* 1958. 102mm diameter. *Courtesy British Council.*

Stoneware bowl with an opaque cream glaze and iron oxide brush work decoration. Made by Henry Hammond. 1967. 305mm diameter.

Stoneware pot with iron underglaze decoration and a grey-green clay matt glaze, fired to 1280°. Made by Henry Hammond in 1976. 152mm diameter.

Stoneware bread crock with an unglazed exterior decorated with tooling and seals. The interior is glazed green. Made in 1951 by Paul Barron. 355mm high.

Paul Barron studied at the Brighton School of Art under Norah Braden (a pupil of Bernard Leach's) from 1937-39. For some years he worked with Henry Hammond at the Oast Pottery, Bentley in Surrey.

Slip decorated lidded stoneware jar made by David Leach. 1979. 305mm high.

Large plate with a wax resist pattern and temmoku and Dolomite glazes. Made by David Leach. 1984. 381mm diameter.

Vase with an oatmeal glaze over an iron-bearing body with four medallions in relief with emblems of the Cross. Made by Michael Leach at the Yelland Manor Pottery, Fremington, Barnstaple, Devon in 1975. 203mm high.

THE LEACH FAMILY

Bernard Leach had certainly started something with his Japanese inspired stoneware. With his drive and dominating personality he influenced generations of students. Any students that turned up to work at the pottery who had ideas of their own soon gave up and went to work elsewhere, though inspired, enlightened and encouraged, for Leach was a broad-minded man. Those whose ideas were less decided were very quickly indoctrinated by the master. Bernard Leach's own sons David and Michael worked with him for a number of years, in fact up until 1956 when they went their separate ways. David modestly said that to begin with he had never thought of doing anything else but working for his father. However this limited vision was short lived and he soon discovered he wanted to develop along his own lines. The alternatives seemed to him were either to branch out independently or to take over the Leach Pottery when his father had finished working. A family crisis precipitated the former decision and this was just as well for Bernard Leach lived to the tremendous age of ninety-two.

David moved to Bovey Tracey and started the Lowerdown Pottery there, gradually getting away from the Leach Pottery image and experimenting with a more personal vision, though his father's influence can still be detected.

Michael Leach worked rather quietly at his Yelland Manor Pottery at Fremington, not making a vast number of pots, but selling them steadily. His father's influence on his work is of course obvious. Sadly he died suddenly in 1985.

David Leach's sons John, Jeremy and Simon are all potters. John Leach was apprenticed to his grandfather and to his father.

Fluted stoneware biscuit barrel with a mottled oatmeal glaze. Derivative of Bernard Leach's fluted barrel jars. Made at the Muchelney Pottery by Jeremy Leach in 1976. 153mm high. *John Leach Collection.*

A facetted teacaddy made of stoneware with an ash glaze on a black slip ground. Fired to nearly 1280°C. Made at the Muchelney Pottery by Jeremy Leach in 1976. 127mm high. *Private Collection.*

Two stoneware pots, fired with sawdust enclosed in the saggar. Made by John Leach 1983/84. 114mm and 127mm high.

He also worked with Ray Finch and Colin Pearson. In 1964 he set up the Muchelney Pottery, near Langport in Somerset where he made oil-fired domestic stoneware of a very traditional English and practical kind, owing nothing to the Oriental influence that had so dominated his grandfather's work. What he has inherited is his grandfather's drive. As a result he has built up a most successful business. In 1976 he turned to the difficult but more exciting wood firing. Since 1972 he has worked with Nick Rees, whom he took as an apprentice. In addition to the domestic stoneware that he makes with such success John Leach has been making some individual pots, still traditional but with a character all his own. These he signs with an initial seal JHL as well as the Muchelney stamp of the pottery.

David's second son Jeremy has also been potting since he was eighteen. After a period of training at the Central School of Art in London, he started up various workshops of his own. He has flair and experimental imagination and his work has been exhibited both here and in Japan, sometimes in conjunction with his father's work. The pottery world will hear more of Jeremy Leach.

Simon Leach is David's youngest son. After doing an apprenticeship at Westlands Helicopters and becoming a skilled lathe operator, he travelled about Europe before starting to work for his father in 1979. In October 1984 he set up his own workshop with his wife Nichola in Alphington near Exeter. He specializes in raku, but makes a range of kitchen stoneware and individual pieces to order.

Two small raku bowls with wax resist pattern and a white crackle alkaline frit glaze on a plain black body. Made by Simon Leach. 1985. 70mm and 85mm high.

Coffee set made by Lucie Rie in brown stoneware with
sgraffito decoration. The interiors of the pieces are covered
with a white glaze. 1969. Coffee pot 178mm high.
Courtesy Council of Industrial Design.

Lucie Rie studied pottery in Vienna and came to settle in
England before the last war. She began by making domestic
ware of a very delicate and individual character with sgraffito
decoration. Latterly she has been making bottles, vases and
other decorative pieces in both porcelain and fine stoneware
bodies. Her work has had a considerable influence on the work
of many potters and is to be seen in galleries and private
collections throughout the world.

Bottle-shaped stoneware vase made by Hans Coper. *c.* 1954.
426mm high. *Crown copyright Victoria and Albert Museum.*

A collection of pots made of white fire clay with added foundry clay and covered in layers of a vitreous slip glaze. Made by Hans Coper in 1968. Height of central foreground pot 172mm.

Hans Coper came to England before the last war. He was trained both as a sculptor and as an engineer, which was perhaps reflected in his work which had a strong sculptural quality at the same time as being intensely precise. To begin with he worked with Lucie Rie, but in 1958 he set up his own workshop in London. In the '60s and early '70s he taught in the Ceramic Department at the Royal College of Art where the students found real inspiration in him and his work. For some time he worked at Digswell House in Welwyn Garden City and then moved to Somerset where he died in 1981. His work is now justly famous and his pots are to be found in galleries and private collections throughout the world. Hans Coper has had more influence on students of pottery than anyone else in the post-war period.

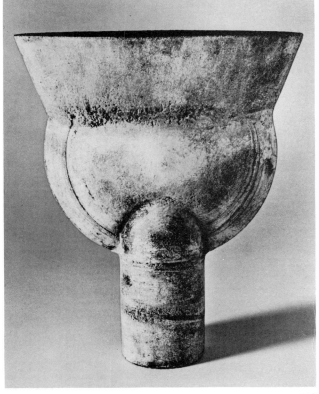

Thistle-shaped pot made by Hans Coper. Made in 1972. 248mm high. *Reproduced by kind permission of Museum für Kunst und Gewerbe, Hamburg.*

Large tin-glazed earthenware bowl with vivid blue colouring and lustre decoration made by Alan Caiger-Smith. 483mm wide. *c.* 1970. *Crown copyright Victoria and Albert Museum.*

Blue-green and grey-green tin-glazed bowl. 330mm diameter. Blue and grey tin-glazed storage jar. 203mm high. Both with brush stroke decoration. Made by Alan Caiger-Smith in 1961 at the Aldermaston Pottery. *Council of Industrial Design.*

Bowl painted in yellow-golden lustre. Smoked lustre
technique on tin-glaze earthenware made by Alan Caiger-
Smith. 1980. 254mm wide.

Alan Caiger-Smith studied painting at Camberwell and then
went to the Central School of Art and Design to study pottery.
He started the Aldermaston Pottery in 1955 and his work has
been shown at many exhibitions all over the world. The thriving
pottery now consists of about half a dozen people. The pots are
made of red Fremington clay and tin-glazed. Some are
electrically fired, but most of them are fired in a slightly
reducing atmosphere in a wood fired kiln, which deepens and
enriches the traditional range of tin-glaze oxide colours. He has
for some time been producing some very beautiful thrice-fired
reduced copper and silver lustre decorated pieces.

Ann Winterson began to learn to make pottery while still at
Cranborne Chase where she was taught by Don Potter. She
went on to Cambridge Art School and then to the Central
School of Art in London. She now works in Barton near
Cambridge. Her pottery is all hand-thrown, using a red
earthenware body with which she achieves surprisingly fine and
delicate results. Much of her work is decorated with copper
cobalt brush work designs and is tin glazed.

Large bowl and two small bowls made by Ann Winterson of
red earthenware, tin glazed and decorated with copper
cobalt. 1979. 241mm and 76mm diameter.

Three stoneware storage jars, the right hand one is greyish in colour, the other two are greenish yellow, with cut decoration. Made by Richard Batterham in 1968. 178mm and 127mm high.

Richard Batterham studied pottery under Donald Potter at Bryanston and then went and worked for two years at the Leach Pottery, before setting up his own workshop at Durweston near Blandford Forum in Dorset. He is one of the few craftsmen potters working on his own, who manages to earn a living entirely by the pots he makes, without spending any time teaching. He produces about 5000 pots a year, each one of which he considers as an individual piece, for he is a perfectionist. His pots are all for domestic use. He uses a number of different clays and different glazes and uses simple incised decoration, resulting in the most satisfying and beautiful pots.

Andrew and Joanna Young met at the West Surrey College of Art and Design. After taking their Art Teachers Certificate Course at Goldsmiths College in London and then working in France and various parts of this country, they set up their workshop near Holt in Norfolk, where they built an 80 cu. ft. oil/wood fired kiln in 1975. They make thrown stoneware which is all raw glazed. Their functional domestic ware has small added touches like sprigged on decorations, nicely turned knobs and scored handles that make it quite out of the ordinary.

A group of raw glazed stoneware made by the Youngs. 1985.
Photograph by David Cripps.

Hand-thrown reduced stoneware jar by David Frith, decorated with a thin temmoku glaze, wax decoration and an ash over-glaze. 1979. 448mm high.

David Frith was trained at the Flintshire College of Technology, Wimbledon School of Art and Stoke-on-Trent College of Art. He started his first workshop in 1963 and began making pressed dishes, trailed and feathercombed on the flat clay, and using an electric kiln. Later he built a wood fired kiln to make reduced stoneware. Since 1975 he and his wife and one assistant have been making their own stoneware bodies by the slip method and turning out a comprehensive range of domestic ware.

Stoneware bottle by Derek Clarkson, fired at 1300° in a reducing atmosphere, using wood ash and kaki glazes with wax brush decoration. 1979. 279mm high.

Derek Clarkson studied at Manchester College and then at Burnley. His major early influence was Harold Thornton (a colleague of Heber Mathews) and then Bernard Leach. After being the head of the ceramic department at Stafford School of Art be became Senior Lecturer at Manchester College of Higher Education. He is now a full time potter. He works mainly in stoneware and is particularly interested in the bottle form. He uses traditional felspathic glazes, temmoku, kaki and celadon.

Raw glazed stoneware teapot and sugar box made by Andrew and Joanna Young in 1980. 149mm and 100mm high.

Michael Casson was trained at Hornsey School of Art. After working for some time in London, he and his wife (also a potter) moved to Herefordshire. He is one of the best known potters in Britain today due no doubt in part to his books and TV appearances. He makes thrown domestic stoneware and porcelain in small runs as well as individual pieces, some of a very impressive size. He is one of the few potters today to use salt glazing. Michael Casson's work can be seen in many public and private collections; he has exhibited widely.

Wood-fired salt glazed jug made by Michael Casson. After throwing, the jug has been dipped in a china and ball-clay slip, the pattern being wiped boldly away. The inside only is ash-glazed. 1980. 610mm high.
See page 287 for a coloured illustration of one of Michael Casson's storage jars.

Walter Keeler was trained at Harrow School of Art and by Victor Margrie and Michael Casson. He established his own studio in 1965 and has since exhibited all over the world. He specialises in salt glazed stoneware, often stained with cobalt. Many of his unusual and very personal shapes derive from metal ware. He still teaches two days a week at the Bristol Polytechnic, but finds the pressure of his own work increasingly demanding.

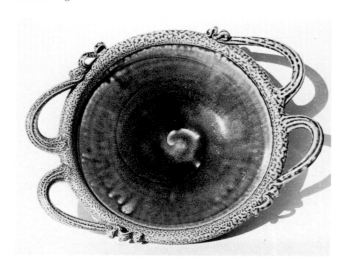

Salt glazed stoneware teapot coloured with cobalt made by Walter Keeler. 1984. 200mm high.

Salt glazed stoneware dish stained with cobalt. Made by Walter Keeler. 1984. 230mm diameter. *Private Collection.*

Planter pot by Peter Stoodley. It has been coiled and then dry-thrown. The inlaid decoration is of black and white vitreous slips. The whole pot has been rubbed with haematite and once-fired to 1250° over a period of three days to avoid bloating. The arrowhead motif arrived by chance from the complicated geometry of converging and diverging meridian lines. 1979. 381mm high.

Peter Stoodley was originally trained as a painter at Bournemouth, then at Goldsmiths College School of Art. He started to make pottery at Camberwell School of Art while taking an ATD course at London University. He began by making planters in response to commissions from architects. His pots are coiled and dry-thrown or else slab-built. He uses a body he makes up himself from equal parts of red terracotta with a mixture of fireclay, felspar, coarse grog and haematite. This is in order to improve the qualities of colour and texture in rather unsympathetic electric firings. He was one of the first members of the Craftsmen Potters Association.

Slab-built pot by Peter Stoodley. The body is a mixture of buff stoneware and red clay fired to 1250° and oxidised. 1979. 216mm high.

The Egg Press was assembled from slabbed and thrown sections, even the screw was turned. A dry wood ash glaze produced a rust-ochre colour. The molten glass was run over a metal former as the potter found the heat shattered the ceramic surface. Made by Delan Cookson in 1977. 432mm high.

Delan Cookson was trained at the Bournmouth College of Art and the Central School of Art and Design in London. He teaches full time at the Buckinghamshire College of Higher Education in High Wycombe and also makes ceramic sculpture, often influenced by mechanical artifacts. He uses all the techniques of throwing, turning, slab-building and press-moulding. His work is highly individual and precisely finished. He has exhibited widely both here and on the Continent and his work is in many collections. He was awarded a Gold Medal at Vallauris in 1974.

In addition to his ceramic sculpture, he also makes short runs of small thrown pots in either porcelain or fine stoneware bodies.

This piece by Delan Cookson evolved from the honeycomb section of a radiator cooling system. The vertical units were individually press-moulded and then luted together in threes. The horizontal linking tubes were extruded. It was made from an iron-stained crank mixture clay and fired in a reducing atmosphere. The surface is granular and of a warm toasted brown. 1980. 130mm high.

Stoneware rimmed dish made by John Smith. One of a series inspired by the classical glazes of China and Japan. He used a combination of three Oriental glazes and a long high temperature reduction firing (1300°). 1980. 305mm diameter.

Patio pots made by John Smith from raw and heavily grogged fireclay with a small percentage of stoneware turnings for extra plasticity. They were thrown in two sections. 1980. Average height 610mm.

John Smith was trained at the Hull School of Art, at Stoke-on-Trent, the University of Bristol and Birmingham Polytechnic. He describes himself as a 'clay worker'. The potter, he says 'condenses natural geophysical time, achieving in a matter of hours what takes milleniums to occur naturally.'

As well as being a designer for the ceramic industry he teaches in the Department of Glass at the Stourbridge College of Technology and Art, thereby adding another dimension to his skill and knowledge. His original approach to design and making things stem from his natural curiosity, vivacity and humour. His experimental studio/workshop is now part of his home in Stourbridge in the West Midlands.

Slip decorated charger made by John Smith of Stourbridge. 1980. 387mm diameter. *Private Collection.*

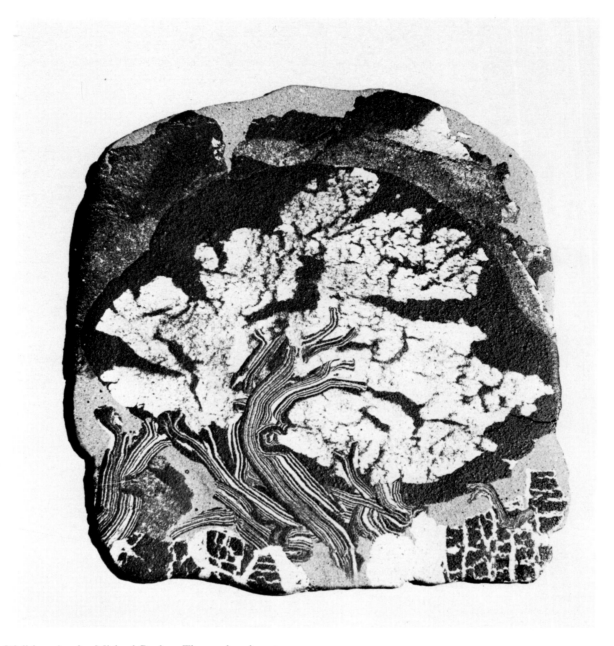

Wall-hanging by Michael Bayley. The unglazed agate
structure expresses perfectly his feeling for fossilised
landscape and natural tree forms. 1979. 863mm high.

Michael Bayley was trained at Hornsey College of Art. He
started his own workshop in 1973 and by 1977 was able to give
up teaching to pot full time.

The natural beauty of remote parts of the countryside have
always had a powerful influence on him and this shows very
clearly in his work. He makes stoneware and semi-porcelain
inlaid and agate ware. His press-moulded or hand-built shapes,
bowls etc., are unglazed and have a wonderfully fossilised
landscape/seascape quality about them. He has exhibited both
in this country and in Germany and his work can be seen in
many public and private collections.

Opposite. Two of Michael Bayley's press-moulded agate ware
bowls. The striking effects of the blending of several tones of
clay mirror his absorbing interest in natural landscape. 1979.
219mm wide.

Standing form by Michael Bayley showing again his use of blended clays to express basic natural form. 1979. 279mm high.

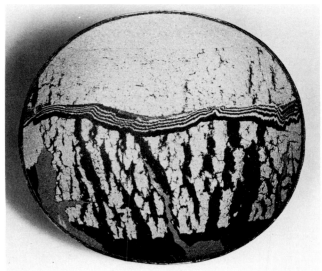

Big Green Jug by Alison Britton. Hand-built of high-fired buff earthenware with a lead sesquisilicate matt glaze. 1979. 350mm high.

Alison Britton studied ceramics at the Central School of Art and Design and at the Royal College of Art, where she was one of a vintage group of students which included Elizabeth Fritsch, Jacqueline Poncelet and Jill Crowley. Alison Britton began by making more tiles than anything else, but has come to prefer making hand-built pots, either slabbed or coiled. The form her pots take inspires the linear decorations with which she embellishes them. Her work shows great solidity and strength. She generally uses a high fired buff earthenware with a lead sesquisilicate matt glaze. She has exhibited widely and her work is in many public and private collections.

Elizabeth Fritsch, after studying the harp and piano at the Royal Academy of Music, went on to the Royal College of Art in 1968 to study ceramics. While there, she came under the influence of Hans Coper. She, like Coper is an intensely sensitive artist and a real perfectionist. Her stoneware pots are coiled and pinched to the limit of thinness and are perfectly balanced in their symmetry or asymmetry. The word classical keeps coming to mind. Her pots, so often inspired by music have an insubstantial and timeless quality. The colours, painted meticulously in slip with a mixture of underglaze industrial colours and oxides are arranged in geometric repeating patterns that are subtle, sometimes surprising and always beautiful. Elizabeth Fritsch feels that to be appreciated to the full her pots should be seen grouped together, for the juxtaposition of the pieces is as important as the shapes and the designs on the pots themselves.

In 1978 there was a travelling retrospective show of her work, entitled *Pots about Music*. She stopped potting to have her second child in 1980 and it was not until 1984 that she returned to the craft with a triumphant show *Pots from Nowhere* at the Royal College of Art. Her range of both colours and shapes have increased as has the atmospheric intensity of her work.

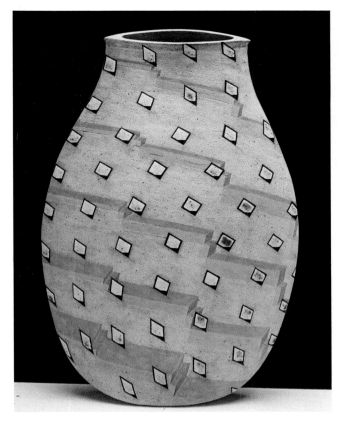

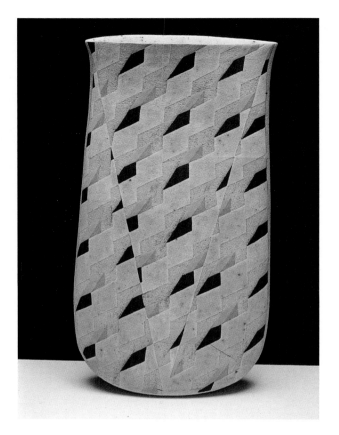

Plate 50. Four of Elizabeth Fritsch's 'Improvised Piano Pots',
1980. The heights range from 203mm to 330mm.
Photograph by David Cripps.

Hand coiled pot of agate clay in salmon, coral and brown colouring with white inlaid design. Made by Felicity Aylieff in 1984. 282mm high.

Hand coiled pot of agate clay in tones of brown and coral, inlaid with bright blue and black. Made by Felicity Aylieff in 1984. 454mm high.

Felicity Aylieff was trained at the Bath Academy and Goldsmiths College. She specialises in hand-built slabbed or coiled pieces in what she says can loosely be described as agate ware, blended clays of different colours, often inlaid with shapes of contrasting clay. She polishes the surface to make a very smooth stone-like finish and rarely uses glazes.

After a career in education, running the Whitechapel Art Gallery and acting as Art Adviser to the East Sussex Education Committee, Betty Blandino started to work full time at Ceramics at St. Hilary, Cowbridge, Wales in 1973. Since then she has had one man shows and taken part in many exhibitions.

Her work is to be seen in many public collections. All her pots are made in stoneware, thin-walled and hand-built using a coiling/pinching technique. They are fired to 1280° in an electric kiln.

Hand-built stoneware pot by Betty Blandino. 1979. 508mm high.

Glynn Hugo was trained at Burton-on-Trent School of Art. After finishing his course he stayed on as a teacher for six years before setting up on his own as a freelance potter. He has been potting successfully ever since. In 1972 he moved to Suffolk. Apart from well designed and finished domestic stoneware he makes interesting individual pieces. He has lately been experimenting with basalt ware and lustre decoration. He has had various successful exhibitions.

306

Sun City. A wall-hanging made by Glynn Hugo.
It is a slab construction in an unglazed stoneware
with a basalt body. Reduction fired to 1300°.
1979. 610mm high.

Circular box and cover made in black basalt with
a golden bird's head on the lid. The interior of
the lower half of the box is glazed with a
transparent glaze. Made by Glynn Hugo. 1980.
90mm high. *Private Collection.*

Shallow bowl on a pedestal made of rather rough black
basalt decorated with incised concentric rings enhanced with
gold lustre. Glazed with a magnesia matt glaze and fired in a
reducing atmosphere to 1300°. Made by Glynn Hugo. 1980.
90mm high. *Private Collection.*

307

Large hand-built raku fired bottle. Made by David Roberts. 1985. 457mm high.

David Roberts was trained at Bretton Hall in Yorkshire. He specialises in hand-built raku fired pieces often of a very large size and of a surprising delicacy. He fires his work to biscuit at about 950°-1000° in electric or gas fired kilns and any decoration is then applied before glazing. His simple geometric designs are created by using masking tape and a latex resist. His glazes are sprayed or poured on and the final raku firing then takes place.

Opposite. Large hand-built raku fired bowl. Made by David Roberts. 1984. 584mm diameter.

Large hand-built raku fired bowl with a latex resist geometric pattern. Made by David Roberts. 1984. 584mm diameter.

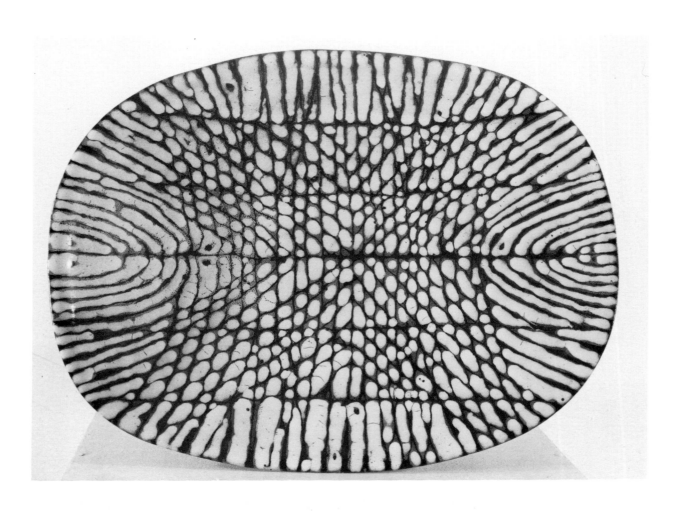

Purple black dish with white tin glaze made by
James Tower in 1980. 508mm diameter.

James Tower studied at the Royal Academy Schools and at the
Slade School of Art. Later he taught at the Bath Academy of
Arts at Corsham. He is now the head of Sculpture at Brighton
Polytechnic. He produces interesting and beautiful hand-built
tin-glazed subjects, many of which are in galleries and
museums. He has regular exhibitions at Gimpel Fils Gallery in
London and also in New York.

Opposite: Dish decorated with white tin glaze on a
purple black background. Made by James Tower in
1979. 508mm wide.

Form, made by James Tower decorated with white
tin glaze on purple black. 1979. 368mm high.

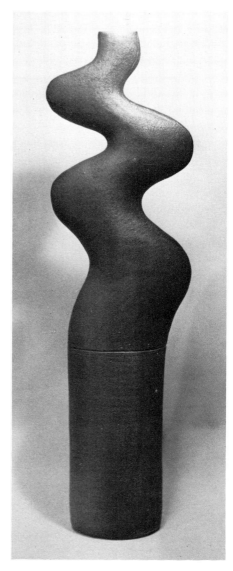

Porcelain bowl by Joanna Constantinidis, pink-orange in colour with black markings. 1978. 140mm high.

Joanna Constantinidis was trained at Sheffield College of Art and now teaches at the Chelmer Institute. She makes thrown porcelain and stoneware, reduction fired. Her work is in many public and private collections. She has had exhibitions both here and in Germany.

Bronze coloured porcelain form, by Joanna Constantinidis. 1978. 397mm high.

Nicholas Homoky was trained at Bristol Polytechnic and the Royal College of Art, where he graduated in 1976. He now teaches at Bristol Polytechnic and has his own studio where he makes individual ceramics, working more as a draughtsman than as a potter. He has evolved a process of making polished inlaid porcelain. He likes to start with basic functional forms, developing them into abstract relationships, but hopefully retaining references to their origins.

A collection of Geoffrey Swindell's porcelain wheel-thrown pots. Those on the top row were all made in 1978 and are 102mm high. Those on the bottom row were made in 1979 and 1980 and vary in height from 102mm to 127mm.

Opposite: Tea and coffee pots made by Nicholas Homoky in porcelain, using a mixture of techniques. The teapot and handle are wheel thrown with slab built lid, base and spout. The coffee pot is completely slabbed with a wheel thrown handle. Both are hand carved and inlaid with black porcelain slip and hand polished after gloss firing to 1260°C. 1980. Height of coffee pot 172mm.

Geoffrey Swindell was a student at Stoke-on-Trent College of Art and then went on to the Royal College of Art. After that he taught at the York School of Art and then at Cardiff College of Art. He has taken part in something like 40 exhibitions and has had some half a dozen one-man shows. His work is in museums and galleries all over the world.

He is at the present time specialising in small delicately thrown porcelain pots. He uses a Dolomite type cream glaze that has a satin-matt texture, the colour is provided by copper carbonate aerographed on under the aerographed glaze. He sometimes adds further colours at enamel temperature firings (730°), for instance, colour in crazing in thin gold and streaky yellow-green, in ready prepared lustre, with a variety of surface tension-breaking solvents. Sometimes he uses a sand-blaster to produce a dry pitted surface texture.

A collection of stoneware cylinders, the centre
section cast aluminium. The sections are treated
in various ways with either metallic black glazes
and copper textured clay or matt white ash glazes
rubbed with copper oxide and fired in a reducing
atmosphere to 1300°. Made by Robin Welch in
1969. Height of largest cylinder is 1,220mm.

A delicate white porcelain bowl made by Jenny Welch in
1980. 220mm diameter. *Private Collection.*

Robin Welch started at the Nuneaton School of Art and went
on to study sculpture at the Penzance School of Art, and pottery
under Michael Leach. After working at the Central School of
Art in London he started his own pottery workshop. In 1963,
with the help of his wife Jenny who had also been at the Central,
he spent three years in Australia establishing a large country
workshop near Melbourne. They returned to England in 1965
and set up their own pottery near Stradbroke in Suffolk.
Robin's work has a strong and essentially sculptural quality and
Jenny, who now works mainly with porcelain, produces
beautifully finished pots of a delicacy and precision rarely seen
today. They are both perfectionists. Their work has been widely
exhibited both here and in Japan and Australia and is much
sought after by collectors. In addition to their special individual
pieces, the pottery turns out useful ware of high quality.

A stoneware bowl, Raku fired, made by Jenny Welch in
1980. 90mm high. *Private Collection.*

Plate 51. Large raku fired stoneware charger with sprayed on cobalt colouring. Made by Robin Welch at his pottery at Stradbroke. 1980. 435mm wide.
Private Collection.
The calm and delicate beauty of this dish is astonishing when the primitive brutality of the raku process is considered. After being thrown, dried, glaze-dipped and sprayed with cobalt, the dish was pre-heated to about 200°C and then transferred to the heart of the kiln with the temperature standing at 800°C. The kiln's temperature was increased to about 1020°C, when it was opened and the dish, now glowing red hot, was taken from it with an immensely long pair of tongs and dropped immediately into a large metal vat full of sawdust. More sawdust was thrown over it. The violent display of flames, sparks and smoke was immediately smothered and a metal lid was put on the container, then a heavy dampened cloth. A reduced temperature atmosphere in the vat was thus achieved. After a few minutes, the dish was taken from the container, hideous, black and still smoking. It was plunged at once into a bath of cold water. When the sizzling had subsided and the dish was cool enough to handle, it was put into another bath of water and scrubbed with a scouring powder and steel wool to remove the ashes of the sawdust still clinging to it. It emerged miraculously clean as it appears in the photograph.

Plate 52. Lustred earthenware bowl made by Sutton Taylor. 380mm diameter. 1985.

Lustred earthenware bowl made by Sutton Taylor. 400mm diameter. 1984.

Sutton Taylor is a self taught potter. He prepares his own clay body and throws his large bowls with the utmost skill. They are then fired three times in a wood fired kiln. The lustred surface is achieved in the third firing. The whole process is laborious and somewhat dangerous, but the results he achieves are most beautiful, inspired as they are by the Hispano-Moresque pottery of the thirteenth century, but used in a way unique and personal to himself.

Lustred earthenware bowl made by Sutton Taylor. 380mm diameter. 1984.

James Campbell studied at Eton with Gordon Baldwin and then at the Royal College of Art from 1960-64. In 1968 he set up a workshop in Herefordshire, where he built a propane fired kiln. Most of his work consists of hand built (coiled, slabbed or thumbed) non-functional pieces fired to stoneware temperature under reduction. His work has been exhibited in London, Glasgow, Denmark, Germany, Italy and Australia.

Slabbed and coiled form by James Campbell, who used a white felspathic glaze containing ball clay and stealite on the body made of potclays and crank mixture. The glaze is creamy in texture and produces iron specks from the clay underneath. The lighter coloured band across the centre of the piece is produced by glaze overlap. Made in 1968. 546mm high.

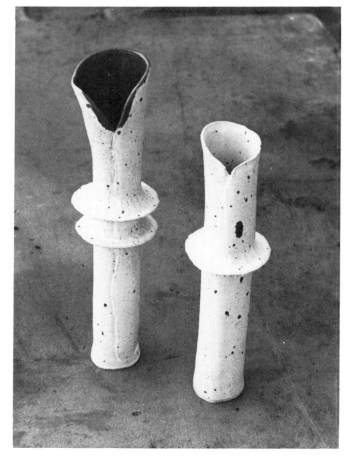

Two slab built tubes with the addition of coiled and pinched flanges. Made of the same clay as the slabbed and coiled form illustrated on the left, with a similar white glaze. The tube on the left has a semi-matt brown/black glaze inside. Made in 1969 by James Campbell. 381mm and 305mm high.

'Formation' shows an amalgam of interests. The airfield line-up imagery shows his obsession with aircraft plus his attraction to repeat pattern quality, stencils and relief surfaces. It was not until some time after this piece was made that David Robinson saw a heat-seeking photograph of aircraft on the ground that was uncannily similar. *c.* 1980. 356mm high.

Ceramic sculpture by David Robinson. 1980. 356mm high.

David Robinson first studied at Sunderland College of Art and then went on to the Royal College of Art. At the present time, in addition to potting and painting, he teaches in the ceramics department at the Bristol Polytechnic.

He has taken part in many exhibitions. He has had a lifelong interest in aircraft and this has inspired some of his more recent work.

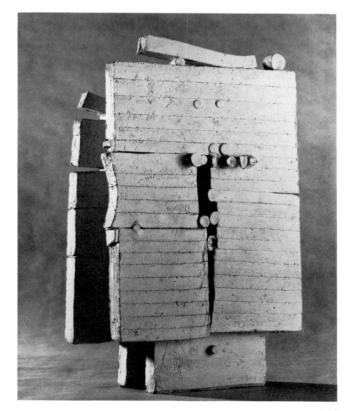

Unglazed stoneware structure by David Robinson. 1969. 356mm high.

Covered bowl with bird on lid, made by Geoffrey Fuller. 1984. 368mm high.
Geoffrey Fuller described his method of working. He first makes his own sprig
moulds with impressed designs, fires them to biscuit and then presses thin slabs of
clay into them which he then applies to the pot. The whole pot is then covered
with a thin white slip and other slips coloured with oxides. The ware is then
brushed with a bi-silicate lead glaze and once fired.

Geoffrey Fuller was born in North Derbyshire in 1936 and educated locally. He
worked in Sheffield as a librarian for twelve years, resigning in 1965 to enter the Art
College on a foundation course. From 1966 to 1969 he was a student at Farnham
School of Art on the Dip. A.D. Studio Ceramics course. He returned to Derbyshire
in 1972 and bought a house and a workshop near Chesterfield. To help finance the
repairs and setting up of the workshop he took on work in part-time teaching, finally
becoming a lecturer on the Vocational Ceramics Course at Chesterfield College of Art.

Opposite: Bower group made in earthenware clay, hand-built form slabs. The
colour comes from the use of metal oxides to produce the greens, browns and
oranges. It is raw-glazed with a clear glaze and once fired. Made by Geoffrey
Fuller. 1985. 460mm high. *Courtesy Miss G. Pertt.*

Two vases of oxidised stoneware, with pressed additions and a grey-green glaze. 1979. 143mm high.

George Rainer was born in China and lived there until he was sixteen. He was trained at Camberwell School of Art and for some years was the head of the Ceramic Department at Bristol Polytechnic. Under his influence this lively and inspiring department was a breeding ground for many of the most talented potters of today. George Rainer makes beautifully finished objects of intriguing form, mainly in stoneware. He has taken part in many exhibitions and his work is to be seen in public galleries and private collections.

Flat vase of oxidised grey stoneware with press-moulded additions. 1979. 146mm high.

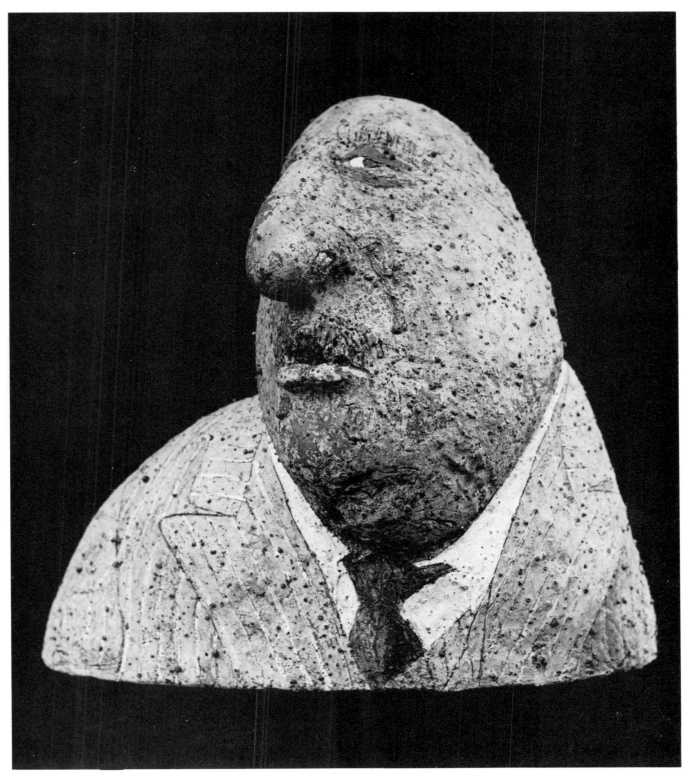

Oxidised stoneware portrait, 'Man in a Pin-stripe Suit'. 1976. 340mm high.

Jill Crowley studied at Bristol Polytechnic and at the Royal College of Art. She is teaching at Morley College and is a Visiting Lecturer at Bristol and Portsmouth Polytechnics. She has had numerous exhibitions in England, on the Continent and in Japan. She works mainly in oxidised stoneware and specialises in ceramic portraits.

The Terrace, slab-built and salt-glazed.
1979. 457mm x 1,220mm.

Ian Gregory was self-taught. He opened
his workshop in 1973. Since then he has
had exhibitions in England, Holland,
Germany and New York. He has lectured
at the Bath Academy at Corsham and the
Medway School of Ceramics. He produces
salt-glazed and slab-built pieces as well as
domestic stoneware and tiles.

Group of buildings slab-built from
Dorset clay, with some of the details
modelled from thrown sections. Wood
fired to 1300° and salt-glazed. 1976.
Maximum height 915mm, each building
approximately 127mm wide.

For further reading

Muriel Rose. *Artist Potters in England*. Faber 1955. Revised edition 1970.
Michael Casson. *Pottery in Britain Today*. Tiranti 1967.
Tony Birks. *The Art of the Modern Potter*. Country Life 1967.
Bernard Leach. *A Potter's Book*. Faber 1969.
Carol Hogben. *The Art of Bernard Leach*. Faber 1978.
Garth Clark. *Michael Cardew*. Faber 1978.
Tony Birks. *Hans Coper*. Collins 1983.
E. Cooper and E. Lewenstein (Ed.). *Studio Ceramics Today*. Craftsmen Potters
    Association of Great Britain 1983.
Peter Lane. *Studio Ceramics*. Collins 1983.
Susan O'Reilly, Jane Taylor and Paul Atterbury. *Artist Potters Now*. Oxford
    County Museum Services 1984.
Betty Blandino. *Coiled Pottery*. A. and C. Black 1984.

26. Factory made pottery 1920-85

'The old bottle kiln is a thing of the past', but they can still be seen at the Gladstone Pottery Museum, Longton, Stoke-on-Trent. *This photograph of their old kilns is reproduced by courtesy of the Gladstone Pottery Museum.*

Cream jug first designed in the 1930s with an Alpine matt glaze and traditional brush-stroke decoration in blue, green, pink and mauve. Made at the Poole Potteries and marked with the backstamp used 1959-66. 70mm high.

The structure and technology of the English pottery industry is changing rapidly. Until the war, there were literally hundreds of potteries – some small and still relatively primitive – some large and forward thinking. During the last quarter of a century, the tendency has been for firms to amalgamate, less to put rivals out of business than to complement each other's activities and to share the ever-growing research and sales organisations. English pottery plays an important part in our economy; the need for export today is as great as it has ever been. Now the industry is in the hands of relatively few groups, though there are some small firms carrying on in the old independent and traditional way. The old bottle kiln is a thing of the past; the Clean Air Act and the use of gas, electricity and oil have made the use of coal obsolete, and the tunnel kiln has taken over. Old, high, congested buildings with dangerously inadequate stairways and fire escapes have been razed to the ground to make room for the long, low buildings that today's production line output needs.

But the complex modern pottery industry is still essentially a craft industry, dependent on the skill of the hand of the worker at each stage of production. In spite of the tremendous advance in mechanization this skill is still very much in evidence, and though each new technical and mechanical advance means the loss of some skilled hand work, and therefore a slight reduction in quality, this is justified by the manufacturers by the fact that they have to increase productivity or go out of business.

Although traditional methods of production are still being revolutionised, as far as design goes, tradition dies very hard indeed. In this century, the designs of the bulk of the pottery that has been made, do not really reflect our way of life and changing tastes; when it comes to our breakfast, dinner and tea services, most of us are escapist. We like to look back at the past, we like what we are used to. Moreover we cannot all afford to scrap our table services every few years; when we do decide to have a change, we want to be assured that we will be able to buy replacements for many years to come. However, there are always some people who want something new, and to whom the latest thing is the best (Josiah Wedwood remarked about this to Thomas Bentley in 1779 – see page 105).

Looking back, the names of three women designers of the 1920s and '30s seem to stand out. These were Truda Adams (later Carter) at the Poole Pottery in Dorset, Clarice Cliff and Susie Cooper working in Staffordshire. All these trend setters had their imitators. Another designer whose work has stood the test of time is Eric Ravilious, a painter and illustrator who worked for Wedgwoods.

Truda Adams was responsible for the first range of brush-stroke

A group of traditional Poole Pottery hand painted pieces. The oxide colours are applied with deft brush strokes to the biscuit ware, already dipped in a special lime aluminium matt glaze, which Poole call 'Alpine'. In the final firing the colours fuse with the glaze giving complete permanence. The patterns are all based on Truda Carter's brush stroke designs which she did in the 1920s and '30s. Blues, mauves, greens, yellow and red are the predominating colours. Largest vase 254mm high. *c.* 1951.

floral patterns that became known far and wide as 'Poole Pottery'. The combination of her choice of pastel colours and the soft tin glaze fitted in with the gentler side of the taste of the 1920s and '30s. Poole pottery was much in demand and shops like Heals in Tottenham Court Road, London stocked many of their designs. In 1931 Truda married Cyril Carter and continued to design for the firm.

Susie Cooper was first employed as a decorator in 1922 by the firm of A.E. Gray and Co., where she stayed until 1929. Grays were solely decorators, they did not make their own pottery but bought it in a biscuit form from other factories, decorated it and often obliterated the impressed factory mark on the bottom of the wares with a transfer printed mark of their own (they used various stylised ships as trade marks). While at Grays Susie Cooper's designs were influenced by Clarice Cliff, she used a great deal of black and orange in banding and in floral designs which, however, were more geometric and less bizarre than Miss Cliff's.

In 1931 Susie Cooper joined Harry Wood and Sons at the new Crown Works, Burslem. Here she was able to design new shapes as well as decorating the ware. Shapes such as her 'Kestrel' range which were decorated with both hand painted and lithographed designs.

She soon sensed a swing in public taste away from the brilliant colours of the previous decade to a much quieter palette and this she

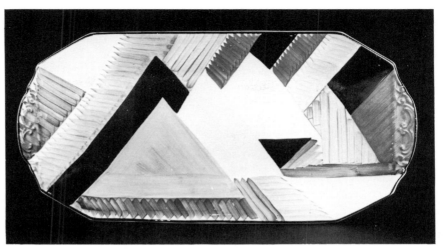

Oblong dish in Art Deco style decorated in orange, brown, green and black by Susie Cooper, and bearing the backstamp incorporating a formalised liner used by Gray's Pottery 1923-31, and the pencilled number 8129. *c.* 1929. 229mm long. *Jasper Pearce Collection.*

exploited to the full. The decorations on these new shapes were of refined gentility, mainly in pastel colours and aimed at the middle class, middle aged market with whom she was immensely popular.

Susie Cooper remained at the Crown works until 1961, producing a vast number of designs. She is still working in a studio at William Adams in Tunstall.

In 1958 the Susie Cooper Pottery joined R.H. and S.C. Plant and in 1966 the group became part of the Wedgwood empire. William Adams of Tunstall was also taken over by Wedgwoods in the same year. Susie Cooper Pottery remained an autonomous unit until the end of 1980.

Though this design was not by Susie Cooper, the leaping deer was a motif much used by her as well as her many emulators in the 1930s. This rather feeble design on a coupe shaped plate is coloured in red, grey and black. Printed backstamp 'Royal Tudor Ware' with a crown and BARKER BROS ENGLAND. A mark used from 1937. 222mm diameter. *Private Collection.*

Coffee pot decorated with the 'Tyrol' design. The lid, spout and handle are yellow and the banding and crosses are blue. Designed by Susie Cooper and marked 'A Susie Cooper Production 1823 and 12' with a raised 30 in a hexagon shape. Early 1930s. 198mm high.
Coffee can and saucer with a graduated green edge and a lithographic design of flowers in pink, mauve and a greeny blue. Marked 'A Susie Cooper Production Crown Works Burslem England', in brown transfer printed capital lettering on the back of the saucer. Saucer 113mm wide. *c.* 1935-9. *Private Collection.*

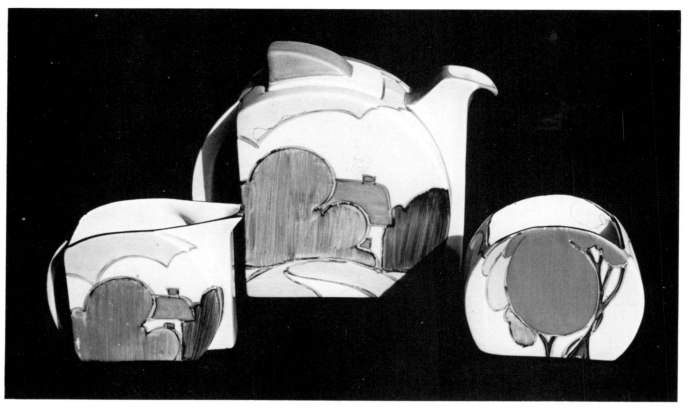

Teapot, sugar bowl and cream jug from an early morning teaset, painted with stylised trees and a cottage in orange, yellow, blue and brown. Designed by Clarice Cliff in her Fantasque range of Bizarre pottery for the Newport Pottery. Teapot 110mm high. *c.* 1930. *Jasper Pearce Collection.*

'Fantasque' design cup and saucer by Clarice Cliff for the Newport Pottery brilliantly coloured in orange, yellow, green and black. *c.* 1931. Cup 65mm high. *Courtesy Castle Antiques (Warwick's Art Deco Shop) Warwick.*

Vase designed by Clarice Cliff and painted in blue, orange and yellow in her Bizarre range for the Newport Pottery. In addition to the usual backstamp is the impressed No 1/188. *c.* 1929. 230mm high. *Jasper Pearce Collection.*

Vegetable dish from a Biarritz 'Modern' design dinner service by Clarice Cliff for the Newport Pottery. Black line decoration on a cream coloured ground. The plates and dishes in this set were all rectangular with a circular or oval depression in the centre. *c.* 1932. 200mm wide. *Courtesy Castle Antiques (Warwick's Art Deco Shop) Warwick.*

Bizarre 'Conical' jug and two coffee cans of the 'Ravel' design in orange, green, yellow and black with a honey glaze designed by Clarice Cliff for the Newport Pottery. *c.* 1933. Jug 100mm high. *Courtesy Castle Antiques (Warwick's Art Deco Shop) Warwick.*

Small deep plate lettered to advertise Clarice Cliff's Bizarre range of pottery and to be used for display purposes. Painted in green, brown and red. Made at the Newport Pottery. *c.* 1930. 162mm diameter. *Jasper Pearce Collection.*

Clarice Cliff started as an apprentice enameller at the age of thirteen. She was obviously a girl of some character with unlimited and uninhibited enthusiasm. At the age of seventeen she moved to A.J. Wilkinson, where she was engaged as a lithographer. She worked very hard, studying in the evenings at various art schools, winning a scholarship to the Royal College of Art where she remained only a short time. By 1928 she had set up a studio in Wilkinson's Newport factory. Brilliantly coloured bizarre designs poured from her, inspired by the work of Frank Brangwyn, Lèon Bakst and the Russian Ballet.

In 1930 she was appointed Art Director of Wilkinsons and by the following year she had a hundred and fifty people working under her. Her work, epitomising the Jazz Age was bought by the Bright Young Things and the stars of stage and screen of the twenties and thirties. It was all thought rather vulgar by their elders.

The 1939-45 war really put an end to Clarice Cliff's 'Bizarre' era,

329

Teapot decorated with the 'Crocus' pattern in orange, mauve, blue and green by Clarice Cliff for the Newport Pottery. 1935. 190mm high. *Courtesy Castle Antiques (Warwick's Art Deco Shop) Warwick.*

Circular 'Bonjour' teapot decorated in green and blue only with a design of hand painted crocuses by Clarice Cliff and made at the Newport Pottery. *c.* 1935. 135mm high. *Courtesy Castle Antiques (Warwick's Art Deco Shop).*

An oblong plate of the 'Biarritz' range, decorated with the 'Rhodanthe' pattern by Clarice Cliff for the Newport Pottery. The colouring is mauve, green, fawn and yellow. *c.* 1936. 225mm wide. *Courtesy Castle Antiques (Warwick's Art Deco Shop) Warwick.*

Earthenware shallow bowl with a polychrome lithographic transfer decoration under the honey glaze. The backstamp reads OPHELIA NEWPORT POTTERY Co. Ltd. Burslem England and is signed 'Clarice Cliff'. *c.* 1938. 199mm diameter. *Private Collection.*

though after the war production was resumed and was carried on until the early 1960s. It is interesting to reflect that Clarice Cliff's twenty-one piece Crocus pattern teaset could be bought in 1930 for the equivalent of £1.15. Further examples of Clarice Cliff's work are shown in colour on page 333.

Myott Son and Co. was the name of another pottery that produced wares in the Art Deco style for the lower end of the market. Myotts had been founded in 1875. In 1971 they were taken over by an American company named Interspace of California, who also purchased Alfred Meakin to form the group Myott-Meakin. In 1982 the company was liquidated and re-formed as Myott-Meakin (1982) Limited.

Jug decorated with orange and brown leaves. Gold transfer mark on the base 'Myott Son & Co made in England' in capital letters and surmounted by a crown. This was the mark used *c.* 1936 by the firm who ran the Alexander Pottery at Stoke from 1898-1902, moved to Cobridge 1902-46 and to Hanley in 1947. 190mm high. *Private Collection.*

Striped brown, green and orange vase of bizarre form made by Myott Son and Co. Ltd. In addition to the crown above the name and Made in England, is the following inscription 'B.A.G. & Co Hand Painted 1766 Regd No 789318', all on a gold transfer on the base. *c.* 1936. 205mm high. *Private Collection.*

Jug of rich, deep cream colour decorated in relief with enamel colours, pink and mauve tulips and yellow primroses with green leaves in enamel colours. Transfer printed mark on the base 'Carlton Ware — registered Australian Design. Registration applied for'. The pieces so marked (between 1935 and 1945) were intended for export to Australia and the registration stopped the Japanese from copying them. *c.* 1935. 260mm high. *Private Collection.*

Vase decorated by Elizabeth Radford with hand painted flowers in pastel colours in the Poole manner. Made by H.J. Wood Ltd. Alexandra Pottery Burslem and signed on the base with a printed signature. *c.* 1935. *Private Collection.*

331

The Old Woman who lived in a Shoe teapot, glazed with a bright yellow glaze with the addition of gilding. Impressed mark on the base LINGARD in a scroll and Tunstall Staffs. Made in England. Lingard Webster and Co. Ltd. of the Swan Pottery Tunstall was founded *c.* 1900. This was probably made in the 1930s. 160mm high. *Private Collection.*

Plate 53. A collection of ware designed by Clarice Cliff, showing the influence of Art Deco, and one Burleigh ware jug. *Courtesy Castle Antiques (Warwick's Art Deco Shop) Warwick.*

Top left: An early 'Bizarre' geometric jug designed by Clarice Cliff for the Newport Pottery. *c.* 1930. 165mm high.

Top right: A 'Fantasque' conical jug decorated with a stylised butterfly, designed by Clarice Cliff. *c.* 1930. 165mm high.

Middle left: A 'Fantasque' vase with a petal top decorated with a stylised cottage and trees by Clarice Cliff for the Newport Pottery. *c.* 1936. 290mm high.

Middle right: A 'Bizarre' design stepped vase on a square base, painted with stylised trees and a café au lait glaze, decorated by Clarice Cliff for the Newport Pottery. Printed on the base specially made for Lawleys. *c.* 1930. 190mm high.

Bottom left: A :Fantasque' bowl painted with stylised flowers by Clarice Cliff for the Newport Pottery. *c.* 1935. 220mm diameter.

Bottom right: Burleigh ware jug with a Parrot handle made by Burgess and Leigh, a Burslem pottery who made many such jugs with decorative handles; the tops were characteristically dotted with black. Marked with one of the printed marks used during the 1930s. 200mm high.

Teapot made in the form of a racing car, covered with a blue glaze and silver lustre. This can also be found in pink and yellow glazes. Impressed mark SADLER˙MADE IN ENGLAND. James Sadler and Sons Ltd. of Burslem was founded *c.* 1899. They made earthenware, specialising in teapots of many fanciful shapes. 1938. 235mm wide. *Private Collection.*

Teapot in the form of a First World War tank with a Churchill like head in a tin hat looking out of the turret. Glazed with a pale turquoise glaze. On the base is the printed mark of SADLER on a ribbon with a crown above and MADE IN ENGLAND below a mark used *c.* 1947 onwards. 160mm wide. *Private Collection.*

Many factories such as Sadlers and the Devonshire Pottery took no notice at all of these current fashions and went their own way making comic teapots and other things in the form of racing cars, tanks or faces, in fact in almost any form (like their 18th century predecessors who made salt-glaze teapots in the form of camels) for the more 'popular' end of the market. The really big established firms continued to produce their traditional wares.

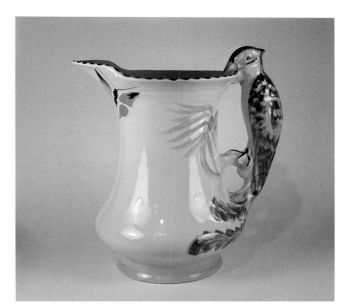

Creamware mug with a lithographed transfer design commemorating Wedgwood's move from Etruria to Barlaston in 1940. The mug shows on the front a profile portrait of Josiah Wedgwood and on either side a formalised kiln with examples of ware. On either side are the dates Etruria 1730 and Barlaston 1940. The new factory of Etruria was not opened until 1769, but Josiah Wedgwood was born in 1730 in Burslem.

Transfer mark on the base 'Wedgwood of Etruria and Barlaston, made in England' and 'Designed by Eric Ravilious' in a rectangle 11mm wide. 102mm high. *Private Collection.*

Eric Ravilious, who had left the Royal College of Art in 1925, had by the late 1930s established himself as an engraver and lithographer.

Wedgwoods approached him with the idea that he should decorate some ware for them. His designs were drawn in pencil and then engraved on copper cylinders by the Wedgwood engravers. Transfer prints were put down on to offset plates and printed by the thousand for applying to the ware.

That the Ravilious designs on cream ware lacked the richness of the eighteenth century Sadler and Green transfer prints must have been largely due to the use of the offset press. His designs included scenes of the Oxford and Cambridge Boat Race, a dinner service called *Persephone* and decorated alphabet jugs, mugs and plates. In 1940 he designed a very handsome commemorative mug to celebrate the removal of the factory from Etruria to Barlaston.

Creamware jug with alphabet designs transferred in black with a washed pink band behind the lettering. Mark on the base, 'Designed by Eric Ravilious' in a rectangle 11mm wide and 'WEDGWOOD Made in England', 1937. 105mm high. *Private Collection*.

A creamware alphabet mug by Eric Ravilious originally designed to have a band of colour behind the lettering. These later versions were printed in either sepia or Indian red. *c.* 1978. 85mm high. Mark on base 'Designed by Eric Ravilious' in a rectangle 24mm wide and 'WEDGWOOD Made in England'.

Souvenir Coronation mug in Queen's ware adapted by Wedgwoods from a design by Eric Ravilious, originally prepared for the Coronation (that never happened) of King Edward VIII. It was re-issued with modifications in 1953 for the Coronation of Queen Elizabeth II. 107mm high. *Josiah Wedgwood and Sons Ltd*.

Booth's version of this blue transfer Willow pattern design, which has been available in many forms and made by innumerable potters ever since Spodes engraved it in the 1780s. This version has a brightly burnished gold edging. Made by Ridgways. *c.* 1955.

This design called *Windsor* was a version of a blue transfer printed design called *Asiatic Pheasants* that was very popular in the nineteenth century. The border is heavier and more ornate than the original. It was still available in the 1960s. Made by Ridgways. *c.* 1955.

An old traditional Mason design now known as *Chartreuse*, transfer printed in outline and hand painted in several greens, yellow and finished with touches of burnished gold. Typical of the designs the Mason factory was producing in the 1820s. Made by Mason's Patent Ironstone China Ltd. *c.* 1956. (And still being made today.) This firm became part of the Wedgwood empire in 1973.

A traditional Wedgwood design called *Napoleon Ivy*, reputed to have been supplied to Napoleon during his exile on St. Helena. The pattern first appeared in 1815 as a hand painted design in shades of green and brown. This version was first produced in 1906 in the form of a grey underglaze transfer print, filled in with rich dark green enamels. It is one of the few designs on earthenware still being made by Wedgwoods today. *Courtesy Josiah Wedgwood and Sons Ltd.*

The 1939-45 war more or less put a stop to the production of any decorated pottery and for years nothing much was available. After the war there was again a hunger for decoration, much of this being satisfied by single colour traditional overall transfer prints in red, green or blue.

The Festival of Britain in 1951 was the end of a period of austerity. In 1953 the Coronation of Queen Elizabeth II was the inspiration for numerous commemorative pieces. Most of these were not very distinguished.

Souvenir Coronation mug in Queen's ware designed for
Wedgwoods by Richard Guyatt in 1953. The lettering inside
and on the base was by John Brinkley, a colleague of
Guyatt's at the Royal College of Art. 107mm high.
Josiah Wedgwood and Sons Ltd.

Souvenir mug of black jasper ware with white applied reliefs
of sporting subjects for a souvenir competition organised by
the Council of Industrial Design. Designed for Wedgwoods
by Richard Guyatt. 1969. 102mm high.

Wedgwood bi-centenary mug. Transfer printed in gold on a
shiny black glaze. Designed by Victor Skellern, Wedgwood's
Art Director, in 1959.

Creamware plate with a black transfer printed design of a Paris quayside restaurant. Marked on the back 'Parisienne made in England'. *c.* 1949. 254mm diameter. *Private Collection.*

Creamware plate, the shape inspired by a television screen with a lithographic transfer design of a fishing boat and gulls in blue, yellow, black and pink. Signed 'Cobelle'. Made by Midwinter. *c.*1950. 242mm diameter. *Private Collection.*
This plate and the one below, in addition to other markings, have a backstamp 'Stylecraft Fashion Tableware by Midwinter, Staffordshire England'.

Plate with a black transfer design called *Homemaker*. Made by Ridgways in 1953. *Private Collection.*

Creamware plate, with a lithographic transfer design of leaves in black, grey, yellow and red under the glaze. Marked 'CAPRI design by Jessie Tait. Stylecraft Fashion Tableware by Midwinter, Staffordshire England'. *c.* 1950. 242mm diameter. *Private Collection.*

'Telly Set' with a black transfer design, marked BESWICK
ENGLAND in a circular form which was one of the post-war
marks used by the firm of John Beswick of Longton, Staffs.
c. 1950. 248mm wide. *Private Collection.*

Creamware plate of a similar shape with a lithographic
transfer design of leaves in Indian red, grey, brown and
yellow under the glaze. *Falling leaves* design by Jessie Tait for
Midwinter. *c.* 1950. *Private Collection.*

The British housewife, having been denied foreign travel throughout
the war period, made up for it by buying any designs that had a
Continental flavour. Paris street scenes and fishing boats found their
way on to pottery for the mass market with such designs as 'Parisienne'
or 'Capri' (an early design by Midwinter's Jessie Tait).

In the fifties the work of Cliff and Cooper had become less popular
and a new trend was setting in. This resulted in a spate of rather feeble
designs, lacking in colour and dominated by the leaf motif (due no
doubt to *Feuilles d'Automne,* a melancholy but extremely popular song
of the period). These inept and often asymmetrical decorations were
used on newly designed rimless or coupe shaped plates, or plates
inspired by the shape of the television screen. Television in fact was
responsible for the potteries producing special oval plates called 'Telly
sets' with an indentation for the cup on one side.

Group of vases designed by A.B. Read working in conjunction with Lucien Myers and Roy T. Holland for the Poole Pottery. 1954. 230-450mm high. *Courtesy Poole Pottery*.

In 1951 A.B. Read RDI was appointed to run a design unit. Alfred Read had already had a successful career as an industrial designer, though he had never worked in the field of pottery. However he soon designed a range of elegant hand painted vases and carafes for the pottery. In 1956 Read left Poole as the result of contracting tuberculosis. He finally severed his connection with the firm two years later.

The *Compact* range of earthenware by the Poole Pottery. This was a carefully thought out range of fifteen pieces designed by Robert Jefferson DES RCA in 1964, to be space and labour saving and versatile enough to fit into any setting. It was oven-proof, stackable and multi-purpose.

Stoneware coffee set designed by Robert Jefferson DES RCA. Dark brown glaze with gold decoration. Made in 1968 by the Purbeck Pottery Ltd. The height of the coffee pot is 260mm. The Purbeck Pottery was started in Bournemouth in January 1966 to produce stoneware tableware, using local clays from the Purbeck Hills. The ware fired to 1250°, is completely vitrified and ovenproof. Normal factory methods are used for the making, decorative techniques rely on the texture and colour of the glazes and on silk screen printing. 85% of the production of this small but extremely go-ahead factory was exported.

Tableware made of china clay, ball clay, flint and hard purple stone. The shape was designed by David Queensberry MSIA HON DES RCA; and the pattern, which is an unusual combination of blue, purple and green called *Spanish Garden*, was designed by Jessie Tait, one of Midwinter's resident designers. First produced 1966. Made by Midwinter Ltd. of Burslem. Midwinter is now part of the Wedgwood empire. *Council of Industrial Design.*

Black basalt coffee set designed by Robert Minkin DES RCA MSIA. Made by Wedgwood *c.* 1965. 250mm high. *Courtesy Josiah Wedgwood and Sons Ltd.*

At the Poole Pottery in Dorset great changes came in with the appointment of Robert Jefferson in 1958, another talented designer whose ideas on shapes and colours altered the whole style of the pottery's output. Cyril Carter retired in 1963 and the following year the firm merged with Pilkingtons. In 1971 both firms were absorbed into the Thomas Tilling Group, but continued as autonomous units.

By the sixties something more positive in the way of colour and decoration was being produced. Jessie Tait designed a successful blue, green and purple range (perhaps inspired by de Morgan tiles) called *Spanish Garden*. The shapes were designed by David Queensbury, the Head of the Ceramic Department at the Royal College of Art.

In the kitchen-ware section, a good deal of rethinking and redesigning was done, with varying degrees of success. Some designs were extremely efficient, especially the ranges of ware intended for easy stacking. But for the most part oven-to-table ware designs have merely made 'polite' the old wholesome casserole, by altering its shape and adding a few flowers or stripes.

A range of stoneware containers made by Doultons for industrial purposes. There
is something extremely satisfying about these well-made absolutely simple basic
shapes. *c.* 1950.
Royal Doulton.

Coffee cans made of fine quality
earthenware, slip-decorated and hand
turned. Called by the makers their
Channel Island range. Top left: Guernsey:
burnt orange. Alderney: French blue or
green. Sark: blue, grey or honey and
black. Jersey: French blue or green.
Shape designed by Judith Onions DES
RCA. Pattern Sark: Martin Hunt DES
RCA. Jersey, Guernsey, Alderney: Judith
Onions. First produced 1967 and made
by T.G. Green Ltd. of Church Gresley.
Council of Industrial Design.
These designs are in the tradition of
Mocha ware, which used to be made by
the same firm. See page 235.

An oven-to-table ware range introduced in 1965, which has a chunky textured quality which is achieved through a combination of moulded relief and new specially developed glazes. This *Pennine* range is in a rich brown colour with amber highlights. It was designed by Eric Owen MSIA, then Wedgwood's chief modeller, and of course made by Wedgwood. *Courtesy Josiah Wedgwood and Sons Ltd.*

A cheese dish from the *Totem* range of designs by Susan Williams-Ellis for the Portmeirion Pottery. This design was made in amber, olive, cobalt and white glazes. *c.* 1962.

Casseroles in the *Sterling* range, designed by Robert Minkin, DES RCA MSIA and made by Wedgwood. It is decorated with a rich chestnut brown glaze. The largest casserole has a capacity of 6 pints. *Courtesy Josiah Wedgwood and Sons Ltd.*

The importance of feminine influence in the design of English pottery has continued in the post-war years with Susan Williams-Ellis, daughter of the architect Clough Williams-Ellis, the creator of Portmeirion in North Wales. Susan and her husband Euan Cooper-Willis started the Portmeirion Pottery at Stoke-on-Trent in 1960, when they took over two potteries, Gray's and Kirkhams. Gray's Pottery, as mentioned earlier, was originally only a decorating business.

343

Plate 54. A selection of tableware designed by Susan Williams-Ellis at the Portmeirion Pottery 1972-84.

Opposite: Soup tureen and ladle in the *Botanic Garden* series. Decorated with an in-glaze coloured transfer design of passion flowers. 1972. 305mm high.

Opposite left: Dessert plate featuring an in-glaze coloured transfer design featuring an aquilegia in the *Botanic Garden* series. This was a later addition to the series in 1984. 217mm diameter.

Opposite right: Dessert plate with in-glaze coloured transfer decoration, the 'Hoary Morning Apple'. One of the *Pomona* series from the *Pomona Britannica* 1818. 1982. 218mm diameter.

Coffee ware in a Greek Key pattern designed by Susan Williams-Ellis of the Portmeirion Pottery. As well as black on white, this design was also made in black and turquoise and black and orange. Height of coffee pot 330mm. *c.* 1965.

Dinner plate with in-glaze colour transfer decoration 'Dog Rose' from the *Botanic Garden* series. Designed by Susan Williams-Ellis at the Portmeirion Pottery in 1972. 216mm diameter.

Kirkham's Pottery had made scientific and chemist's pottery and it was the direct and simple shapes of this type of ware that originally inspired Miss Williams-Ellis to design her early ranges of kitchen ware.

Since 1972 the Portmeirion Pottery has produced some of the most original, colourful and collectable pottery that has been made since the 1939-45 war. Susan Williams-Ellis is an artist and designer of great talent and imagination, and inspired by the beautiful hand-coloured engravings in late eighteenth and early nineteenth century herbals and botanical, entomological and ornithological works has produced three immensely successful series. The first of these, 'Botanic Garden' named after Erasmus Darwin's poetic work, was produced in 1972, followed by 'Birds of Britain' and in 1982 by 'Pomona', the latest of the designs. Susan Williams-Ellis has also designed and modelled the shapes of all the individual pieces.

The success of the venture can be measured by the increase in employment from a relatively few people in 1960 to over 200 today. Portmeirion pottery is exported all over the world. Their wares will surely be collectors' items for the future.

345

Some pieces from the *Heirloom* range, designed by the design team and made at the Hornsea pottery in 1967. The range is produced in three colours, brown, blue and green. The Hornsea pottery began in a very small way just after the last war; it now employs nearly two hundred people and the output is somewhere about 70,000 pieces a week, many of which are exported all over the world. The designs are lively, the colours brilliant and the ware is very well made.

Earthenware mug with a honey-coloured glaze and silk screen transfer design in Indian red and black designed by John Smith of Stourbridge to commemorate the opening of the new City Museum at Stoke-on-Trent. It is based on a traditional slipware design. A limited edition of 500 was produced by the Hornsea Pottery in 1979. 90mm high. *Private Collection*.

The actual silk screen transfer design for the City Museum, Stoke-on-Trent commemoration mug. 76mm high.

'Walking' series of ware with the feet painted in various colours including yellow, black and blue. Designed by Roger Mitchell and Danka Napiorkowska and produced by Carlton Ware Ltd. *c.* 1980. Height of teapot 197mm.

Dovecot and Malachite tea and coffee sets. The Dovecot is pale and dark pink with blue and touches of ochre with gold lines. The Malachite set is green with ochre and black with gold lines. Both sets were designed by Roger Mitchell for Carlton Ware Ltd. *c.* 1978. Coffee pot 280mm high.

Egg cup with feet decorated in black with pink lustre patterns. Designed by Roger Mitchell and Danka Napiorkowska. Backstamp on base of foot CARLTON WARE ENGLAND LUSTRE POTTERY 1973. 60mm high.

A recurring feature of English pottery design is an inherent humour, evident in the past in salt-glazed pew groups, slipware chargers, Obadiah Sherratt groups and Martin ware jugs and today in the work of some modern studio and commercial potters. One such commercial pottery is Carlton Ware Ltd., with their 'walking' series of eggcups, teapots, etc.

There are one or two other potteries who have seen the possibilities for humorous pots. Richard Parrington and Swineside Ceramics are two very small firms who have, during the last decade established themselves by their witty, often wayward productions. They have found markets for their wares both at home and abroad.

As for the established potteries, many with great names, these are either satisfying their customers' demands by making earthenware in traditional patterns, or, and this has become a marked trend in the last few years, they have turned over to the manufacture of bone china.

347

A teapot in the form of a seated Gorilla, slip cast in white earthenware and glazed in brown. Green glazed leaves are held between his lips. 1985. 166mm high.

White pottery teapot entitled 'The White Hunter', glazed with a black shiny glaze, and the firewood is brownish ochre. 1982. 187mm high.

'Corgi and Beth' teapot made of white earthenware enamel coloured with brown hair, ochre corgi and carmine lips. The corgi serves as a spout. Impressed on the base 'Exile Ceramics 1981 TEA by Appointment'. 222mm high.

All the slip-cast pots on this page were designed and made by Richard Parrington at Nettlestead Green, Kent.

White pottery money box entitled 'Sheikh Yermoney', decorated with touches of silver lustre, blue and black. 1982. 210mm high.

Richard Parrington is a potter who began his training at the Central School of Art and Design, but by experience, found his own way of working. He was originally inspired by the mass produced ornaments made for working people in the nineteenth century. Subsidising himself by part-time teaching he started up his own pottery some six years ago, making everyday things into useful ceramic objects. Miniature dustbins became storage jars, a crocodile handbag became a teapot, so did the kitchen clock. He has a most original and quirky way of looking at life, sometimes disconcerting but often extremely funny. He now makes his slip-cast pots in a small workshop in Kent, firing them in a low thermal mass kiln. He has two assistants and sells his work through Trade Fairs and several retail outlets in London. He also exports much of his work to Japan, the United States and Europe.

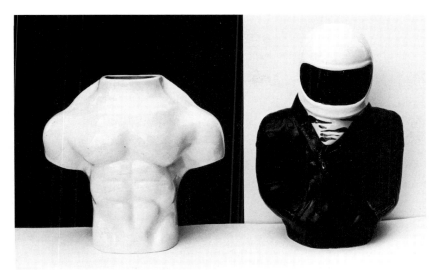

Vase in the form of a torso, 205mm high and a container in the form of a leather-jacketted motorcyclist, the head is the lid. Coloured with black and a touch of yellow. *c.* 1979-80. 265mm high.

Teddy Boy coloured in black and yellow. *c.* 1979-80. 230mm high.

All the slip-cast pots on this page were designed and made by Martin Bibby at Swineshead Ceramics, Leyburn, Yorkshire.

Burglar moneybox coloured in black and ochre. *c* 1980. 130mm high.

Pieces from two sets of tableware. To the left white earthenware teapot and jug with red and black linear decoration, teapot with blue lid and blue and pink decoration. 1982. Jug is 185mm high.

Martin and Judy Bibby are another enterprising young couple who met as students at the Hornsea College of Art. They set up a small pottery, Swineside Ceramics, in 1979, making amusing pieces poking fun at the then fashionable 'macho' look. They have continued to produce tongue-in-cheek pieces as well as an abstract range of tableware, all of which they export. The business has outgrown its original premises and has moved to a small industrial estate at Leyburn in Yorkshire where they now employ five people, including themselves.

Lithographic transfer decoration for the Potteries Willow Plate, produced by the Gladstone Pottery Museum to commemorate Stoke-on-Trent's 60th year as a City, its 75th year as a Federation of Six Towns and the Gladstone Pottery Museum's 10th year. The design is by Peter Brears. 1985. 216mm diameter. *Courtesy the Gladstone Pottery Museum.*

In 1985 the Gladstone Pottery Museum produced their Stoke-on-Trent commemorative plate, summing up in an amusing way the art and industries of the Potteries. The manner in which Peter Brears has interwoven his railway train, Spitfire aeroplanes, coal mine, canal boat and bottle kilns, belching out orange trees rather than smoke, combines a fine feeling for the Chinoiserie and the Willow Pattern tradition and a pleasant degree of wit. The Spitfires, which first flew in 1935, commemorate Reg Mitchell, their designer, who was born and educated in Stoke.

For further reading

Peter Wentworth-Shields and Kay Johnson. *Clarice Cliff*. L'Odeon. London 1976.

Jennifer Hawkins. *The Poole Potteries*. Barrie and Jenkins 1980.

Paul and Kathy Niblett. *Hand Painted Gray's Pottery*. City Museum and Art Gallery, Stoke-on-Trent. 1983. 2nd impression.

Robert Stirling. *Carlton Ware Naturalistic Patterns of the 1930s and 1940s*. Antique Collecting, May 1984.

Neil Fletcher. *Sixty Glorious Years. The Work of Susie Cooper O.B.E.* Antique Collecting, October 1984.

Ann Eatwell. *Susie Cooper. Her Pre-War Productions 1922-1939*. Victoria and Albert Museum Album 5. De Montfort Publishing Ltd. 1986.

Robert Harling. *Ravilious and Wedgwood*. Dalrymple Press. London 1986. Catalogue entries by Maureen Batkin and Robert Dalrymple.

Bibliography

GENERAL

Books listed for further reading at the end of each chapter have also been included in this bibliography. Titles of magazine articles, booklets and small catalogues have not been repeated. In this first section, the books are listed in chronological order.

Simeon Shaw. *History of the Staffordshire Potteries*. Hanley 1829. Reprint Wakefield 1970.

William Chaffers. *Marks and Monograms on Pottery and Porcelain*. Reeves and Turner 1863. 13th Edn. London 1912.

Llewellynn Jewitt. *The Ceramic Art of Great Britain*. 2nd Edn. London and New York 1883.

L.M. Solon. *The Art of the Old English Potter*. New York 1886. Reprinted by E.P. Publishing Ltd. Wakefield 1976.

G.W. and F.A. Rhead. *Staffordshire Pots and Potters*. Hutchinson. London 1906.

Josiah C. Wedgwood. *Staffordshire Pottery and its History*. Sampson Low, Marston and Co. London 1913.

J.F. Blacker. *The ABC of Collecting Old English Pottery*. Stanley Paul. London 1920.

J.F. Blacker. *The ABC of Nineteenth Century English Ceramic Art*. Stanley Paul. London n.d.

G. Woolliscroft Rhead. *The Earthenware Collector*. Herbert Jenkins. London 1920.

Bernard Rackham and Herbert Read. *English Pottery: its Development from Early Times to the end of the Eighteenth Century*. London 1924. Reprinted E.P. Publishers 1973.

Bernard Rackham. *Mediaeval English Pottery*. Faber London 1948.

Reginald G. Haggar. *English Country Pottery*. Phoenix House. London 1950.

Bernard Rackham. *Early Staffordshire Pottery*. Faber London 1951.

R.J. Charleston. *Roman Pottery*. Faber. London 1953.

George Savage. *Pottery through the Ages*. Penguin Books. Harmondsworth 1959.

Hugh Wakefield. *Victorian Pottery*. Herbert Jenkins. London 1962.

John and Jennifer May. *Commemorative Pottery 1780-1900*. Heinemann. London 1972.

Austwick, J. and B. *The Decorated Tile*. Pitman House. London 1980.

Ball, A. *The Price Guide to Pot-Lids and other underglaze Multi-colour Prints on Ware*. Antique Collectors' Club. Woodbridge 1980.

Barnard, Julian. *Victorian Ceramic Tiles*. Studio Vista. London 1972.

Catleugh, J. *William de Morgan Tiles*. Trefoil. London 1983.

Clarke, H.G. *The Pictorial Pot Lid Book*. Courier Press. London 1960.

Cooper, Ronald G. *The Pottery of Thomas Toft*. Leeds City Art Gallery. 1952.

Cooper, Ronald G. *English Slipware Dishes*. Tiranti. London 1968.

Coysh, A.W. *British Art Pottery 1870-1940*. David and Charles. Newton Abbot 1976.

Cross, A.J. *Pilkington's Royal Lancastrian Pottery and Tiles*. Richard Dennis. London 1980.

Eyles, Desmond. *The Doulton Lambeth Wares*. Hutchinson. London 1975.

Garner, F.H., and Archer, Michael. *English Delftware*. Faber. London 1948. Revised edition 1972.

Grant, Captain M.H. *The Makers of Black Basaltes*. William Blackwood. Edinburgh 1910.

Haslam, Malcolm. *English Art Pottery*. Antique Collectors' Club. Woodbridge 1975.

Henrywood, R.K. *Relief-Moulded Jugs 1820-1900*. Antique Collectors' Club. Woodbridge 1984.

Howard, G.E. *Early English Drug Jars*. Medici. London 1931.

John, W.D. and Baker, W. *Old English Lustre Pottery*. The Ceramic Book Company. Newport 1951.

Lewis, John and Griselda. *Pratt Ware: English and Scottish Relief Decorated and Underglaze Coloured Earthenware 1780-1840*. Antique Collectors' Club. Woodbridge 1984.

Lipski, Louis, Ed. and Augmented by Michael Archer. *Dated English Delftware Tin Glazed Earthenware 1600-1800*. Sotheby Publications.

Lockett, Terence A. *Collecting Victorian Tiles*. Antique Collectors' Club. Woodbridge 1979.

Mountford, Arnold. *The Illustrated Guide to Staffordshire Salt-glazed Stoneware*. Barrie and Jenkins. London 1971.

Oswald, Adrian, Hildyard, R.J.C. and Hughes, R.G. *English Brown Stonewares 1670-1900*. Faber. London 1982.

Ray, Anthony. *English Delftware Pottery in the Robert Hall Warren Collection Ashmolean Museum, Oxford*. Faber. London 1968.

Thomas, E. Lloyd. *Victorian Art Pottery*. Guildart. London 1975.

Thorne, A. *Pink Lustre Pottery*. B.T. Batsford. London 1926.

Towner, Donald. *Creamware*. Faber. London 1978.

Williams-Wood, C. *Staffordshire Pot Lids and their Potters*. Faber. London 1972.

POTTERY FIGURES

Balston, Thomas. *Staffordshire Portrait Figures of the Victorian Age* with a supplement by John Hall (1963). Faber. London 1958.

Earle, Cyril. *The Earle Collection of Early Staffordshire Pottery.* A. Brown and Sons. London and New York 1915.

Haggar, Reginald. *Staffordshire Chimney Ornaments.* Phoenix House. London 1955.

Haggar, R.G. *English Pottery Figures 1660-1860.* Tiranti. London 1947.

Hall, John. *Staffordshire Portrait Figures.* Charles Letts and Co. London 1972.

Mackintosh, Sir Harold Bt. *Early English Figure Pottery.* Chapman and Hall. London 1938.

Price, R.K. *Astbury, Whieldon and Ralph Wood Figures and Toby Jugs.* John Lane. London 1922.

Pugh, Gordon P.D. *Staffordshire Portrait Figures of the Victorian Era.* Barrie and Jenkins. London 1970. Antique Collectors' Club. Woodbridge 1987.

Read, Herbert. *Staffordshire Pottery Figures.* Duckworth. London 1920.

POTTERIES

Baines, J.M. *Sussex Pottery.* Fisher Publications 1980.

Baker, John C. *Sunderland Pottery.* Tyne and Wear County Council Museums 1984.

Bell, R.C. *Tyneside Potteries.* Studio Vista. London 1971.

Brannam, Peter. *A Family Business: The Story of a Pottery.* Barnstaple 1982.

Eyles, Desmond. *Royal Doulton 1815-1965.* Hutchinson 1965.

Grabham, Oxley. *Yorkshire Potteries, Pots and Potters.* 1916. Reprinted 1971. S.R. Publications.

Hawkins, Jennifer. *The Poole Potteries.* Barrie and Jenkins. London 1980.

Kidson, J.R. and F. *Historical Notices of the Leeds Old Pottery.* Leeds 1892.

Lawrence, Heather. *Yorkshire Pots and Potters.* David and Charles. Newton Abbot 1974.

Mayer, J. *The Art of Pottery with a History of its Progress in Liverpool.* Liverpool 1873.

Pountney, W.J. *Old Bristol Potteries.* Arrowsmith. Bristol 1920. Reprint 1972.

Roussel, Diana Edwards. *The Castleford Pottery 1790-1821.* Wakefield Historical Publications 1982.

Smith, Alan. *Liverpool Herculaneum Pottery 1796-1840.* Barrie and Jenkins. London 1970.

Lloyd-Thomas, D. and E. *The Old Torquay Potteries* n.d.

Towner, Donald. *The Leeds Pottery.* Cory, Adams and Mackay. London 1963.

POTTERS, DESIGNERS AND THEIR WORK

Copeland, Robert. *Spode's Willow Pattern and other Designs after the Chinese.* Studio Vista/Christies Cassall. London 1980.

Dawson, Aileen. *Bernard Moore, Potter.* London 1982.

Dennis, R. *William and Walter Moorcroft 1897-1973.* London n.d.

Drakard, David and Holdway, Paul. *Spode Printed Ware.* Longman. London 1983.

Falkner, Frank. *The Wood Family of Burslem.* London 1912. Reprinted E.P. Publishing Ltd. Wakefield 1972.

Godden, Geoffrey A. *Mason's China and the Ironstone Wares.* Antique Collectors' Club. 1984.

Haggar, R.G. *The Masons of Lane Delph.* Printed for Geo. L. Ashworth by Percy Lund Humphries. London 1952.

Haggar, R.G. and Adams, E. *Mason Porcelain and Ironstone 1796-1853.* Faber. London 1977.

Harling, Robert. *Ravilious and Wedgwood.* Dalrymple Press. London 1986. Catalogue entries by Maureen Batkin and Robert Dalrymple.

Haslam, Malcolm. *The Martin Brothers Potters.* Richard Dennis. London 1978.

Hayden, Arthur. *Spode and his Successors.* Longman. London 1925.

Hillier, Bevis. *The Turners of Lane End.* Cory, Adams and Mackay. London 1965.

Jewitt, Llewellynn. *The Wedgwoods, being a Life of Josiah Wedgwood.* London 1865.

Mankowitz, Wolf. *Wedgwood.* Batsford. London 1953. Reprinted by Spring Books 1966.

Meteyard, Eliza. *The Life of Josiah Wedgwood.* Hurst and Blackett. London 1865.

Wedgwood, Josiah C. *A History of the Wedgwood Family.* London 1908.

Wentworth-Shields, Peter and Johnson, Kay. *Clarice Cliff.* L'Odeon. London 1976.

Whiter, Leonard. *Spode.* Barrie and Jenkins. London 1970.

Williams, S.B. *Antique Blue and White Spode.* Batsford. London 1943.

STUDIO POTTERS

Birks, Tony. *The Art of the Modern Potter.* Country Life. London 1967.

Birks, Tony. *Hans Coper.* Collins. London 1983.

Blandino, Betty. *Coiled Pottery.* A. and C. Black. London 1984.

Casson, Michael. *Pottery in Britain Today.* Tiranti. London 1967.

Clark, Garth. *Michael Cardew.* Faber. London 1978.

Cooper, E. and Lewenstein, E. (Ed.) *Studio Ceramics Today.* Craftsmen Potters Association of Great Britain. London 1983.

Hogben, Carol. *The Art of Bernard Leach.* Faber. London 1978.

Lane, Peter. *Studio Ceramics.* Collins. London 1983.

Leach, Bernard. *A Potter's Book.* Faber. London 1969.

O'Reilly, Susan, Taylor, Jane and Atterbury, Paul. *Artist Potters Now.* Oxford County Museum Services 1984.

Rose, Muriel. *Artist Potters in England.* Faber. London 1955. Revised edition 1970.

DICTIONARIES, ENCYCLOPAEDIAS AND CATALOGUES

Coysh, A.W. and Henrywood, R.K. *The Dictionary of Blue and White Printed Pottery 1780-1880.* Antique Collectors' Club. Woodbridge 1982.

Godden, Geoffrey A. *Encyclopaedia of British Pottery and Porcelain Marks.* Herbert Jenkins. London 1964.

Godden, Geoffrey A. *An Illustrated Encyclopaedia of British Pottery and Porcelain.* Herbert Jenkins. London 1966.

Lockett, T.A. and Halfpenny, P.A. (Ed.). *Stonewares and Stone Chinas of Northern England to 1851.* City Museum and Art Gallery, Stoke-on-Trent 1982.

Lockett, T.A. and Halfpenny, P.A. (Ed.). *Creamware and Pearlware.* City Museum and Art Gallery, Stoke-on-Trent 1986.

Mankowitz, W. and Haggar, R.G. *The Concise Encyclopaedia of English Pottery and Porcelain.* Andre Deutsch. London 1957.

Rackham, Bernard. *Catalogue of the Schreiber Collection, Vol. 2 Earthenware.* Victoria and Albert Museum 1930.

Rackham, Bernard. *Catalogue of the Glaisher Collection of Pottery and Porcelain in the Fitzwilliam Museum, Cambridge,* Cambridge 1934. Antique Collectors' Club. Woodbridge 1987.

Savage, G. and Reilly, R. *The Dictionary of Wedgwood.* The Antique Collectors' Club. Woodbridge 1980.

Walton, Peter. *Creamware and other English Pottery at Temple Newsam House, Leeds.* Manningham Press. Bradford and London 1976.

Willett, Henry. *Catalogue of a Collection of Pottery and Porcelain illustrating Popular British History.* H.M.S.O. 1899.

AMERICAN COLLECTIONS

The Burnap Collection. William Rockhill Nelson Gallery, Kansas City, Missouri 1967.

The Colonial Williamsburg Foundation. There is no catalogue of the ceramic collections in general, but a very thorough catalogue of the Delft ware at Colonial Williamsburg is in preparation by John C. Austin. Also a smaller book on the Slip ware collection is being prepared by Leslie Grigsby, both are due to be published in 1987.

The Delhom Gallery Guide: English Pottery. Mint Museum, Charlotte, North Carolina, 1982.

The Henry Francis du Pont Winterthur Museum, Delaware. There is no catalogue of the ceramic collections in general, but a book dealing with the tin-glazed wares is in preparation by Phillip H. Curtis, scheduled for publication in 1987. Further catalogues of the rest of the English ceramic collection are planned to follow in due course.

Index

357

Index of subjects from museum collections

* Mentioned in text but not illustrated.